THOMAS HARDY:
The 'Dream-country' of his Fiction

THOMAS HARDY: THE 'DREAM-COUNTRY' OF HIS FICTION

by
Anne Alexander

VISION
and
BARNES & NOBLE

Vision Press Limited
Fulham Wharf
Townmead Road
London SW6 2SB

and

Barnes & Noble Books
81 Adams Drive
Totowa, NJ 07512

ISBN (UK) 0 85478 166 8
ISBN (US) 0 389 20712 8

Library of Congress Cataloging-in-Publication Data

Alexander, Anne.
  Thomas Hardy: the 'dream-country' of his fiction.

  Bibliography: p.
  1. Hardy, Thomas, 1840–1928—Criticism and
interpretation. 2. Landscape in literature. 3. Dreams
in literature. 4. Archetype 'psychology' in literature.
5. Psychoanalysis and literature. I. Title.
PR4757. L3A44   1987   823'.8   86-28842
ISBN 0-389-20712-8

Printed and bound in Great Britain by
L.R. Printing Services Ltd.,
Crawley, W. Sussex.
Phototypeset by Galleon Photosetting,
Ipswich, Suffolk.
MCMLXXXVII

Contents

Acknowledgements

Grateful acknowledgements are due to Dr. Rosemary Sumner, who patiently and critically steered my progress towards the writing of the original thesis for the Master of Philosophy degree of the University of London. Thanks are also due to tutors at the Polytechnic of North London; without their exceptional care I could not have reached that stage.

1

'Dream-country'

When Thomas Hardy 'disinterred the old' name for the tract of
country in which much of his fiction was to be set, he 'thought
to reserve' the name of Wessex 'to the horizons and landscapes
of a partly real, partly dream country' of his own imagining. To
his regret, 'the dream-country has, by degrees, solidified into a
utilitarian region which people can go to, take a house in, and
write to the papers from.'[1] Casterbridge, the focal town of this
fictional world, is 'a dream-place'. It is 'not a photograph in
words' depicting Dorchester—'not even the Dorchester as it
existed sixty years' before. He could not 'absolutely contradict'
the idea 'that "Casterbridge" is a sort of *essence* of the town as
it used to be, "a place more Dorchester than Dorchester
itself"', but even this he 'could not quite perceive'.[2] Hence, he
explicitly asks 'all good and idealistic readers to forget this'
'utilitarian region', and to consider the significance of the
'dream-country'.

It is strange that interest in the 'real' should have eclipsed
interest in the 'dream-country' of Hardy's fiction; for, even
while Hardy was writing fiction, the limits of 'realism' were
being vigorously discussed.[3] One modern critic in this tradition,
David Lodge, reminds us that a writer of fiction 'cannot avoid
selection and emphasis, and the aesthetic effects which follow'.[4]
He regards 'language' and not the 'real' world as 'the novelist's
medium': 'whatever he does, qua novelist, he does in and
through language'; language is 'used to create a certain texture
and tone which in themselves state and define' the 'reality' of
the fictional world they describe. He suggests that language is
thus 'forced, through conscious manipulation, into all those

larger meanings' which form the most meaningful 'reality' of the fictional world.[5]

Lodge writes here of 'conscious manipulation' of language. Later he concedes that the author's control of his language is incomplete; for 'words come to the writer already violated by other men, impressed with meanings derived from the world of common experience.'[6] Others, such as Frye and Fiedler,[7] have suggested, further, that unconscious, mythic meanings may be suggested, even when the writer is oblivious to them.[8] The writer is no less unique for this. The dimensions of the unconscious, mythic world are immense. Infinite perspectives upon it are possible. Hence, 'in reading each novel . . . we enter a unique linguistic universe.'[9] A writer's genius might be perceived in terms of his sensitivity to the unconscious and his skill in translating its symbols into that language which creates 'texture and tone', and hence creates the 'reality' of the writer's fictional world.

Hardy sees Art as a conscious 'disproportioning' of physical 'realities' in order 'to show more clearly *the features that matter* in those realities' (emphasis his).[10] Yet he also describes as 'Mystery'[11] his quest 'to intensify the expression of things . . . so that the heart and inner meaning is made vividly visible'.[12] He seeks to convey '*the deeper reality underlying the scenic*, the expression of what are sometimes called abstract imaginings' (emphasis his). He suggests that 'Nature is played out as a Beauty, but not as a Mystery.'[11] He shows how Nature's defects can become 'the basis of a hitherto unperceived beauty, irradiated by "the light that never was" on their surface, but [which] is *seen to be latent* in them *by the spiritual eye*' (emphasis his).[13] That 'spiritual eye' seeks to distinguish between 'the real' and 'the visible'.[14] It perceives 'the sorriness underlying the grandest things, and the grandeur underlying the sorriest things'.[15] It perceives 'the old material realities' as 'shadowy accessories' to 'the true realities of life, hitherto called abstractions'.[16] These 'abstractions' include spiritual insights. He searched fervently 'for God for fifty years'.[17] He studied 'all the researches of the Psychical Society'. He is so 'anxious' to believe that he 'would give ten years of his life . . . to see a ghost'.[18] Yet, though he has 'panted for response', 'none replies'.[19] Nor can he find conclusive proof that there is nothing there. Hence, an intense spiritual curiosity continues to inspire his Art, probing the unconscious to express through that Art more, perhaps, than he consciously knows.

Not only can Hardy's spiritual conflict inspire his Art: he can seek a kind of resolution of that conflict through his Art. In *The Dynasts*, Hardy dramatizes a conflict between the disbelieving mind (the Spirit of the Years), and the urging heart (the Spirit of the Pities). As Bailey suggests,

> in thought he had much in common with the Spirit of the Years, who is presented as a stoic philosopher informed by science, but in feeling he had more in common with the compassionate Spirit of the Pities. His feeling attracted him towards the supernatural and the psychic.[20]

The theme pervades his non-fictional writings. He strives to express his 'hope' and 'dream' of achieving 'an alliance between religion . . . and complete rationality . . . through the inter-fusing effect of poetry'.[21]

Perhaps it is because his spiritual searching directs his Art so acutely that he can trust his artistic instincts to decide which 'impressions' of the physical world are significant; for he claims that 'unadjusted impressions have their value.' Nonetheless, while 'humbly recording diverse readings of its phenomena as they are forced upon us by chance and change',[22] he also endeavours 'to give shape and coherence' to this 'series of seemings or personal impressions'[23] through his choice of language. He illustrates patterns of behaviour. He suggests provisional philosophies. At times, he even states his opinion explicitly. Nonetheless, some of his most powerful scenes, such as the evocation of Egdon Heath in *The Return of the Native*, may make us feel that his Art derives from a 'consciousness, infinitely far off, at the other end of a chain of phenomena, always striving to express itself, and always baffled and blundering, just as the spirits seem to be'.[24]

In effect, he is an 'irrationalist . . . on account of his incon-sistencies'. 'His impressions . . . frequently change.' He cannot claim 'permanent convictions' because his spiritual seeking has not yet ceased.[25] His perspective upon his dream-life endorses this: 'my dreams are not . . . coherent'; they 'generally end by my falling down the turret stairs of an old church owing to steps being missing'.[26] He is 'utterly bewildered to understand how the doctrine that, beyond the knowable, there must always be an unknown, can be displaced'.[27] In a sense, then, he does 'believe' 'in spectres, mysterious voices, intuitions, omens, dreams, haunted places, etc., etc.', seemingly seeking here signs and symbols of the unconscious through which aspects of the 'unknown' may be revealed.[27] He was concerned when 'forget-fulness . . . weakened the facts out of which the tale' of *The Withered Arm* 'grew': 'imperfect memories insensibly formalize the fresh originality of the living fact—from whose shape they slowly depart. . . .'[28] Geographical and circumstantial details are comparatively unimportant; but the vision of the incubus is crucial: it suggests, not only the source, but also the impact, of the evil and how it is deflected away from Rhoda's lover to create a chain of injustice. 'The stories are but dreams, and not records'; but even irrational traditional tales can offer insights into the human condition. These Hardy is anxious to preserve. (See Appendix 1.)

While these insights are preserved, he retains hope for improving the human condition: hence *The Dorsetshire Labourer*, his letter to Rider Haggard, and his recognition and appreciation of the work of William Barnes.[29] The nature and thoroughness of Hardy's research into the human condition is suggested by his approach to archaeology. Dewar regards Hardy as 'a most accurate observer' who 'was struck by the haphazard way in which numerous vestiges found in Durnovaria were treated' by contemporary archaeologists.[30] He notes the intensity of Hardy's drive 'towards piecing together and reconstructing these evidences into an unmutilated whole' in

> a worthy attempt to rehabilitate, on paper, the living Durnovaria of fourteen or fifteen hundred years ago—as it actually appeared to the eyes of the then Dorchester men and women, under the rays of the same morning and evening sun which rises and sets over it now.

Dewar comments,

> if archaeology could but dare to deal with the peoples of the past, rather than their sometimes too dry bricks and stones, we might gain for humanity something that was lost to archae-ology when Thomas Hardy decided to devote his genius to literature.[30]

Hardy does not abandon empirical research; he goes beyond it. He shares and admires Barnes's interest in 'investigations of Roman remains, theories on the origin of Stonehenge, and kindred archaeological matters'.[31] He also notices that evidence of the existence of primitive Man is closer and more widespread than was generally imagined.[32] He responds by wandering 'in nocturnal hours' when 'the episodes and incidents associated therewith come back more readily to the mind.'[33] He appreciates Stonehenge as 'a sacred possession', respects 'the associations of the place' and 'confesses to a liking for the state of dim conjecture in which we stand with regard to its history'.[34] He advocates protecting Stonehenge from weathering by planting a forest to replace the original primeval forest which may have surrounded it. Clearly he wishes to intensify its atmosphere. Only 'in dull, threatening weather', at dusk, 'on a day of heavy cloud' or 'on moonlight nights' can he 'get lights for the chapter' in *Tess* which epitomizes Man's innate cruelty as preserved in religious rites. Then Stonehenge seems to be 'the hub of olden Wessex', and a 'mysterious relic' which 'belongs to all England'.[34] It is as if this monument which defies objective scientific or historical analysis[35] may symbolize for Hardy, by that very defiance, the neglected significance of the irrational, unconscious world in our striving to comprehend the human condition.[36]

This is the kind of experience through which Hardy strove to educate his 'spiritual eye', rather than through the 'contradictions and futilities' of 'philosophic systems'.[37] Twenty-six years earlier he noted that 'he has read well who has learnt that there is more to read outside books than in them.'[38] He believes that 'Experience *un*teaches—(what one at first thinks to be the rule in events)'[39] and that 'theories' can only be relevant within a 'narrow region' of human 'experience'. Hence, he is 'content with tentativeness from day to day'.[40] Hardy's short story, *A Tryst at an Ancient Earthwork*[41] conveys in detail an experience like that in the 'dim light' at Stonehenge; here, however, an earthwork is visited by night. The opening chapters of *The Return of the Native* suggest a similar atmosphere. Whether or not the sun shines there, the reader regards the country through a strangely subdued light—as if the reader were regarding a 'dream', or kind of projection from an unconscious world.

11

Considering the extent of Hardy's awareness of his own artistic method, Virginia Woolf's oft-quoted comment upon Hardy's Art seems limited. That 'blur of consciousness, that halo of freshness and margin of the unexpressed which often produce the most profound sense of satisfaction' is indeed a hallmark of Hardy's Art. Maybe, like many writers, Hardy was not quite aware of what he did, 'as if his consciousness held more than he could produce'. However, he *was* aware of the deep spiritual search which inspired his Art. Moreover, he did not just *leave* 'it for his readers to make out his full meaning and to supplement it from their own experience'[42]; it was a vital characteristic of his Art that it should inspire them to do so. His despair at readers' failure to recognize the 'dream-country' of his fiction shows this; the creation of the 'dream-country' would have no purpose unless it inspired the awakening of the readers' unconscious through association with the 'experience' of his Art.

Hardy encourages readers to relate to the 'dream-country' in this way by suggesting a human dimension to that 'dream-country'; indeed, the human dimension is the vital quickening factor of the 'dream-country' without which it would have little meaning. Even the initial description of Egdon Heath in *The Return of the Native* encourages the reader to identify with its human characteristics: the chapter heading emphasizes its 'Face'; the second paragraph extends the image, giving the face a 'complexion'. A chain of response is thus initiated so that the reader focuses upon the human characteristics of that 'complexion' in the subsequent description—the power to 'sadden', the 'frowning', the causing of 'shaking and dread'. And yet, the distortion of straightforward personification is immediately apparent: Man cannot sadden 'noon'; not Man, but storms, are spoken of as 'frowning'; Man has no power to 'intensify the opacity of a moonless midnight to a cause of shaking and dread'. However, recalling the nature of Hardy's spiritual seeking, it seems reasonable to suggest that he is hinting at that God in whose image Man was made, who might do these things. By evoking that expectation and then failing to acknowledge that God, Hardy suggests the frightening vacuity of a godless universe. At the same time, through its seemingly human characteristics, Hardy makes us curious to discover what makes Egdon so awesome, so spiritually alive.

Egdon is symbolizing something indefinable, yet discernible, which has power to change the expected course of Nature—to add 'half an hour to evening' or to 'retard the dawn'. That same 'something' can 'intensify' natural darkness in a way which both inspires and simultaneously represents human fear. It can both transmit to Man a sense of storms to come and simultaneously represent that sense. Its power to 'sadden noon' is profoundly ambiguous: maybe noon is physically darker than it should be; maybe the drabness of the heath only makes it seem so; maybe the poverty of human life upon Egdon makes it seem so only through the filter of human sensibilities; maybe human suffering and human evils can influence the cosmos so far as to effect change as dramatic as the darkening of noon.[43] The range of possibilities is endless; the explanation is never complete. And yet, for all its vagueness, we are indeed convinced that this is 'precisely' the 'point' of its 'great and particular glory' when it could 'tell its true tale' (I, I, paragraph 3). The persistent personification throughout the chapter encourages further convictions—that the fictional Egdon symbolizes some nodal point of existence where Man and the cosmos are inextricably related; that the light of noonday consciousness is blighted, incomplete, and that something in Man is helping to cause, or to 'intensify', that blight. Thus, even before a human character enters the scene, the reader feels that he is exploring a human 'mystery'.

Thus, the 'human' dimension of Egdon seems to represent Man's archetypal nature. Egdon seems to be 'a place perfectly accordant with' that nature—'neither ghastly, hateful, nor ugly: neither commonplace, unmeaning, nor tame; but like Man, slighted and enduring; and withal singularly colossal and mysterious in its swarthy monotony'. And yet Egdon suggests, too, a single man in that, 'as with some persons who have long lived apart, solitude seemed to look out of its countenance' (I, I, paragraph 8) and in that it has 'a lonely face, suggesting tragical possibilities' (same paragraph). For it is through an individual consciousness that Man's archetypal nature is explored. A writer of fiction can communicate to his readers no more of his spiritual adventure than images which tap and awaken his readers' unconscious in complex, ambiguous ways; Hardy's ability to communicate at this level, to awaken the reader so successfully, is remarkable.

The first character to tread Egdon is described in detail (I, II, paragraph 1). Later he will develop into the character of Eustacia's grandfather. However, he is to be far from the central character of the book, characterized more by his failure to act positively than by any motive force in the novel. Hence, as the novel develops, we are left musing as to why he is introduced first of all the human characters, and why Hardy imprints his appearance so vividly upon our minds. By contrast, Venn and Thomasin crucially affect the action of the novel and yet are introduced as mere passers-by along the 'path of' the 'old man' across Egdon. Indeed, Thomasin is invisible, asleep, and dreaming. Eustacia, the most dynamic character of all, is not introduced until later in the chapter, and then merely as a speck in the scene which meets the reddleman's eye, while the other creators of confusion—Mrs. Yeobright, Wildeve and Clym— are not introduced until after the heath-folk.

It is generally accepted that this is Hardy's characteristic way of creating the human as well as the natural environment; he moves from the panoramic to the close-up, like a precursor of modern film technique. However, considering the perspective from which Hardy has inspired us to respond to Egdon, a further explanation is possible: the 'old man' arises from Egdon in the same way as Jung describes such a figure arising from dreams—a figure who 'symbolizes the spiritual factor'.[44]

Jung refers to this 'old man' as 'wise' but immediately qualifies this label, warning of its possible moral ambiguity. Similarly, Eustacia's grandfather is a pleasant old man of no ill-repute. He is in the background at this and other times of trouble—Eustacia's later conflict over Clym and Wildeve, the missed letter, and her final departure to her death. His contrasting, too-passive rôle recalls Hardy's criticism that, 'whatever may be the inherent good or evil of life . . . men make it much worse than it need be.'[45] A servant boy recognizes the destructive potential of Eustacia's state of mind and takes it upon himself to hide her grandfather's pistols; the grandfather does not. Yet her inner forces are clearly potentially destructive. Her story demonstrates this. They destroy her, they destroy others, and they bring out the worst in heathfolk such as Susan Nunsuch. Thus, the 'old man' seems to epitomize Man's archetypal failure to recognize this destructive potential, and hence his failure to take active steps to restrain it.

When Eustacia first appears as a speck in Venn's view she is already involved in that web of destructive activity, though we do not know it. Consciousness of this evolves only gradually. That speck appears to develop, according to 'first instinct', into 'one of the Celts who built the barrow'—now dead beneath it—'a sort of last man among them, musing for a moment before dropping into eternal night with the rest of his race'. Next she is seen as, not dead, nor extinct, but as inanimate—a 'form . . . motionless as the hill beneath'. (Perhaps there is a hint that she emanates from it.) Next she appears as human, but as subordinate to the scene in which she is set: 'Above the plain rose the hill, above the hill rose the barrow'; only at the last does her 'figure' appear. Nonetheless, that figure is important. It provides 'a perfect, delicate, and *necessary* finish . . . to the dark pile of hills'. It 'seemed to be the only obvious justification of their outline. Without it, there was the dome without the lantern; with it the architectural demands of the mass were satisfied.' The result is a 'scene . . . strangely homogeneous, in that the vale, the upland, the barrow, and the figure above it amounted only to unity'. Not until Chapter VI, after we have become acquainted with the novel's entire Wessex cast, are we introduced to Eustacia as a character. Until then she is but a remote 'figure'—not even recognizably female. Yet, not only does she complete the 'unity' of the Egdon scene; she is its 'focal point'.

Thus, Hardy withholds our interest in her as a character until we have developed an awareness of her as like 'the motif of the unknown woman . . . "the anima"— . . . a personification of the animated atmosphere'.[46] The more we are aware of this perspective, the deeper will be our interest in her, as a character, when she does appear; for we will balance her destructive behaviour against a sense of her as a puppet manipulated by destructive forces within herself which she does not understand. Those forces are at the root of much of the 'Trouble' with which 'Humanity' generally goes 'Hand in Hand'. If we perceive this, how much deeper will be our experience of her own deepening awareness that she is other than she would wish to be, and how much deeper our sensitivity to her final anguish upon the heath.

15

Thomas Hardy: The 'Dream-country' of his Fiction

While Eustacia seems to be 'a personification of' Egdon's 'animated psychic atmosphere',[46] that early personification of Egdon seems to be a preparation for our perception of this human drama. Of dreams, Jung suggested that such a 'personification always indicates an autonomous activity of the unconscious. If some personal figure appears we may be sure that the unconscious is beginning to grow active.'[46] Similarly, as Egdon develops enigmatic human characteristics, as the 'old man' and Eustacia appear, perhaps we are witnessing Egdon as it might appear in a dream—a dream which inspires a vision of the unconscious striving to become conscious, in order to resolve the persistent archetypal problems of humankind. The beginning of the novel suggests but the beginning of such a perception. By the time of Eustacia's final anguish we have become intensely involved: the dream has become a part of ourselves. Then, in the 'storm' and 'wind', Egdon becomes for us 'the home of strange phantoms'; it is

> found to be the hitherto unrecognized original of those wild regions of obscurity which are vaguely felt to be compassing us about in midnight dreams of flight and disaster, and are never thought of after the dream till revived by scenes like this. (*RN*, I, I, p. 13)

The affinities with Jung are remarkable enough considering that Hardy was writing half a century before Jung. More interesting still are the affinities between Hardy's 'dream-country' and other theories regarding the nature of dreams, both before and since. In this I see further testimony to the sincerity of his spiritual search, the acuity of his 'spiritual eye', and the accuracy with which he communicates consequent 'seemings' through his Art.

For example, Hardy ascribes to Tess a 'fancy' that her soul may travel outside her body while alive (III, XVIII, p. 158). The idea echoes 'the fantastical' theory of dreams. Evans suggests that this

> has declined somewhat in recent years (it is probably the oldest of the theories), but it is still very widely held, even if in a pseudosophisticated form. This theory is really a great set of subtheories, all more or less plausible according to one's upbringing and inclination; but, at the root, all are manifestations

16

of a single theme: during sleep, the soul or spirit is free to leave the body, and dreams are the soul's adventures during its free roaming.[47]

The idea invites comparison with the spiritual 'adventures' which educated Hardy's 'spiritual eye' and inspired the creation of the fictional Egdon.

Evans testifies to the ancient importance of dream language, from the beginning of written history, to a variety of cultures.[48] He relates this interest to evidence that the physical world was perceived as 'mortal and transient'—the spiritual world as 'perpetual—in the most important sense the *real* world'.[49] For centuries, the Church has been wary about taking dreams seriously. However, Evans suggests that it was not until the nineteenth century that Church and Science firmly and finally united in ridiculing the significance of dreams.[49] Hardy lived through this time. He appears to uphold contemporary ideas. Yet his spiritual conflict suggests that too much is being suppressed. Hardy is not alone in this. The idea of the 'unconscious mind' was

> floating around in nineteenth-century literature decades before [Freud] began to work with it. The poet Wordsworth seems to have been the first to use the word in the English language around 1800, and the German equivalent, meaning roughly 'unconscious', was commonly used in philosophy and in the early psychological literature.[50]

Thus, even scientists could not dismiss the 'dream' world for long; rather, the new psychological sciences were to arise in an attempt to redefine it in scientific terms. Hence the affinities between Hardy and Jung (and Freud).

The affinities between Hardy's 'dream-country' and Evans' modern dream theory are more remarkable. In this age it is natural enough for Evans to describe the workings of the 'dream' world in terms of 'The Computer Theory'. He notes 'major themes revisited by the collective unconscious'. He suggests that we 'regard them as vital programs to which all human beings feel the need—unconsciously—to return'.[51] He concludes that

> all [the] most commonly experienced dreams elicited from my surveys are indeed linked to fundamental drives, needs,

aspirations, fears and anxieties. The main programs are re-inspected more regularly than sub-programs because they are literally central to the business of being human. . . . Dreaming, then, is a reminder—or perhaps reaffirmation—of what it is to be human.[51]

If this is so, perhaps it shows why Hardy felt it necessary to create a 'dream-country' in order to express the contemporary crisis in thinking about the nature of Man and his relationship with the Universe. Nor is it surprising if, in so doing, he expresses important archetypal themes with particular relevance to contemporary issues.

Thus, even primitive archetypal perspectives upon the dream world may illuminate the process by which Hardy creates his 'dream-country'. When Hardy initiated us into awareness of Egdon's 'true tale' (*RN*, I, I), the experience suggested a strange, yet highly meaningful, confusion between people and things. What Clodd saw, in superstitions, as a 'barbaric idea which confuses persons and things' struck Hardy as being 'common to the highest imaginative genius—that of the poet'.[52] Indeed, it is possible to see several parallels between a 'primitive' 'spiritual world view' and the art of Hardy's fiction.[53]

One parallel concerns modern ideas on the limitations of 'realism'. Long after Hardy, Rank was to argue that it is 'increasingly recognized . . . that primitive man was less realistically orientated than is modern man'; he 'projected his soul into his total reality and universe' so that 'dream and reality coincided completely'. Indeed, he saw 'the dream' as 'a higher reality'.[54] Such was 'the compulsion to bring reality into agreement with spiritual belief', Rank argues, that primitive man 'neutralized' contradictions 'by adjusting reality to suit the dream'.[55] We might consider this absurd. Yet, in conceding the limitations of 'realism', we recognize a similar 'correction'. We can even respect this 'higher reality' as being more important than the physical 'reality' which is 'adjusted . . . to suit the dream', as in Hardy's fictional representation of Egdon.

Another parallel concerns the inspiration and creation of symbols. The creator of literature selects and illuminates aspects of physical 'reality' to communicate his sense of a 'higher reality'. He is keenly aware of the limitations of language. He is keenly aware of the limited nature of the perceptions which he strives to convey through language. He needs symbols.

Symbols extend the senses beyond the grasp of reason; as Jung suggests, 'because there are innumerable things beyond the range of human understanding, we constantly use symbolic forms to represent concepts we cannot define or fully comprehend.'[56] According to Jaffé, 'the history of symbolism shows that everything can assume symbolic significance. . . . the whole cosmos is a potential symbol'; 'Man, with his symbol-making propensity, unconsciously transforms objects or forms into symbols (thereby endowing them with great psychological importance) and expresses them in both his religion and his . . . art.'[57]

To appreciate the scope and significance of this unconscious activity, we need to regard the unconscious as

> not [like the 'subconscious' of Freud] merely a glory-hole of repressed desires, but a world that is just as much a vital and real part of the life of an individual as the conscious 'cogitating' world of the ego, and infinitely wider and richer.

This 'unconscious' may be continually active, continually creating symbols, as a product of striving to make sense of life in terms of the other five more easily recognizable senses. Dreams are a means of communicating those symbols.[58] 'Through dream symbols', Jung suggests, it is possible to learn 'to understand again the forgotten language of the instincts'.[59] Maybe the symbol-creating function of literary art is rooted in an unconscious ability to share a 'primitive' 'spiritual world view' as perceived in dreams, although the modern mind is no longer consciously aware of it.

Support for this idea may be found in comparing the power and significance of specific symbols as they occur in literature with those suggested by the 'primitive' 'spiritual world view' of primitive religion and of dreams. A symbol, by its very nature, will never convey exactly the same meaning either on any two separate occasions or to any two separate people; yet some do appear to have come to have similar associations in different contexts. Then they tend to be recognized as 'archetypes'. They are aspects of what Evans would regard as 'major themes revisited by the collective unconscious'—'vital programs', 'central to the business of being human'.[51]

19

The symbol of the horse, for example, can have powerful significance in literature. Its power was especially recognized and illustrated by D. H. Lawrence, for example, in *The Rainbow* and *Women in Love*. However, perhaps because Hardy's use of the 'horse' symbol is less outspoken than Lawrence's, its significance seems to have escaped comment.

The 'Darling' of *The Woodlanders* offers a nexus of symbolic significance. Her existence in the novel assumes the nature of a symbolic horse in a dream; it closely parallels, in significance, the horse of which a client of Jung's dreamt, even though the contexts of the two horses are quite different.[60] Darling is a gift from Giles to Grace (XI), given in expectation of her hand in marriage, just before Giles's hopes fail on account of his fall in fortune. Giles has taken great 'care' that the horse should be suited to Grace: 'she has been used to carry a lady', is 'quiet', 'twenty-one, and very clever for her age' (XI, p. 88). Giles's name for the horse, and this description, increasingly associate the horse with Grace. Similarly, in the dream, the horse is identified with the 17-year-old girl dreamer.

By the time of Darling's next appearance, Fitzpiers has married Grace and has ungratefully taken advantage of her father's hospitality (a hospitality which Giles would have appreciated keenly had he married Grace). Now Fitzpiers 'constantly used' Darling, 'the animal having turned out a wonderful bargain in combining a perfect docility with an almost human intelligence' (XXVIII, p. 209). The associations with Grace are still clear, though increasingly complex in their implications. It is immediately clear that Darling is as much a 'bargain' as Grace. As the consequences of her father's attitude are brought to consciousness, we recall Grace's previous resentment at being regarded as a 'chattel' by her father. The perverse abuse of Grace is epitomized when Fitzpiers uses the horse to deceive Grace; he claims that he can 'take much shorter cuts on horseback' to visit patients, when 'he had, in fact, taken these riding exercises for about a week, only since Mrs. Charmond's absence; his universal practice hitherto having been to drive' (XXVIII, p. 209). The rides on the horse have, of course, been to visit Mrs. Charmond, despite her efforts to discourage emotional involvement by staying away from home. Graces senses that all is not well; but it is some time before she grows conscious of the full implications (when Mrs. Charmond confesses in the dark wood) (XXXIII, p. 251). Thus the horse-rides come to symbolize aspects of Grace's unconscious life, in terms of growth in sexual awareness regarding herself and others: like the 'dream' horse, Darling now 'represents the non-human psyche, the subhuman, animal side, the unconscious',[60] not only with respect to Grace, but also with respect to the complex 'Great Web' of sexual and emotional relationships within the world of *The Woodlanders*.[61]

With this widening of meaning grows an increasing awareness of Fitzpiers' character. He seems to regard himself as a sexual hero. However, he is a poor horseman. He could not pursue Mrs. Charmond if Darling did not have the 'qualities' which he so valued for this perverse reason. Thus, Darling is used as his 'beast of burden' (in both a moral and a physical sense)—a rôle 'closely related to the mother-archetype (witness the Valkyries that bear the dead to Valhalla, the Trojan horse, etc)'.[60] At the same time, the horse is, increasingly, a symbol of that wider complex web of sexual and emotional relationships in which Fitzpiers plays a dynamic and destructive part. As such, his riding of Darling has further symbolic implications: as Jung suggests,

> as an animal lower than man it represents the lower part of the body and the animal impulses that rise from there. The horse is dynamic and vehicular power: it carries one away like a surge of instinct. It is subject to panics like all instinctive creatures who lack higher consciousness.[60]

Fitzpiers' riding of Darling affects, even infects, the atmosphere of Little Hintock in a psychic as well as a sexual way. 'The unprecedented exhaustion of Darling', after a night of hard riding, 'was sufficient to develop a whole series of tales about equestrian witches and demons, the narration of which occupied a considerable time' (XXVIII. pp. 209–10). Still Darling's condition suggests the moral and psychic distress of which Grace is not conscious. It also suggests Fitzpiers' neglect and abuse of Grace. Later, Hardy emphasizes the double burden upon Grace of father and husband, as Melbury guides Darling

> through the copse where Winterborne had worked, and into the heavier soil where the oaks grew: thence towards Marshcombe

Bottom, intensely dark now with overgrowth, and popularly supposed to be haunted with spirits.

Here, as Melbury supports him (literally now), Fitzpiers unveils his secret hope that Grace may die from the illness that has been precipitated by his own behaviour. Then he would marry Mrs. Charmond (XXXV, p. 263). Thus, another dimension to Darling's symbolic significance has evolved. Fitzpiers' deceit seems to have precipitated a disturbance in the atmosphere. Hintock folk, like Mr. Melbury, do not normally take seriously the possibility of adultery. Hence, while they remain unconscious of the moral source of that disturbance, they recognize a vague impression of evil, of psychic disturbance, and try to translate it into consciousness through the form of supernatural tales. These supernatural tales through which the evil is expressed seem to incorporate symbols from a collective unconscious—symbols which recall the symbolic horse of the dream as interpreted by Jung, the horse which 'has to do with sorcery and magical spells—especially the black night-horses which herald death'.[60] Just as 'real' aspects of the physical world inspire the creation of Hardy's fictional 'dream-country', including the creation of Darling, similarly, the—to them—'real' horse, Darling, seems to inspire the so-called 'primitive' mind of the Hintock folk to create these symbols.

Thus Hardy uses their recourse to supernatural tales to suggest the extent to which Wessex folk have retained a valuable instinctive sense of danger. On the other hand, their limited comprehension of John South's obsession leads them to seek and carry out Fitzpiers' misguided and fatal advice. They recognize that South believes that the tree 'is exactly his own age, that it has got human sense, and sprouted up when he was born on purpose to rule him, and keep him as its slave'. They even recall that 'others have been like it afore in Hintock' (XIV, p. 107). Perhaps, if centuries of oppression and subsequent suppression had not eroded their confidence in their instincts, they would not merely notice these phenomena, but would respond to them more accurately.

Jung suggests that 'most of us have consigned to the unconscious all the fantastic psychic associations that every object or idea possesses.' He suggests that the primitive, on the other hand, is still aware of these psychic properties; he endows animals, plants or stones with powers that we find strange and unacceptable. . . . a tree may play a vital part in the life of a primitive, apparently possessing for him its own soul and voice, and the man concerned will feel that he shares its fate[62]

—for 'in the primitive's world things do not have the same sharp boundaries as they do in our "rational" societies.'[63] Like South, 'many primitives' even

assume that a man has a "bush soul" as well as his own, and that this bush soul is incarnate in a wild animal or a tree, with which the human individual has some kind of psychic identity.[64]

Moreover, 'if the bush soul is a tree, the tree is presumed to have something like parental authority over the individual concerned.'

'Parental' commands might be expected to be for South's own good and for the good of family and friends. If 'injury to the bush soul is interpreted as injury to the man',[65] it would be clear that hacking at the tree could not help South. Rather, Hardy makes us feel that they should perceive South's fear of the tree as a warning to act *against* the voice of temporal authority—to *change* the position regarding the lifeholds. It is therefore characteristic of Giles that he is the one who cuts down the tree when he has power to change the leases and has most to lose from their termination. It is also characteristic of him that, while doing so, he fails to act positively to avoid losing Grace and the opportunities for life and fecundity which she represents. Instead, he chooses the remain in that 'Niflheim fogland'—that mythic representation of the fate of men like Giles who die of sickness (or old age) rather than in the fight for survival (XIII, p. 100).[66] That myth expresses our unconscious recognition that such a man is indeed likely to suffer the kind of death Hardy has him suffer. In other words, when 'the whole wood seemed to be a house of death' (XLIII, p. 336) at his demise, the 'dream-country' environment is reflecting the eventual bringing to consciousness, in symbolic form, of this earlier, unconscious recognition.

Thus may the 'dream-country' of Hardy's fiction evoke perceptions which seem to parallel Jungian ideas of a 'primitive' 'spiritual world view'. Thereby, Hardy suggests the tragic deterioration of the Wessex villagers' competence in interpreting their instincts. Fitzpiers' studies of 'nervous illness' do not redress the balance. Rather, they seem ineffectual, if not evil.

All this implies a third important parallel between the 'primitive' 'spiritual world view' and Hardy's fictional art: that between the mythological roots of literature and the symbols and archetypes expressed by the unconscious in dreams. Here, it is possible to regard Hardy's fictional world as if there were a 'primitive' mind 'telling of a dream as though it were an actual event experienced in the past by one's forebears, or in the present by one's contemporaries'. Rank suggests that, originally,

> out of such stories grew myths, fairy tales, and historical fables, which not only worked over the same spiritual motifs as the dream, but corresponded to obviously dreamed events or to accounts of dreams as altered by subsequent action.

Rank then shows how it is possible to trace 'their development into heroic myths'.[67] He exemplifies the North American Indians, whose 'dreams comprised their sole source of mythology and prevailed in many of their narratives'.[68] The relationship between myth and literature is now well recognized; not so this relationship between dream and myth.

Jung suggests that 'so far as the collective unconscious contents are concerned, we are dealing with archaic or . . . primordial types, that is, with universal images that have existed since the remotest times'[69]; it seems that similar images are evolved in creating the 'dream-country' of Hardy's fiction. For example, the 'tree' which proved an important symbol in *The Woodlanders* might be regarded as relating to the 'ceras mundi' myth; for so many branches are generated from it in terms of the far-reaching consequences of South's death that the tree might be regarded as the root of the action of the rest of the novel. Similarly, the 'fire' image of *The Return of the Native* (I, III, p. 23), in a section entitled *The Custom of the Country*, is not only an ancient tradition shared by many past religions. It is also 'the instinctive and resistant act of man when, at the winter's ingress, the curfew is sounded throughout Nature' indicating 'a spontaneous Promethean rebelliousness against the fact that this recurrent season shall bring foul times, cold darkness, misery and death. . .'. It is also a warning of the archetypal human struggle we are to expect the novel to unveil when Eustacia's fire tempts Wildeve to start the wheel of destructive consequences.

The temptation-scene itself is another of those 'universal images'. It is met again in the second chapter of *The Woodlanders* where Marty's temptation foreshadows the later temptation of Suke, Grace, and Felice, by Fitzpiers. Two golden sovereigns tempt Marty, like 'a pair of jaundiced eyes on the watch for an opportunity' (III, p. 18). The scene seems to anticipate the money questions which are later to pervert the judgement of those characters who have more than enough—such as Felice, Fitzpiers, Melbury, and Grace. As a result, those characters cause suffering to themselves; moreover, they cause suffering to those who, consequently, lose even the little that they had (Giles and Marty). Thus Hardy uses the 'temptation' myth to question the materialistic value-systems of the times.

He also uses it to evoke an archetypal awareness that the 'spiritual' value-system inverts this destructive, materialistic value-system. Those two sovereigns are not, themselves, Marty's tempters. However, they 'suggest' 'two jaundiced eyes' because the image of their ower has become fused with the objects with which he tempts Marty; and we are struck by the truth of her accusation that he '[goes] on like the Devil to Doctor Faustus' (II, p. 15). Thus Hardy uses recognizable religious myths to draw attention to this universal image of the temptation myth. When we hear of the evil purposes to which Mrs. Charmond is likely to put Marty's hair, when we hear the tempter try to utilize Marty's fear of Mrs. Charmond's power, when we recall that we have already been warned of the 'very clever and learned young doctor' who lives nearby 'not because there's anybody for'n to cure there, but because they say he's in league with the devil' (I, p. 10), instincts are aroused, warning us that this Mephistophelian strain is likely to be developed with destructive consequences as the novel proceeds.

As soon as Marty cuts her hair she is struck by a deeper consciousness of the seriousness of the act. As in a dream, the ancestral memory seems to delve deeper, unveiling the Norse precursor of the medieval Christian Mephistophelian myth— 'Loke the Malicious' (III, p. 23). Thus Hardy suggests her striving to comprehend the significance of what she has done.[70]

Her subsequent sleepless night and confrontation with Giles in the early morning suggest her sense that her present predicament is worse than before. Through thus recalling the depth and universality of the Mephistophelian character, Hardy emphasizes its 'reality' and its danger. Man has an instinctive fear of delving into the unknown, whether it be the unknown of the unconscious or the unknown of the prehistory. There is something frightening about relating Marty's experience back to a dead, almost-forgotten religion of 'Teutonic forefathers' now extinct (III, p. 18); it seems to suggest that she may share their fate of oblivion and extinction.

The more the relevant Teutonic myths are unveiled, the more justifiable this kind of reaction seems. Loki was 'intimately connected with the infernal world . . . reminiscent of Mephistopheles. . . . Authors of poems about him . . . connected him with the Devil, particularly as presented in the medieval Christian tradition.'[71] Although he 'was intimate with the great gods, who came to him for advice . . . he often rounded upon his masters'.[72] Yet, despite all the evidence of his 'malignity'[71]— 'his name [appearing] more often than any other' in Norse mythology[73]—the gods, like Man, never learned from these warning myths not to trust him. Nor were 'the goddesses . . . safe from his malice and deceit, as several stories show',[71] among them that of Marty's 'own ancestral goddess' (III, p. 23), Sif, who was but one of many whom Loki boasted of having seduced.[74]

In *The Woodlanders*, however, a significant fusing of the seduction and the 'rape of the locks' (III, p. 23) is suggested; instead of Loki himself, on one occasion, seducing Sif, and on another occasion cutting off her hair as a senseless joke, here, Marty is seduced into inflicting the injury upon herself. This is only possible because Marty is cornered by poverty and insecurity. She has to support her dying father and herself. Like Giles, she too will become homeless (XIII, p. 95) when her father dies. She, too, will be thrown upon the mercy of Mrs. Charmond. Hence, her fears are justified, and her tempter utilizes them in order to force his will upon her. The tempter is even more calculated, callous, and terrifying than Loki in that he is able to tempt Marty into this act of self-injury. Yet this power is a distinctive thread in the novel; it seems to imply that both Giles and Marty are driven towards self-annihilation.

Hardy's narrative has evolved far from the original myth; yet the seduction remains associated with the 'rape' of the 'locks'. Mrs. Charmond's treatment of Marty (and Giles) is echoed in the common assumption that 'she had treated cavalierly' (XXI, p. 158) her neglected lover. Her reputation seems to express a general 'impression' that there is something false about her. Her false hair objectifies this. Marty seems to assume that, in making Fitzpiers conscious of the false hair, she is making him conscious of a false beauty. To some extent she is proved right; the knowledge does precipitate their final rupture. While pursuing Fitzpiers on account of that letter she is killed by that former lover. Thus, ultimately, Mrs. Charmond suffers from the ramifications of that destructive power with which she pressurized Marty (and Giles).

Mythic ramifications such as these seem to underlie the structure of this novel. They encourage a sense of how apparently 'lonely courses' may be 'part of the pattern in the great web of human doings then weaving in both hemispheres from the White Sea to Cape Horn' (III, p. 24). In 1886, while writing this novel, Hardy noted that 'the human race [was] to be shown as one great network or tissue which quivers in every part when one point is shaken, like a spider's web if touched.'[75] It seems likely that he was thinking of this novel, for, through it, we are indeed sensitized to recognizing how far-reaching the effects of a character's behaviour may be. Yet Fitzpiers' and Grace's inconsiderate behaviour, at the end, suggests that neither has experienced permanent character change; each has recognized partially, and then forgotten, the consequences of their respective forms of selfishness. Furthermore, just as those Norse gods never learnt to distrust Loki, Grace has not learnt to distrust Fitzpiers. Thus the significance of the Loki myth is perpetuated.

Through the reservations of the woodlanders, Hardy finally brings these perceptions to consciousness. Nonetheless, their perspectives are limited too. Through Creedle, Hardy suggests that Grace should have 'been faithful' to Giles. Yet none of them pays much heed to Marty, though she exemplifies faithfulness, and truly appreciates that Giles was 'a good man' who 'did good things' (XLVIII, p. 380). Thus, as the party passes

27

by church and graveyard, Hardy focuses, finally, upon the neglected Marty, attending Giles' grave. Thus he suggests an archetypal image of Man's failure to recognize and to foster such values. This is his final word in the novel. In these values, belittled still, he yet seems to wonder whether there may be hope for humankind.

The final words of the novel serve to re-emphasize that earlier awesome 'house of death' image of the woods, which seemed to evoke the myth of the weeping of all Creation at Balder's death.[76] Here, Hardy has Melbury contrast the nature of Giles's and Mrs. Charmond's deaths. Thus he reminds us of her rôle in that 'great web' of human behaviour which led, ultimately, to the death of this 'good man'. She seems to represent the long tradition of temporal authority which has influenced the shaping—or rather the cramping—of Giles's character, and hence has influenced his behaviour. The 'Niflheim fogland' which 'involved' Giles (XIII, p. 100) is also the place to which Balder was banished.

Moreover, Loki's responsibility for Balder's death bears comparison with Fitzpiers' part in that 'great web'. As Grace and her father move towards a final decision to reject Giles's suit, they walk through 'the fabled Jarnvid wood' (VII, p. 56) traditionally inhabited by Loki. Giles follows them. Too late, he finds that he has been, unwittingly, 'bidding against Melbury' (p. 59). In the next chapter, Grace is drawn towards Mrs. Charmond. She discusses Fitzpiers with her. Giles's party follows. Thereafter Mr. Melbury's mind is set against Giles's suit. Of course, Fitzpiers has, as yet, done nothing to influence that decision; but the mythic substructure seems to imply that he will—especially as Chapter VII begins with those 'kaleidoscopic dreams of a weird alchemist-surgeon, Grammer Oliver's skeleton, and the face of Giles Winterborne' (p. 55), which 'brought Grace Melbury to the morning of the' day of that walk in the Jarnvid-like wood. Thus, in using a form of the Loki myth to encourage sympathy for Giles, Hardy exposes deficiencies in the society to which Fitzpiers and Mrs. Charmond adhere.

It is possible, then, to perceive this 'great web' of apparently 'lonely courses' as a weaving together of the threads of archetypal myths into a new fabric. Jung was later to refer to this 'ability to reach a rich vein of such material and to translate it effectively into . . . literature' as 'one of the hallmarks of what is commonly called genius'. In recreating those myths so that they are peculiarly appropriate to his times, Hardy exemplifies, too, how 'completely new thoughts and creative ideas can also present themselves from the unconscious—thoughts and ideas that have never been conscious before.'[77] Marty's temptation and Giles's involvement with that 'Niflheim fogland' are archetypal problems; but at the same time Hardy emphasizes how social pressures encourage that tendency to make archetypal problems 'much worse than [they] need be'.[78] He shows Fitzpiers' archetypal seductive activities and Felice's vanity as especially dangerous when backed by temporal authority and social prestige. Grace fails to learn to distrust Fitzpiers, as the Norse gods failed to learn to distrust Loki; but the marriage laws encourage her to distort her judgement, just as, indirectly, they encourage Fitzpiers to persist in his destructive, Loki-like behaviour. Thus the 'seemings' evoked by Hardy's 'dream-country' are more than new tales upon archetypal themes; 'they represent' too his 'impressions of the age'[24] in which he lives. Thus they can evoke his criticisms of that age.

While using myth to draw attention to these destructive tendencies, Hardy also suggests a sense that renewal is possible—that things could be different. Marty's communion with Nature and her powers of encouraging the trees to grow, suggest an affinity with a fertility goddess; her physical under-development and social insignificance suggest the stunting of her powers: she seems doomed to alienation and subsequent extinction. Similarly, Sif is presumed to have been 'a fertility goddess whose importance had diminished by the time that this myth was recorded'.[79] Other references to Teutonic myths seem to confirm this association. As Marty opened the door of her house[80] 'the night in all its darkness met her flatly on the threshold, like the very brink of an absolute void, or the ante-mundane Ginnung-Gap believed in by her Teuton forefathers.' Of course, 'her eyes were fresh from the blaze, and here there was no street lamp or lantern to form a kindly transition between the inner glare and the outer dark' (III, pp. 18–19). Nonetheless, so alone is Marty in her time of temptation that she sees the world in terms of a despairing nihilism—as an 'absolute void'. Yet despair often precedes hope, and the 'Ginnung-Gap' is not the final, hopeless chaos it appears. It refers to a time ' "in the beginning [when] there was neither sand, nor sea, nor salt waves, nor the earth below, nor the sky above; there was a yawning gulf and nowhere did grass grow." '[81] It is 'antemundane'; it precedes Creation and the beginnings of life and fertility. Eventually, grass does grow, and, in consequence of the procreative activity of the god Ymir, human life and fertility begin.

Our initial response to Marty's experience of this 'Ginnung-Gap' is also reflected in Teutonic legend. Beyond that Ginnung-Gap, 'to the north, is a realm called Niflheim. It is' contrastingly cold—'packed with ice and covered with vast sweeps of snow'. Yet 'in the heart of that region lies the spring Hvergelnir . . . the source of eleven rivers'. At the beginning of Creation 'the rivers . . . streamed into the void' of the Ginnung-Gap.

> The yeasty venom in them thickened and congealed like slag and the rivers turned to ice. That venom also spat out drizzle—an unending dismal hagger that, as soon as it settled, turned into rime. So it went on until all the northern part of the Ginnung-Gap was heavy with layers of ice and hoar frost, a desolate place haunted by gusts and skuthers of wind.[82]

A reader aware of the Teutonic myths (as is Hardy) is not going to expect renewal to be easy. However, the significant factor is this: conscious knowledge of those myths does not change the nature of the reader's response to this scene. So skilfully does Hardy create atmosphere, it seems as if the briefest references to these myths, enshrouded in appropriate imagery, are sufficient to evoke unconscious ancestral memories of the myths.

To know these myths is to know that the 'first spring' and 'human life' are to evolve from that Ginnung-Gap eventually.[83] Rebirth is possible. Spring may follow winter. It is worth striving towards that possibility. Characters such as Oak, in *Far from the Madding Crowd*, perceive this. Here, however, the only clue Hardy offers to suggest that Marty's despair might precede rebirth is his use of that word 'ante-mundane'. Yet his placing of this passage so near to the beginning of the novel might suggest that it was still just possible for Man to redirect his strivings towards such a rebirth—that things could be different. At the same time, Hardy symbolizes the subsequent 'distinct manifestation of morning in the air' in terms of 'the bleared white visage of a sunless winter day' which 'emerged like a dead-born child'. The woodlanders' 'eyes stretched to [this] sky to forecast the weather for the day' (IV, p. 26). In this context, Hardy leads us to forecast that Marty's 'dead-born' hopes symbolize the unlikeliness of such a rebirth within the context of the novel.

Although rebirth is unlikely, Hardy continues to suggest that possibility. Marty's self-destructive act emphasizes how the pressures of life seem to have driven from Marty any potential sexual attractiveness. Marty needs the money offered for her hair; but the timing of her final decision to part with it suggests that she also intends that act to symbolize her despair at ever attracting Giles's love. Yet she has not despaired, nonetheless. She still desires him. She is to write a letter designed to divert Giles's interest away from Grace, towards her, by re-uniting Fitzpiers with Grace. Thus, Hardy seems to develop that original Sif-like image of Marty—to suggest Marty's hope that her powers of fertility might be renewable. He is developing, too, the idea that the Ginnung-Gap precedes rebirth, rather than, as it seemed at first, ultimate despair. Giles is 'involved' 'in that gloomy Niflheim or fogland' (XIII, p. 100) from which rivers flow with such ghastly effect into the Ginnung-Gap which involves Marty.[82] When Hardy suggests how Giles 'might have won' Grace, had he 'immediately come down from the tree' (XIII, p. 100), he shows how Giles's character and actions confirm that involvement. Hardy is also indicating, directly, one way in which Giles might have averted the destructive impetus of his life. Yet, through evoking Giles's unconscious affinity with Marty, Hardy also offers a vague sense of other constructive possibilities.

Mary Jacobus shows how Hardy's association of Giles with Balder, and the thwarting of seasonal cycles, suggests that the 'coming of Spring is not to be re-enacted' through him.[84] However, while there may be destructive 'irremediable' ills within Nature, the coming of Spring cannot be thwarted by them. By associating Giles with the disturbance in seasonal cycles, Hardy encourages us to consider carefully the distinction between 'irremediable' and 'remediable' ills. Through encouraging us to seek out areas of human responsibility, Hardy suggests areas where change is possible. Giles's own conflict with Mrs.

Charmond shows how he shares with Marty the debilitating effects of social pressures, even to the extent that both their homes are involved. However, only he has the opportunity, the responsibility, to avert their loss. He mishandles it. Giles's and Marty's shared communion with Nature and their power of encouraging the trees to grow suggests that Giles shares, too, Marty's image of possible fertility. However, Marty is the passive partner; she holds the saplings while Giles lays their roots so as to encourage growth. Unless Giles takes the initiative to redirect his life, Marty's quest is hopeless. And there is as little chance of Giles learning to love Marty as there is that Marty's initial despair may prove a preliminary to rebirth. And yet, the apparent contradiction between the possibility and the thwarting of rebirth persists. Eventually, even Grace grows conscious that

> Marty South alone, of all the women in Hintock and the world, had approximated to Winterborne's level of intelligent inter-course with Nature. In that respect she had formed his true complement in the other sex, had lived as his counterpart, had subjoined her thoughts to his as a corollary. (XLIV, p. 340)

Thus Hardy goes to great lengths to weave into the novel this sense of what might have been had Giles (in particular) realized his potential. He shows that Giles is unconscious of the extent to which he is allowing social pressures to condition what he is. Moreover, Giles's sense that existing marriage laws could not be superseded epitomizes his inability to perceive that things could be different. Through reference to Giles's unfulfilled potential Hardy accompanies social criticism with a sense that human nature retains the potential for change.

Marty's communion is with the potential Giles. Although his memory lives on, through her, the initial despairing nihilism seems to have proved the final reality; Marty seems to be going the way of her ancestral goddess. But that evocation of social criticism and of how things could be different, survives them. Even when those specific social questions are resolved, the underlying archetypal human problems will remain; literature seems to include a kind of history of how they are reshaped into new and perplexing forms in each generation. That correlation between the spirits of Marty and Giles lives on too. It illustrates the regenerative potential of humankind. Thus it is part of that history of human troubles. The two aspects seem to be inextricably interwoven in the fathomless unknown of the collective unconscious and the unknown of prehistory, symbolized in the chaos of the Ginnung-Gap.

The Ginnung-Gap of *The Woodlanders* has clear affinities with the Egdon Heath of *The Return of the Native*. It is as if, in striving to develop the potential of the 'dream-country' Egdon, Hardy has left Wessex behind altogether—as if the 'dream-country' Egdon was a springboard for this development. But this is not so. In *The Woodlanders*, as the title reminds us, Hardy focuses upon the relationship between the woods and their human occupants. From the tree which haunts South like a tree-soul to the time when the whole wood reflects Giles's death, this relationship is firmly in the foreground, despite the significant mythic background.

As Mary Jacobus suggests, 'the source of Fitzpiers' rootlessness' seems to be his ignorance of the relationship between the woodlanders and their environment.[85] Instead, he studies medicine in association with demonology. Thus Hardy seems to associate Fitzpiers with that choice of tree which led to the barring of the Tree of Life. As he and Felice represent temporal authority, it seems that the laws which prevent Giles and Marty from finding the Tree of Life are founded upon humankind's misguided attempts to define for itself the nature of good and evil.

From the perspectives of both sets of characters, Hardy encourages us to consider how far humankind is culpable for the almost hopeless state of this world, for 'the veil of depression (Schwermuth) which is spread over the whole of nature'.[86] Hardy implies that Fitzpiers learns little by focusing upon the human brain; but Hardy unveils a great deal as he focuses, instead, upon the human spirit, as symbolized in *The Woodlanders*, in ramifications of that archetypal 'ceras mundi' myth.

Hardy's concern that readers ignored 'dream-country' aspects of his fiction prompted a reconsideration of the limits of 'realism'. It became clear that literary art involves the creation of symbols, however far a writer aspires towards 'realism'. In this, it also appeared that the creation of literary art could be related to an unconscious ability to share a 'primitive' 'spiritual world view'. The mythological roots of literature seemed related to the process through which myths are re-enacted in dreams, and Hardy could be seen to have recreated archetypal myths into new forms in his fiction. These serve to criticize society, and to inspire the reader to change society—in order to renew life's constructive potential.

This kind of activity might be discerned in a range of literary art. An early precedent is the ancient heroic poetry of the Norse tradition. Here poets allude to countless myths and characters of traditional history with which they assume their audience to be conversant; in so doing, they create a new myth which illuminates contemporary problems through a new perspective on traditional history. For example, *Hamthismal* and *Atlakvitha* must have inspired an audience to recognize how violence can destroy an entire family, or race, or civilization. It must have inspired them to think how to avert the destructive impetus of their own times. It may affect us similarly.

Hardy's re-creation of archetypal myths seems inspired by his yearning to find solutions to the contemporary and archetypal trials of humankind. In this they relate to important structures in his fiction. Clym aspires to reform social laws and improve the quality of life of ordinary folk. Oak seems to strive to improve the quality of life with little reference to general social reform. On the other hand, Jude seems to aspire to change social laws, assuming that an improvement in the quality of life will follow. Hardy emphasizes the hopelessness of such a task, within the span of one generation; but Jude's efforts do inspire us to think about the need for, and to seek the means of, such change: they suggest the dawn of twentieth-century consciousness. I suggest that the efforts of such characters might be regarded as a kind of spiritual adventure, to which the reader may be attuned. In this sense, a further parallel between the creation of literary art and that unconscious ability to share a 'primitive' 'spiritual world view' might be that both can involve a kind of spiritual adventure or quest.

Sometimes, that spiritual adventure seems entirely negative. In *The Woodlanders*, Hardy dramatizes the stunting of intrinsically fertile human activity. 'The Unfulfilled Intention, which makes life what it is' epitomizes this; it was 'as obvious' in the woods

> as it could be among the depraved crowds of a city slum. The leaf was deformed, the curve was crippled, the taper was interrupted; the lichen ate the vigour of the stalk, and the ivy slowly strangled to death the promising sapling. (VII, p. 56)

In tracing the development of heroic myth from dream, Rank suggested that, 'like the fairytale hero, the strong-willed individual was not content with taking the dream passively, but had to act it out and to perish in his attempt at immortality.'[87] In this sense, Giles might be regarded as an anti-hero, who fails to recognize that need to act out the dream.[88]

Much in the 'dream-country' of Hardy's fiction confirms this impression of overwhelming powers stunting the possibilities for spiritual growth—for learning from, for interpreting constructively, instinctive knowledge which arises from the unconscious. If a pessimistic spirit seems to dominate his fiction, perhaps it is partly because Hardy feels honour-bound to represent thus the spiritual state of the modern world. Yet he does also offer hints that renewal is possible.

Jung suggests that 'if some personal figure appears' within a dream, 'we may be sure that the unconscious is beginning to grow active'[46]; a similar process was observed in the early chapters of *The Return of the Native*: in this sense, the appearance of a personal figure within Hardy's fictional 'dream-country' may represent the beginning of such a spiritual adventure. That is not to say that characters will necessarily be learning from their own dreams; the characters are part of the dream and live in the 'dream-country'. They learn about life from what are, to them, the physical 'realities' of that 'dream-country'. In this they resemble the so-called 'primitive' who strives to translate, not only symbols which appear in dreams, but also their conscious experience of 'symbolic thoughts and feelings, symbolic acts and situations'.[89]

We recognize—if only unconsciously—that there are 'symbolic thoughts, feelings, . . . acts and situations' in our everyday lives. Thus, we can believe in and identify with the similar experiences of characters within the 'dream-country' of Hardy's fiction. Consequently, as we follow and respond to the spiritual adventures of the characters, we may recognize, beyond the geographical Wessex, the 'higher reality' of the 'dream-country'. Thus, we may share an awareness of Egdon as our own 'home of strange phantoms'—as that

> hitherto unrecognized original of those wild regions of obscurity which are vaguely felt to be compassing us about in midnight dreams of flight and disaster, and are never thought of after the dream till revived by scenes like this. (*RN*, I, I, p. 13)[90]

NOTES

1. Thomas Hardy's Preface to the New Wessex edition of *Far from the Madding Crowd* (1912).
2. F. E. Hardy, *The Life of Thomas Hardy* (Macmillan, 1975 edn.), Ch. XXX, p. 351.
3. See, for example, Miriam Allott, *Novelists on the Novel* (1959; Routledge Paperback edn., 1965), especially pp. 27–30; 40–53; 68–105; 130–33; 158; 174–75; 215; 216; 244–45.
4. David Lodge, *The Language of Fiction* (Routledge & Kegan Paul, 1966), p. 42.
5. Ibid., Preface, p. ix.
6. Ibid., p. 47.
7. See N. Frye, 'Credo', *Kenyon Review XIII* (Winter 1951), and L. A. Fiedler, 'Archetype & Signature', in J. L. Calderwood and H. E. Tolliver's *Perspectives on Poetry* (Oxford University Press, 1968).
8. See also W. K. Wimsatt, *The Verbal Icon*, section on 'The Intentional Fallacy' (University of Kentucky Press, 1982).
9. Lodge, p. 69.
10. F. E. Hardy, p. 229.
11. Ibid., p. 185.
12. Ibid., p. 177.
13. Ibid., p. 114.
14. Ibid., p. 186.
15. Ibid., p. 171.
16. Ibid., p. 177.
17. Ibid., p. 224.
18. William Archer, 'Real Conversations', *The Critic* XXXVIII (April 1901), 309–18, particularly 313–14.
19. T. Hardy, *The Complete Poems* (Macmillan, 1979), p. 50. 'A Sign Seeker'.
20. J. O. Bailey, *Thomas Hardy and the Cosmic Mind* (University of Carolina Press, 1956), Ch. 1, p. 2.
21. T. Hardy, *The Complete Poems*, 'Apology For Late Lyrics and Earlier', pp. 561–62.

22. Ibid., p. 84, Preface to 'Poems of the Past and Present', August 1901.
23. Preface to first edn., *Jude the Obscure* (August 1895; Macmillan paperback edn., 1978), p. 23. See too F. E. Hardy, Ch. XXXIII, p. 375. See, too, I. Gregor, *The Great Web: The Form of Hardy's Major Fiction* (Faber, 1974), p. 33.
24. Archer, p. 316, quoting T. Hardy.
25. F. E. Hardy, Ch. XVII, p. 209. See too Ch. VI, p. 83: Hardy writes similarly 21 years previously.
26. M. Millgate, *Thomas Hardy: A Biography* (Oxford University Press, 1982) Ch. 27, p. 551, footnote.
27. F. E. Hardy, Ch. XXXIII, p. 369.
28. Preface to *Wessex Tales*.
29. 'The Dorsetshire Labourer', *Longman's Magazine* (July 1883), 252–69. Also in *Thomas Hardy's Personal Writings*, ed. Harold Orel (Macmillan, 1967), p. 174ff. Hardy illustrates why it would have been unjust to expect farmworkers 'to remain stagnant and old-fashioned for the pleasure of romantic spectators'. Yet Hardy sees the means of change as unnecessarily destructive. He decries the 'less intimate and kindly relation with the land he tills than existed before enlightenment enabled him to rise above the condition of a serf who lived and died on a particular plot, like a tree. . . .' He regrets the fact that they have 'lost touch with their environment, and that sense of long local participancy which is one of the pleasures of old age. . . .'
    Letter to Mr. (afterwards Sir) Rider Haggard, March 1902, F. E. Hardy, Ch. XXVI, p. 312. Again, Hardy decries past hardships and approves improved conditions and wages. Yet he abhors the consequent loss of 'village tradition—a vast mass of unwritten folk lore, local chronicle, local topography, and nomenclature [which] is absolutely sinking, has nearly sunk, into eternal oblivion. . . . there being no continuity of environment in their lives there is no continuity of information. . . . for example, if you ask one of the workfolk . . . the names of surrounding hills, streams; the character and circumstances of people buried in particular graves; at what spots parish personages lie interred; questions on local fairies, ghosts, herbs, etc, they can give no answer: yet I can recollect the time when the places of burial even of the poor and tombless were all remembered, and the history of the parish and squire's family for 150 years back known. . . .'
    T. Hardy, 'The Rev. William Barnes B.D.', *Athenaeum* (16 October 1886), 501–2. Reprinted in *Thomas Hardy's Personal Writings*, p. 101ff. Barnes grew up and wrote of a similar rural area to that of Hardy's Wessex. Hardy shows great interest in and respect for Barnes' achievements. '. . . Born . . . 1800 . . . a complete repertory of forgotten manners, words, and sentiments, . . . turned to such good use in his writings on ancient British and Anglo-Saxon speech, customs and folklore. . . .'
30. H. S. L. Dewar, F.R.A.I., Introduction to Hardy's paper on 'Some Roman-British Relics found at Max Gate, Dorchester', published in *Dorset Monographs*, No. 6, by The Dorset Natural History and Archaeological Society (Dorchester, 1966). Paper originally read by Hardy at the 1884 Dorchester Meeting and subsequently appeared in the *Proceedings of*

the Dorset Natural History and Antiquarian Field Club, Vol. XI, pp. 78–81 (Dorchester, 1890).

31. As 29, iii, *Athenaeum*, 502. *Thomas Hardy's Personal Writings*, p. 102.
32. T. Hardy, 'Maumbury Ring', *The Times*, 9 October 1908, 11. Reprinted in *Thomas Hardy's Personal Writings*, p. 226–27.
33. Ibid., p. 227.
34. Ibid., p. 196ff. *Shall Stonehenge Go?*, interview, *Daily Chronicle*, 24 August 1899, 3.
35. See, for example, Francis Hitching, *Earth Magic* (Picador, Pan Books, 1978); R. J. C. Atkinson, *Stonehenge* (Pelican, 1960); G. S. Hawkins, *Stonehenge Decoded* (Souvenir Press, 1966); and G. S. Hawkins, *Beyond Stonehenge* (Hutchinson, 1973).
36. F. E. Hardy, Ch. XXVI, p. 309. 'My own interest lies largely in non-rationalistic subjects, since non-rationality seems, so far as I can perceive, to be the principle of the Universe. By which I do not mean foolishness, but rather a principle for which there is no exact name, lying at the indifference point between rationality and irrationality.'
37. F. E. Hardy, Ch. XXVI, p. 310.
38. Ibid., Ch. VII, p. 107.
39. Ibid., Ch. XIV, p. 176.
40. Ibid., Ch. XII, p. 155.
41. In *A Changed Man and Other Tales*, pp. 169–84.
42. *Virginia Woolf: Collected Essays* (Hogarth Press, 1966), Vol. I, p. 258.
43. This invites comparison with the noon-day eclipse at the Crucifixion.
44. C. G. Jung, *Archetypes of the Collective Unconscious*, Collected Works, Vol. 9. i, Bollingen Series XX, translated by R. F. C. Hull, 2nd edn. (Princeton University Press, 1968), pp. 215–16.
45. F. E. Hardy, Ch. XVIII, p. 230.
46. C. G. Jung, 'Individual Dream Symbolism in Relation to Alchemy', *Dreams* (Princeton/Bollingen Paperbacks, 1974), Part IV, p. 128.
47. C. Evans, 'Dreams—a functional theory', *Electronics and Power* (August 1968), reprinted from *Trans-Action* (Washington University, St. Louis, 1967), 323–25. This extract 323.
48. C. Evans, *Landscapes of the Night* (Gollancz, 1983), ed. and completed by Peter Evans, Ch. 5.
49. Ibid., Ch. 6, p. 52.
50. Ibid., Ch. 8, p. 86.
51. Ibid., Ch. 18, p. 192.
52. F. E. Hardy, Ch. XVIII, p. 230.
53. Otto Rank, *Psychology and the Soul*, translated from the German *Seelenglaube und Psychologie* by W. D. Turner, Perpetua edn. (A. S. Barnes, New York, 1961), pp. 95; 98.
54. Ibid., p. 12.
55. Ibid., p. 99.
56. C. G. Jung, *Man and his Symbols* (Picador, Pan Books, 1980), Part I: 'Approaching the Unconscious', p. 4.
57. Aniela Jaffé, 'Symbolism in the Visual Arts', Part IV of *Man and his Symbols*, p. 257. This section is written with specific reference to 'visual

art', but readers may agree that the 'art' of literature is, similarly, an agent of Man's 'symbol-making propensity'.

58. C. G. Jung, *Man and his Symbols*, p. viii.
59. Ibid., p. 37.
60. C. G. Jung, *Dreams*, Part III: 'The Practical Use of Dream Analysis', translated by R. F. C. Hull. This dream is on p. 106; Jung's comment p. 107. (Also in Collected Works, Vol. 16, Bollingen Series XX.) Jung suggests here that ' "Horse" is an archetype that is widely current in mythology and folklore. As an animal it represents the non-human psyche, the subhuman, animal side, the unconscious. That is why horses in folklore sometimes see visions, hear voices, and speak. . . .'
61. Ibid. Commenting on the 'mother' archetype which parallels the 'horse' archetype, Jung comments: 'This is no individual acquisition of a seventeen-year-old girl; it is a collective inheritance, alive and recorded in language, inherited along with the structure of the psyche and therefore to be found at all times and among all peoples.'
62. C. G. Jung, *Man and his Symbols*, Part I, p. 30.
63. Ibid., p. 31.
64. Ibid., p. 6.
65. Ibid., p. 7.
66. Larousse, *World Mythology*, ed. Pierre Grimal (Hamlyn, 1974), pp. 364–65.
67. Otto Rank, 'Dream And Reality', p. 99.
68. Ibid., p. 100.
69. C. G. Jung, *Archetypes of the Collective Unconscious*, pp. 4–5.
70. C. Evans, *Landscapes of the Night*, Part IV: 'The Quest for Inner Space', Ch. 20, on 'the ability to use dreams to solve problems', p. 229.
71. Larousse, p. 379.
72. Ibid., p. 373.
73. Ibid., p. 378.
74. Kevin Crossley-Holland, *The Norse Myths* (Andre Deutsch, 1980), p. 198. See also, Larousse, p. 378.
75. F. E. Hardy, Ch. XIV, p. 177.
76. See Dale Kramer (ed.), *Critical Approaches to the Fiction of Thomas Hardy* (Macmillan, 1979), No. 7, Mary Jacobus, 'Tree and Machine: *The Woodlanders*', pp. 118–19. Or see Matthew Arnold's poem, *Balder Dead* (1855).
77. C. G. Jung, *Man and his Symbols*, p. 25.
78. Archer, pp. 309–18.
79. Crossley-Holland, p. 198.
80. The house may suggest Marty herself in this context. Compare Jung's dream where he himself was symbolized by his home. See *Man and his Symbols*, pp. 42–4.
81. Larousse, p. 362.
82. Crossley-Holland, p. 3.
83. Larousse, p. 362. Note that the healing 'rivers come from the south'. Cf. Marty's surname.
84. Dale Kramer (ed.), p. 119 and pp. 122–23.
85. Ibid., p. 132.

86. Ibid., pp. 130–31. Jacobus refers to James Sully's *Pessimism* (1877), 'which Hardy seems to have read while working on this novel in 1886'.
87. Otto Rank, p. 101.
88. The 'Niflheim' which 'involves' Giles is also a 'land of the dead', the 'furthest region of the goddess Hel', where men who died of old age or sickness were presumed to go, as opposed to the Valhalla—the reward of heroes who died fighting. See Larousse, pp. 364–65.
89. C. G. Jung, *Man and his Symbols*, p. 41, but coincidences can be taken too seriously..
90. Perhaps 'the only adventure that is still worthwhile for modern man lies in the inner realm of the unconscious psyche', M. L. Von Franz, 'The Process of Individuation', from *Man and his Symbols*, p. 228.

2
Man and Environment

Through a kind of 'spiritual adventure' as defined towards the end of Chapter 1, Hardy uses the 'dream-country' to suggest the nature and development of individual characters. Insofar as these characters illuminate the creative process, it is useful to isolate this aspect of the novels. This approach also prepares the reader to consider how Hardy uses the 'dream-country' to suggest relationships between Man and Woman (Chapter 3) and between Man and Society (Chapter 4).

1. Gabriel Oak

Through the 'dream-country' perspective of *The Return of the Native* and *The Woodlanders* Hardy suggests a kind of mythic vision of archetypal problems. He emphasizes those which are exacerbated by contemporary social ills. He hints at areas where those ills might be eased. Past, present and future are thus fused as in the manner of a dream.

Yet in his earlier novel, *Far from the Madding Crowd*, a reference to Oak as Thor is merely a passing metaphor (XV, p. 114), and social criticism is less pertinent. Ultimately, Oak overcomes the social factors which affect Bathsheba's attitude and exacerbate Oak's struggle. It is tempting to compare Oak with Giles—to show how Oak illustrates Man's potential when not repressed by Society. Yet Hardy does not suggest that we should compare them. Here, in making success seem possible, Hardy distracts us from considering that there can be much wrong with society. Rather, he suggests an archetypal sense that 'life is a battle-ground. It always has been, and always will be; and if it were not existence would come to an end.'[1] He also illustrates his idea that 'whatever is the inherent good or evil of life, it is certain that men make it much worse than it need be.'[2] Oak strives to reverse that tendency. In this, Hardy seems to suggest that Oak is a kind of hero in the archetypal sense of epitomizing a relatively successful struggle for survival.

As a good farmer and loving friend, Oak exemplifies qualities in which Hardy perceives hope for humankind. Despite Oak's 'misfortunes, amorous and pastoral' (VI, p. 52), he strives to save Bathsheba's ricks from fire. Although, subsequently, he suffers because of her bailiff's 'nervous dread of loving his neighbour as himself' (VII, p. 59), Oak, by contrast, senses Fanny's 'very deep sadness' and gives her a shilling. Despite his own ruinous loss of sheep, and despite having been dismissed for advising Bathsheba as a friend, he utilizes his rare skill to save her flock of dying sheep. Despite all her destructive behaviour, he eschews all bitterness. 'That Bathsheba was getting into toils' on account of Troy 'was now a sorrow greater than' his misery at losing her for himself, 'and one which nearly obscured it' (XXIX, p. 194). Even when she marries Troy, Oak puts 'the best face on the matter' because that 'would be the greatest kindness' (XXXV, p. 239). Thus Oak exemplifies a positive 'way . . . of enduring things' (XLIII, p. 295). Thereby, he overcomes much of the destructive potential of Nature. Even so, he is 'deeply troubled' by his apparent 'powerlessness' (XLII, p. 292) further to divert destructive forces towards constructive ends, although, at this stage, his strength of character earns him material success. Moreover, Bathsheba's fate hinges upon Oak's persistent determination 'to counteract' her miserable circumstances, whatever their origin. Thus Hardy illustrates the potential of those qualities which Oak exemplifies.

Hardy seems to suggest that Oak develops these qualities through working out a constructive approach to suffering. The beginning of the novel is optimistic, cheerful, lighthearted. Oak seems already to have arrived. Finally, of course, his amorous and pastoral ambitions are fulfilled; but most of the novel describes a long period of suffering during which such an outcome seems almost unthinkable. Soon after the pain of his rejection by Bathsheba, Oak looks down over the precipice: the 'dead and dying . . . mangled carcasses' of 200 lambing ewes signify the extinction of all his hopes. His 'thankfulness' that Bathsheba had rejected his suit does not diminish his suffering: 'I shall do one thing in this life—one thing certain—that is, love you, and long for you, and keep wanting you till I die' (IV, p. 42) he has declared. 'There is no regular path for getting out of love' (V, p. 44); love only exacerbates the suffering. Moreover,

> Gabriel's energies, patience, and industry had been so severely taxed during the years of his life between eighteen and twenty-eight, to reach his present stage of progress, that no more seemed to be left in him. (V, p. 47)

His despair is reflected in his observations upon the 'oval pond' 'by the outer margin of the pit'; over a pool which 'glittered like a dead man's eye' 'hung the attenuated skeleton of a chrome-yellow moon, which had only a few days to last'. Jung suggests that 'water is the commonest symbol of the unconscious'; 'psychologically . . . water means spirit that has become unconscious.'[3] Oak seems to recognize in that 'pit' an image of his own unconscious, its death-like pallor reflecting his despair, the 'dead man's eye' a subjective reflection of the despairing perspective with which he regards the natural scene.

Yet he notes too 'the morning star dogging [the moon] on the left hand'; and,

> as the world awoke a breeze blew, shaking and elongating the reflection of the moon without breaking it, and turning the image of the star to a phosphoric streak upon the water. All this Oak saw and remembered. (V, p. 47)

Through the 'breeze' which changes the contours of the apparent death-omens Hardy seems to suggest Oak's dawning awareness that despair need not be inevitable. Jung suggests that 'the opening up of the unconscious always means the outbreak of intense spiritual suffering'[4] through which it is possible to 'begin to seek a way out and to reflect about the meaning of life and its bewildering painful experiences'.[5] Hardy's evocation of a 'dream-country' illustrates just such an initial process; it also shows how Hardy can translate that experience into a recognizable form to which the reader may respond.

Jung also suggests that the beginning of a spiritual journey 'is almost invariably characterized by one's getting stuck in a blind alley or in some impossible situation.'⁶ However, through an 'experience of symbolic reality'⁷ such as Jung describes, Oak finds a way forward to resolve his depression. He visits the hiring-fair because he needs to work to live; he is also striving to re-integrate with the world from which his suffering has alienated him. The path is hard. He acknowledges that he has taken chances—farming without insurance and with an un-reliable sheepdog. Now he has to join other 'labourers waiting upon Chance' (VI, p. 49). Chance seems to continue to thwart him—shepherds being in demand while he proposes service as a bailiff, bailiffs being in demand after he has taken trouble and expense to adapt to the idea that he may offer service as a shepherd. The 'promising look and character' which had been the 'strength' upon which a dealer had granted his mortgage no longer benefit him. Other farmers will not take the chance Oak took with George's son. They will not offer work to a shepherd who has failed on his own farm. Yet, as if recalling his vision, Oak finds a way through his disgrace and failure, adapting again; as an itinerant musician he earns enough to see him through the night and on in the direction of the next day's hiring-fair. Having used a 'dream-country' environment to suggest Oak's change of attitude, Hardy uses the hiring-fair experience to show Oak working out a practical philosophy. Hence, when Hardy tells us that 'Gabriel was paler now', that 'his eyes were more meditative, and his expression more sad', we can sympathize with and relate to Gabriel's experience much more deeply than we might have done otherwise. For Hardy has thereby conveyed Oak's innermost feelings as he 'passed through' that 'ordeal of wretchedness which had given him more than it had taken away' until

> there was left to him a dignified calm he had never known before, and that indifference to fate which, though it often makes a villain of a man, is the basis of his sublimity when it does not. And thus the abasement had been exaltation, and the loss gain. (VI, p. 49)

By recognizing his own partial responsibility, Oak has found the strength of mind and purpose to triumph over a fate which had at first seemed wholly attributable to Chance. Next day,

awaking 'somewhat suddenly' to hear of a 'mistress' 'as proud
as Lucifer' and 'very vain' (VI, p. 53), 'Gabriel slipped out of
the waggon unseen . . ., turned to an opening in the hedge,
which he found to be a gate, and mounting thereon . . . sat
meditating' (VI, p. 54). He descends from the archetypal gate
'about to walk on' along his original path. Only for unselfish
reasons does he change course. Not only does he take the
initiative to save the burning ricks; he takes upon himself the
hardest, most skilful, dangerous, and unpleasant rôle astride the
rick. While Hardy shows that Oak's struggle is against forces in
the physical environment, he also uses supernatural imagery to
suggest the intensity of that struggle. As a consequence of Oak's
constructive and practical attitude, his quest for work in the
service and proximity of his beloved is unexpectedly fulfilled.

Now Oak began to perceive 'that he was not alone'. He has
joined 'a great company—whose shadows danced merrily up
and down'. He seems to have a rôle among them, creating order
out of a 'remarkable confusion of purpose' (VI, p. 55). Thus he
finds a 'way back to a world in which he is no longer a stranger'.[7]
It is as if he has experienced a spiritual as well as a practical
realization that, having learnt to cope with personal distress, he
has a rôle to play in alleviating human distress other than his
own.

The fire which 'glowed on the windward side, rising and
falling in intensity like the coal of a cigar' (VI, p. 54) suggests a
new sexual theme—in harsh contrast to the enduring affection
associated with Oak. This new theme is associated with evil
omens, with 'knots of red worms, . . . imaginary fiery faces,
tongues hanging from lips, glaring eyes, and other impish
forms'. Here, supernatural imagery does not only suggest
struggle; Hardy seems also to suggest that the fire may be a
projection of Oak's unconscious recognition that there are
destructive forces virulent in Weatherbury even harder to
quench than literal fire. Again, Hardy's evocation of a 'dream-
country' environment encourages the reader to identify with
Oak and with Oak's spiritual progress, even though the reader
barely knows how this happens or why he experiences a more
than natural course of events.

At this stage, Oak was 'obliged to some extent to forgo
dreaming in order to find the way' through this new environment.

Even so, 'he reached the churchyard, and passed round it under
the wall where several ancient trees grew. . . . When abreast of a
trunk which appeared to be the oldest of the old, he became
aware' (VII, p. 60) of a figure whose 'very deep sadness' (VII,
p. 62) seems to represent that of the archetypal deceived
maiden, that 'oldest of the old' sorrows.

That deceit represents an evil of which the world seems
hardly aware; cold, indifferent Nature dwarfs Fanny's significance as she tries to attract Troy's attention (XI). His fellows'
'peal of laughter' is identified with Nature's indifference
through being 'hardly distinguishable from the gurgle of the
tiny whirlpools outside' (p. 96). So far does mirth blind even
women to awareness of that evil that they can weep with regret
at the soldiers' passing, oblivious to the implications as 'they
pranced down the street playing "The Girl I Left Behind Me".'
Nor do the soldiers play regretfully or contritely, but 'in glorious
notes of triumph' (X, p. 90). Even when aware of the implications, society's 'disapproval' of Troy's 'morals' is 'frequently . . .
tempered with a smile' (XXV, p. 172), while his 'system of
ethics'—to be 'moderately truthful towards men, but to women'
to lie 'like a Cretan'—is 'above all others calculated to win
popularity at the first flush of admission into lively society'
(XXV, p. 171). (Similarly, amusement at Loki's mischief
distracts us from the severity of his evil. See Chapter 1.)

The wry irony of Hardy's tone may encourage the reader to
dismiss those deeper implications. However, there is a contrary
sense in which Hardy also encourages us to share Oak's
growing awareness of Fanny's sorrow, of the vulnerability of
that 'slight and fragile creature' who is deceived by one she
believes to be 'a man of great respectability and high honour'
(XV, p. 117). There is a sense, too, that characters speak truer
than they are consciously aware when they idly reflect that 'evil
do thrive so in these times that ye may be as much deceived in
the cleanest shaved and whitest shirted man as in the raggedest
tramp' (VIII, p. 75). Thus Oak's churchyard experience seems
to initiate a subterranean current of thought and feeling which
conflicts with the overt current of the novel at this stage and yet
which may ultimately prove the deeper reality.

That very same evening, as Oak physically and symbolically
shares the cup with the villagers in Warren's Malthouse, a

sense of latent evil is drawn towards consciousness. Joseph Poorgrass's reaction illustrates the impact of the revelation regarding Bathsheba's bailiff (VIII, p. 77). 'The newsbell' and the lone magpie[8] seem to relate to Fanny's disappearance. His extraordinary suspicion that she has 'burned' seems to relate her disappearance to the omens suggested by the recent rick fire. (Yet no one suspects 'murder', despite the 'newsbell': curiously, that is to be the fate of her deceiver.) Around the barracks Nature may appear coldly indifferent, but the psychic atmosphere of Weatherbury seems disturbed. Meanwhile, Oak is 'busy with fancies, and full of movement, like a river flowing rapidly under its ice' (VIII, p. 79). He seems to be striving to comprehend the situation in order to help control it. He thinks of the books he may need: practical books for farming, and spiritual guides—*Paradise Lost* and *The Pilgrim's Progress*. In this, he contrasts with the anti-hero Fitzpiers, who reads books on the black arts and who 'much preferred the ideal world to the real, and the discovery of principles to their application' (*W*, XVI, p. 119). Oak's spiritual quest is integrated with practical reality. He is the 'only one man in the neighbourhood' who 'knows the way' to save Bathsheba's dying herd of sheep (XXI, p. 145), and the only man awake and sober enough to save the ricks from the storm. The value of this work would not have been under-estimated in a rural community which relied heavily upon its own agricultural produce for its survival, even if its significance was ignored by Troy. Oak was striving, not only for Bathsheba, but for the rural community, for human-kind in general (XXXVI, p. 247).

Before either of these events, Oak is kept extremely busy with a 'terrible trying' lambing (XV, p. 112) with a 'good few twins' (p. 113). It would have been understandable if Oak had been bitter about working in order that Bathsheba should so prosper, considering the fate of his own lambing ewes. On the other hand, had he been pleased to perceive her profit, this too would have been believable, knowing Oak's character. Yet neither he nor Poorgrass regard the situation in practical terms. Rather, the lambs are 'too many by half'. The lambing is 'very queer . . . this year' and prolonged for longer than usual (p. 113). In this, Oak seems to endorse the general view that these things are signs of a disturbed atmosphere.[9]

Despite Oak's protestations, he knows that Bathsheba's 'pride and vanity' make her and her community vulnerable (p. 114). The theme of vulnerability persists in the tragic pathos between the lines of Fanny's letter, which shows Fanny's limited awareness of the dangers of entering into a sexual relationship with the irresponsible Troy. Cain Ball's dramatic announcement, just then, of the twinning of yet two more ewes, seems to suggest that irresponsible human behaviour has unleashed the evil signified by the disturbed atmosphere. Hardy has the community acknowledge Oak's ability to help, not only with the lambing, but also, with the disturbance it signifies—because he is an 'extraordinary good and clever man' (p. 115).

By contrast, the 'unruly' behaviour of the bees seems to suggest the nature of Bathsheba's passion (XXVII, p. 184). The difficulty posed by the bees' random choice of 'the uppermost' bough (p. 184) seems to hint at that complication of affairs caused by her inconvenient instinctive reaction to Troy. As the instincts of the bees coincide in that apparently random choice, Hardy suggests 'a process somewhat analogous to that alleged formation of the universe, time and times ago' (p. 184). In this, Hardy seems to suggest that the surrounding narrative describes an archetypal pattern of behaviour.

Hardy admires Bathsheba's proud and independent spirit— up to a point; for he regrets how it leads her to reject the values Oak represents. In rejecting the advice of a reliable, genuine, loving friend (XXIV, p. 165; XXIX, p. 198), she allows destructive forces within her to convince her that she has 'nobody in the world to fight my battles for me'. His advice backfires; she feels driven towards that very fate which both she and Oak fear.

Thus, during her 'fearful journey' (XXXV, p. 239) to Bath, Weatherbury is stunned, 'quiet as the graveyard in its midst . . . the living . . . lying well-nigh as still as the dead' (XXXII, p. 213). Dream and reality seem fused as Maryann, alone in Bathsheba's 'crannied and mouldy halls', 'turned in her bed with a sense of being disturbed. . . . The interruption . . . led to a dream, and the dream to an awakening, with an uneasy sensation that something had happened' (XXXII, p. 213). Bathsheba's distress, her flight with the horse, its assumed theft, and Oak's fruitless pursuit, seem to be part of that dream. (See Chapter 1 on the significance of dream horses.) Even by day, and a fortnight later, Nature's 'drought', human silence, and 'a dreadful bodement' seem to sustain an aura of psychic shock, that 'unlucky token'—a dropped and broken doorkey— inspiring Maryann to 'wish miss'ess was home' (XXXIII, p. 221).

Here, as in a dream, the cosmos within and without seem to be one. The storm which follows is natural enough after this 'dry and sultry' weather (XXXVI, p. 243). Yet the 'sinister aspect' of the night and the 'lurid metallic look' of a moon which casts 'impure light' upon the consequently 'sallow' fields seem also to suggest a psychically inevitable culmination of Bathsheba's and Weatherbury's tension. Oak recognizes and constructively interprets Nature's signs that

> thunder was imminent, and taking some secondary appearances into consideration, it was likely to be followed by one of the lengthened rains which mark the cease of dry weather for the season. Before twelve hours had passed a harvest atmosphere would be a bygone thing. (XXXVI, p. 243)

He despairs of alerting Troy to the signs. He despairs of the seductive influence of Troy's personality over the Weatherbury men. Yet he persists in interpreting Nature's signals. To him the 'large toad' is a 'direct message from the Great Mother'; the 'huge . . . slug' is 'Nature's second way of hinting to him that he was to prepare for foul weather' (XXXVI, p. 246). While 'the creeping things' warn of 'a cold, continuous rain' (p. 247), the 'two black spiders reminded him that . . . one class of manifestation . . . that he thoroughly understood . . . was the instincts of sheep.' Their 'terror of something greater than the terror of man' warns of a storm; its direction is indicated by their unanimous turning away from that source. Thus, 'natural' explanations do not make the situation less fearful; rather, 'every voice in nature' (p. 246) clamours to warn Oak of 'this complication of weathers (which), being uncommon, was all the more to be feared' (p. 247).

There is, of course, nothing supernatural in Oak's inter- preting ability. Even Conjuror Fall foretells the weather, as does Oak, through reading signs in Nature—'by the sun, moon and

stars, by the clouds, the winds, the trees; likewise by the cats'
eyes, the ravens, the leeches, the spiders, and the dung-mixen'
(*MC*, XXVI, p. 188). Marty foretold 'a fine day tomorrow' on
the grounds that the birds 'are acroupied down nearly at the
end of the bough. If it were going to be stormy they'd squeeze
close to the trunk' (*W*, IX, p. 73). Oak has no access to
supernatural power; rather, he shows exceptional strength of
character. Weatherbury remains stunned by the impact of
destructive forces. Only Oak is neither asleep nor intoxicated.
He has learnt from experience and from the vision of the pond
within the pit, to interpret natural signs constructively, as
warnings of trouble which might, with a struggle, be averted,
rather than destructively, fatalistically, as omens.

The natural dignity of mankind is suppressed within the
ancient centre of farm life—the barn; harvest celebrations come
to a 'painful and demoralizing' (p. 248) end with a 'debauch'
which 'boded ill' (p. 249); meanwhile, Oak works to avert the
destruction of which Nature has offered warning. Having learnt
from his personal misfortunes not to take unnecessary chances,
he extinguishes the 'expiring lights' (p. 249). He also makes
himself a lightning conductor (XXXVII, p. 252); the precaution
proves a wise one. Yet, despite precautions, despite his early
awareness and interpretations of Nature's warnings, Oak still
has a long, hard struggle to defend the ricks; Hardy describes
the scene in language which, to say the least, suggests a grim
trial of character (p. 249). When destructive forces are virulent,
Man is tempted to sleep, as does Weatherbury here. Yet Oak
has learned that this is the very time when Man must struggle
the most. 'Some monster' of a cloud seems to be frightening
away the 'faint cloudlets'. That wind with 'teeth' of a 'dragon'
and 'parted lips' suggests that, once more, while Oak is under
extreme pressure, a terrifying, destructive spirit seems to be
ruling an 'infuriated universe'. Through the 'haggard', 'sick'
night 'came finally an utter expiration of air from the whole
heaven in the form of a slow breeze, which might have been
likened to a death' (p. 250). Thus Oak seems to be struggling
against forces which could drive Man to extinction.

Oak is awakened by seeing signs of danger—Bathsheba only
by hearing the thunder when it comes. Yet, even she is of more
use than the rest of the community which sleeps until all is over.

The apparent proximity of death accounts for Bathsheba's urge to explain to Oak the moral confusion which led to her marrying Troy (XXXVII, p. 256). However, as they work together, Hardy describes the lightning in a way which recalls Troy's part in initiating the destructive forces which paralyse Weatherbury. Troy once likened his sudden passion for Bathsheba to lightning (XXVI, p. 180). Its present silver gleam recalls his seductive sword play (XXVIII). Neumann suggests that 'lightning is the characteristic symbol for' a 'surprise attack' by the Archetypal Masculine.[10] Oak and Bathsheba seem to relate the two; hence, Oak's subsequent 'musing' upon the 'story', and upon her ability 'to speak more warmly to him tonight than she had ever done whilst unmarried and free to speak as warmly as she chose' (XXXVII, p. 257). Clearly, Bathsheba respects Oak more as she realizes more fully the destructive potential of the storm; she respects Troy less as she realizes the importance of the tasks which Troy has neglected. However, Hardy suggests her developing awareness in a way which resembles the awakening of consciousness as experienced in a dream.

That awakening involves more than a recognition of past and present situations; it also involves a sense of premonition regarding likely consequences. The 'poplar in the immediate foreground' (XXXVII, p. 251), which is struck down by lightning, illustrates the scale of destructive forces beyond Oak's control. It may also remind us of Troy, who is in the foreground at the farm, both in terms of personality and in terms of responsibility for the present trouble. No longer does lightning illustrate Troy's seductive powers; rather, it suggests destructive forces being conducted through him, finally leading to destructive consequences for himself, as well as for Fanny, Bathsheba and the rest of the community. Oak and Bathsheba share the experience of 'the shadow of that tree' 'drawn in black on the wall of the barn' (p. 253) wherein Troy and the men lie in drunken sleep. 'The flash' which follows is 'almost too novel for its inexpressibly dangerous nature to be at once realized'; 'they could only comprehend the magnificence of its beauty.' Thus, again, we are reminded of Troy's seductive powers. It is followed by a 'perfect dance of death'. 'The form of skeletons . . . mingling together in unparalleled confusion' recalls the disturbed heifers, and the initial confusion of the Weatherbury community at the rick fire. The 'snakes of green', the 'grisly forms' which fail to kill Oak only because of his precautionary conductor, 'the spring of a serpent and the shout of a fiend'—all seem to suggest the evil unleashed in 'an infuriated universe' (p. 253). Or, rather, Hardy uses the storm to suggest the development of the characters' unspoken perceptions that Troy's reckless behaviour has initiated trouble and confusion. Now the evil has taken root, it spreads relentlessly, independently of Troy (but see also Note 11). It seems that it will become increasingly hard for human intervention to subdue it.

There are natural reasons why 'Oak had hardly time to gather up these impressions into a thought.' Nonetheless, Hardy implicitly suggests that Oak is aware of impressions which might develop into conscious thought; thus Hardy implies that Oak has responded to the symbolic implications of his present environment. Perhaps his perception of 'how strangely the red feather of [Bathsheba's] hat shone in this light' suggests a recognition that there are startling and dangerous aspects to her personality too and that she shares responsibility for this condition. (We may recall the significance of her lost hat in the context of Oak's courting (II, pp. 25, 29) and of Troy's (XXVII, p. 185). As Jung suggests, in the context of a dream, it seems that 'the hat ... epitomizes the personality' and the removal of hats the 'emergence of the unconscious'.[12]) The simultaneous splitting by lightning of 'the tall tree on the hill', accompanied by 'a stupefying blast, harsh and pitiless', leaving 'a sulphurous smell' which 'filled the air', and the resultant 'silent' atmosphere, 'black as a cloud in Hinnon' (p. 254), emphasize Weatherbury's consequent spiritual condition.

Once these destructive forces have burnt themselves out, Hardy seems to say, the final stage of Oak's spiritual journey can begin: 'a change in the wind' and 'disastrous rain' (p. 257). No longer will Oak be 'fighting against fire', as when he first came to Weatherbury, but against the 'water' which, perhaps, relates to Bathsheba's spiritual condition of misery and regret (XXXVIII, p. 258). It takes time for the destructive flames to burn themselves out and for healing and renewal to begin; hence 'the wind [which] snarled round every corner, the trees [which] rocked to the bases of their trunks, and the twigs [which] clashed in strife'. Hardy shows that Oak is suffering too, 'the water . . . tracking cold and clammy routes down his back' as he strives to prevent human misery as far as he can; in this combined fight, first against fire and now against the misery of the 'cold, continuous rain', he has 'never had such a struggle in my life' (p. 259). However, since overcoming his personal misfortune, he has 'the repose of a man whom misfortune had inured rather than subdued' (p. 260) and 'a way . . . of enduring things' (XLIII, p. 295) which has brought him through both stages of Weatherbury's troubles to the benefit of Bathsheba and the community, and to the ultimate fulfilment of his original aspirations, 'both amorous and pastoral'.

Unlike Giles, Oak succeeds in diverting destructive forces to constructive ends as far as is humanly possible. Through this experience, Hardy suggests the archetypal spiritual development of a 'hero' as reflected in the 'dream-country' environment. Yet practical experience is intrinsic to that development. Oak is the one character in the novel who interprets rationally and acts upon Nature's signs. Through Oak, Hardy shows that Nature is indifferent to Man and that there are logical explanations for most happenings in the world of Man and in the world of Nature. And yet, Hardy also uses Nature to externalize Oak's thoughts and feelings regarding the nature and origins of Weatherbury's troubles. Constantly, the tone shifts between these two perspectives. Simultaneously, Hardy evokes both a 'real' and a 'dream-country'.

As in a dream, ideas which are evolving from the unconscious towards consciousness are expressed in terms of a symbolic environment. By acknowledging and responding to those symbols, the reader can share in that process and identify more deeply with Oak and his community. Thus Hardy encourages us to become involved in Oak's spiritual development. Oak is but one character in the novel, but much of the action is treated from his point of view. Furthermore, he provides a kind of centre of consciousness of the novel from which it is possible to perceive some of the archetypal problems of humankind as exemplified by a fictionalized 'sheep-farming' community in early Victorian England.

Through using the 'dream-country' to suggest character development Hardy releases the mythic potential of the novel, opening up the question of an evolutionary link between heroic fable and literary art. We cannot know how far Hardy was aware that his own spiritual quest influenced his art in this way. And, only by drawing attention to moments of particular emotional intensity in the novel, can it be read thus. Moreover, it is possible to read the novel without consciously perceiving this dimension. Even so, this approach does illuminate the relationship between Hardy's art and experience; it shows how the 'dream-country' through which it is expressed may have evolved from Hardy's creative unconscious.

2. *Jude Fawley*

In contrast to *Far from the Madding Crowd*, a 'series of seemings'[13] evoked by Hardy in *Jude the Obscure* provokes powerful social criticism. Here Hardy uses a 'dream-country' to suggest glimpses into a state of being independent of the social structures which can prejudice moral judgement. Thus he encourages a renewed moral consciousness. To a large extent he suggests this process of renewal through the development of his characters. In particular, he focuses upon the shifting consciousness of Jude Fawley, exposing the sterile hypocrisy of institutionalized religion, the academic and social pride which fed the system, and the inconsistencies and trappings of a sexual morality which failed to fulfil its archetypal purpose—the prevention of unnecessary human suffering and the protection of the innocent and vulnerable.

Perhaps it is easier now than in Hardy's time to perceive how that hinterland of 'seemings' is given 'shape and coherence' in this novel. Enough of the social problems evoked are as yet unresolved for the modern reader to identify with Hardy's social criticism. On the other hand, modern readers do not feel themselves to be objects of Hardy's direct criticism as did his contemporary readers. Hence, modern readers can identify with Hardy rather than with those he criticizes. They are therefore, perhaps, more willing to listen and to examine the source of their response. At the same time, our attention is less likely to be diverted from this examination by the intensity of our reaction to those social ills which seem less immediate, less pertinent, than they once did.

This shift in the audience's likely reaction to the social factors involved may have enhanced our awareness of 'dream-country' aspects of the environment. While in *Jude*, as elsewhere,[14] Hardy encourages constructive change, the changes which have made Jude's environment 'ugly' are destructive. The modern environment is a recognizable product of the processes of change to which Hardy refers. However, the specific changes described are less familiar to us, the shock they provoke less potent, than to his contemporaries. Moreover, they are ostensibly beyond our control. More immediate is the sense in which Hardy is using the environment to reflect a destructive current which he perceives in the character of humankind.

Hardy's paradoxical treatment of change in *The Woodlanders* suggests a similar perspective. Hardy acknowledges the constructive potential of Fitzpiers' scientific studies and broadened horizons: that Fitzpiers could have turned 'his great talents to good account' had he 'had more principle' (XLIV, p. 339). Yet Fitzpiers' prescriptions for South's illness hasten his demise; for he misinterprets the psychological basis of South's traditional sense of affinity with his environment. Through Fitzpiers and Mrs. Charmond, Hardy shows how dangerous it can be when those in positions of authority are alienated from the environment. He shows that the increasing alienation of humankind from the environment can be a destructive form of change. In *The Woodlanders* the possibility of survival and renewal is preserved—just—through Giles's and Marty's empathy with the environment and through suggestions of their mythical lineage. (See Chapter 1.) However, in *Jude*, this destructive current seems to have overwhelmed human society; no one now perceives those 'associations' (p. 33) with 'invisible ones of days gone by' (*W*, XVII, pp. 128–29)—neither in terms of ancestral environment, nor in terms of mythical lineage. (See *Jude*, I, I, pp. 30–1; I, II, pp. 33–4.)

Hardy's main character is introduced as a child who can relate to his environment only through sympathy with the sufferings of rooks (I, II, p. 34), worms and trees (p. 36)—because they, like Jude, are victims of that destructive current in human society. Jude's employer—a newly exalted representative of that society (I, II, p. 37)—punishes him for this sympathy. The violence of that punishment encourages us to awaken, through Jude, to consciousness of a sickening disharmony in the world, reflected in his sense that 'all around you there seemed to be something glaring, garish, rattling, all the noises and glares hit upon the little cell called your life and shook it, and warped it' (I, II, p. 38). Maybe there are 'flaw[s] in the terrestrial scheme' (p. 36); but Farmer Troutham certainly exacerbates them. During the beating, Hardy tells how Troutham has 'subscribed' to 'the brand-new church tower just behind the mist . . . to testify his love for God and man' (p. 35). We can hardly miss the social criticism. Nor can we fail to perceive that, to some extent, Jude's relationship with his environment reflects his relationship with society.

Jude's environment changes little as he grows up. However, successive perspectives upon that environment evoke a sense of a 'series of seemings', and so create the impression of a kind of 'dream-country'. To some extent, the character of Jude is created out of, and is an expression of, the complex web of 'seemings' which inspires the novel. Discussion of the relationship between Jude and his environment can, therefore, clarify and deepen our comprehension of those 'seemings'. It is also a crucial preliminary to considering Hardy's use of the 'dream-country' to suggest relationships between Jude and Arabella, and especially between Jude and Sue (Chapter 3), as well as the relationship between Man and Society (Chapter 4).

In Jude Fawley, Hardy creates a character whose ambitions seem almost designed to evoke consciousness of specific social ills. Maybe his failure to come to terms with an apparent 'doom or curse of hereditary temperament'[15] affects his spiritual as well as his sexual aspirations. However, Jude's tragic death is more than the ultimate expression of the difficulty of the task he sets himself; through the bitterly ironical context of the Remembrance celebrations (VI, XI, p. 423ff) Hardy also cauterizes our consciousness with 'impressions' of those areas where social reform is necessary.

Hardy emphasizes the primacy of character over social criticism.[16] Lodge's argument that neither Jude nor Sue could 'have achieved happy and fulfilled lives' even if the social ills of their times were cured[17] reminds us that Hardy acknowledges

flaws within human character as well as within society. However, society exacerbates those flaws within human character,
instead of encouraging—or even allowing—Jude to triumph
over them by developing more constructive aspects of his
character. Thus, we sympathize deeply when Jude feels driven
'to commit suicide' (VI, IX, p. 411), although we also recognize
that he is, thereby, deliberately abandoning the struggle against
destructive forces within him and without. The counterpoint
between the rejoicings of the Remembrance celebrations and
Jude's quoting of Job intensifies the social criticism, although
we may recognize that Job, unlike Jude, eventually overcame
his extreme and justifiable despair. The product of these conflicting perspectives is suggested more explicitly through Jude's
frustration and anger that, after all his striving, he should be
reduced to this antithesis of his original aspirations.

Yet there is more to Jude than his 'failure' to manoeuvre
social barriers or to overcome flaws of character. To some
extent he might be considered 'a sort of success as a frightful
example of what not to do; and so illustrate a moral story' (VI,
I, p. 345); but the bitter tone here encourages us to consider
alternative perspectives. Certainly Hardy perceived this as a
'moral work'.[18] And in his opinion 'the highest tragedy . . . is
that of the WORTHY encompassed by the INEVITABLE'—
not that of 'immoral and worthless people' (emphasis his).[19]
Hardy encourages us to admire Jude for refusing to 'follow
uncritically the track he finds himself in, without considering
his aptness for it'. Jude believes that, having considered 'what
his aptness of bent may be', he should 're-shape his course
accordingly' (VI, I, p. 345). 'Man and senseless circumstance'
may seem to destroy Jude; he may fail to find a way to fulfil his
potential, but that does not invalidate the constructive potential
of the idea. 'Arabella's and Vilbert's survival, while better
people are driven to neurotic and compulsive remarriage, madness, and death' may 'reinforce our impression of man's
devolution'.[20] However, it may also anger us into a determination that 'better people' should be encouraged to continue
Jude's abandoned struggle to redirect that destructive current.
In *Far from the Madding Crowd*, the development of character
expressed the archetypal struggle to redirect destructive energies,
both within and without. Here, Hardy evokes a renewed moral

consciousness of that struggle, and shows how unnecessarily difficult it has become.

Thus, we can respond to Jude as a 'worthy' character, even though, from the time that Arabella throws the pizzle and the 'war . . . between flesh and spirit' begins, self-degradation and self-destruction are increasingly evident. Indeed, Hardy deliberately strove to build the novel out of such 'contrasts' as that 'between Jude the saint' and 'Jude the sinner' (n. 15: Letter II). He hoped that 'the throwing of the pizzle, at the supreme moment of his young dream' would 'sharply initiate' 'the contrast between the ideal life a man wished to lead, and the squalid real life he was fated to lead. . . . The idea was meant to run through the novel' (n. 15: Letter I). Were Hardy to continue to divorce the 'saint' striving towards 'the ideal life' from the 'sinner' leading a 'squalid real life', the reader would relate to Jude less keenly. This would have been crucial to Hardy, who believed 'the idea' to be of archetypal, universal significance—'to be discovered in *every*body's life, though it lies less on the surface perhaps than it does in my poor puppet's' (emphasis his).

Hardy emphasized that 'the "grimy" features of the story' were meant to show this contrast; but they also illustrate the painful difficulty of the resultant conflict within Jude. In *Far from the Madding Crowd* it was possible to sense the development of Oak's character through his reflections upon the environment. Jude's 'grimy' environment may seem to suggest only the failure of his efforts. Rather, however, Hardy's use of environment has become a complex and sensitive barometer of this paradoxical human struggle. The ugliness of Marygreen is a metaphor for destructive currents in human society. Its ugliness also serves as a projection of Jude's own feelings, expressed in symbolic form, as in a 'dream-country'. At the same time, Hardy specifically tells us that this environment holds meaning for Jude of which he is almost entirely unconscious (I, II, p. 33). Through shifting these perspectives upon the environment, Hardy suggests the extent to which Jude is mistaken in believing that Christianity can satisfy the 'yearning of his heart to find something to anchor on, to cling to' (I, III, p. 45).

Hardy shows that Jude's ideals are not quite as he imagines them; they are only an approximate expression of his yearning to discover, and to be able to be true to, himself. From the beginning, Jude assumes that the ideals of his only friend coincide with his own. Thus he focuses his thought upon Phillotson that first foggy morning when, lonely and tearful, he looks deep into the ancient well.[21] Hardy emphasizes that the well is 'as ancient as the village itself' and 'probably the only relic of the local history that remained absolutely unchanged' in a village where houses and trees—symbols of the lives of villagers, including his own ancestors—have been destroyed. As in a dream, the scene seems to indicate a searching into the unconscious self. Thus Hardy suggests that Jude's loneliness prevents him from perceiving clearly the true nature of that quest.

Hardy does believe that Christminster should admit working-class men. He emphasizes that Jude is suited to academic life; his ill-health confirms Jude's claim that he 'was never really stout enough for the stone trade'; on the other hand, as his conversations confirm, he 'could accumulate ideas, and impart them to others' (VI, X, p. 418). Hardy also seems to suggest that Jude could have played a particular rôle in academic life; for, from his own particular perspective, he could perceive the need and scope for regeneration of that life.[22] In effect, Jude does fulfil this rôle, as if he were next in the line of those 'phantoms' of Christminster (II, I). However, he is broken and disillusioned by the time there are 'schemes afoot for making the University less exclusive and extending its influence' (VI, X, p. 418). Through suggesting this experience, Hardy hopes to hasten that change.

As it is clearly appropriate for Jude to pursue his educational goals, it may appear contradictory for Hardy to associate them, from the beginning, with Jude's misdirected spiritual quest. Yet, in so doing, Hardy questioned the time-honoured assumption that the prime function of a university education was preparation for entry into the Church. Initially, Jude does not perceive any conflict between his religious and educational goals. His response to the 'phantoms' of Christminster seems to suggest that education might help him to realize his spiritual identity. Yet it becomes increasingly clear that his spiritual identity cannot be moulded to conform with the Christian traditions represented by Christminster.

The ancient well seems to have deep spiritual significance—at least, for Jude; the contemporary church seems to have none—for anyone. It incorporates no record of the 'site' of the 'original church'. Its builders have 'obliterated' the graves of Jude's ancestors. In suggesting that these are 'commemorated' only temporarily (I, I, pp. 30–1), Hardy suggests that humanity may be on the brink of losing sight of its archetypal roots forever. In 'echoing' through 'the mist' the beating of Jude by a major benefactor (I, II, p. 35), the contemporary church is associated with the perverse and cruel materialistic values of Jude's society. Yet this society also governs, and therefore perverts, the spiritual and intellectual ideals of ancient Christminster: hence the ironical tone when Jude idealizes Christminster as a 'city of light' (p. 45) and a 'heavenly Jerusalem' (p. 40).

Jude's perspective upon Christminster reflects his limitations in assessing his spiritual identity. Furthermore, by projecting that limited assessment of himself upon Christminster, he is inviting collapse when Christminster fails him. His faith in the power of prayer seems superficial and alien to his true nature. That faith seems to derive from the socially acceptable versions of Christianity presented in tracts. Hardy ridicules these ideas through the suggestion that the only reason certain prayers were unanswered was that the breeches of the man who prayed 'were made by a wicked Jew' (p. 40). Amusement turns to ill-ease as we realize that an impressionable boy has been influenced by this un-Christian, illogical, yet typical enough religious attitude. The reader may feel correspondingly uneasy when Jude's prayer is apparently answered. This ironic context further intensifies that unease about Jude's idealization of Christminster as a 'city of light'—a centre of such religion—as does that open question, whether Christminster is 'directly seen, or miraged in the peculiar atmosphere' (p. 41). In this context, the re-veiling of that 'vague city . . . in mist', the disappearance of the sun, the sudden extinguishing of light and replacement by a 'funereally dark' 'foreground' serve as 'impressions', or as symbolic expressions, of Jude's unconscious acknowledgement that his spiritual quest is misdirected.

The alarming wildness of Jude's imaginative response to his environment at this time reinforces this impression. The 'chimaeras' he sees in 'the hues and shapes' of near objects reflect the dangerous inaccuracy of his 'gigantic dreams' concerning Christminster. At the same time, they reflect his innate ability to relate the archetypal warnings enshrined in myths and legends to his personal spiritual situation, through projection into the environment, as in a dream. At an instinctive level, he can respond to the implications; for on their account he is 'anxious', inspired to 'descend' his real and yet archetypal ladder and to start 'homewards at a run'. Yet he tries not to think of the archetypal, demonic giant-figures instinctively aroused by the immediate environment, instead of recognizing in them warning expressions of the dangers of his misdirected spiritual quest.

Unconscious impressions seem to approach consciousness when Jude realizes that, having 'become entirely lost to his bodily situation', 'only . . . a rough recalling' could bring him back to it (p. 43). The reservations of an anonymous carter add substance to Jude's previously unconscious reservations (p. 44). The Tower of Babel and prostitutes are fruits of Christminster's 'tree of knowledge' (p. 45). Yet Jude suppresses his awareness of the biblical significance of that tree. Years later, 'a hunchbacked old woman of great intelligence, who read everything she could lay her hands on' (I, V, p. 54), encourages him with idealistic tales 'of the romantic charms of the city of light'. However, the pathetic irony of his efforts to channel his intelligence into old churches and the strangeness of the encounter, seem to suggest that the woman might be a projection of Jude's own misguided ideals. Again, it suggests, too, his unconscious reservations about those ideals. But Jude is too eager for encouragement to allow those reservations to approach consciousness.

While Hardy suggests that Jude over-rates Christminster, he also shows how Christminster under-rates Jude. He illustrates the strength of Jude's character as he pursues his educational goals. Overcoming his despair regarding Vilbert, he utilizes the coincidence of Phillotson's sending for his pianoforte to send for grammars. Overcoming his despair on finding his idealization of a grammar as a 'secret cipher' (I, IV, p. 49) to be an illusion, he devotes himself to study, despite his lack of free time, and despite the objections of others. Overcoming his shock on finding that his natural inclinations divert him towards pagan moon-worship, he intensifies his resolve by training as an apprentice in order to be able to earn a living at this site of learning. Each stage also suggests a warning of which Jude fails to grow conscious. If Vilbert's word is untrustworthy, his encouragement of Jude is meaningless. If education is not the acquisition of a 'secret cipher', but a hard personal struggle, even the books studied at Christminster can be, at best, no more than a guide. If his studies lead him towards pagan moon-worship, maybe a bishopric is not his innermost desire. Thus, while Hardy encourages us to admire the qualities of character illustrated by Jude's efforts to attain his educational goals, he simultaneously intensifies our uneasiness about Jude's conscious definition of those goals.

This paradox culminates in Jude's unquestioning assumption that his social aspirations are compatible with his declared aim of 'leading a pure, energetic, wise Christian life' and with Christminster's religious ideals. At this moment, the sharp smack of a pig's pizzle introduces a further complication which Jude has hitherto failed to consider—his sexuality. Thus, the incident draws towards consciousness 'the slight sounds of voices and laughter that had mingled with his dreams' (I, VI, p. 58). It is as if his sexuality—perhaps his most powerful instinct—has been suppressed for so long that it must ultimately be forced into consciousness, exposing his most vulnerable point. Thus, it obviates 'commonsense' (p. 61). His unexpected helplessness and the ominous atmosphere which accompanies their walk combine to suggest that his sexual aspirations are as misguided as his spiritual aspirations, while he pursues each without reference to the other.

Jude's vulnerability to Arabella's ploys is, perhaps, a peripheral concern, compared with his vulnerability to sexual forces within himself over which he seems powerless: the 'compelling arm of extraordinary muscular power' which 'seized hold of him . . . which had nothing in common with the spirits and influences which had moved him hitherto', which

> seemed to care little for his reason and his will, nothing for his so-called elevated intentions, and moved him along as a violent schoolmaster a schoolboy he has seized by the collar in a direction which tended towards the embrace of a woman for whom he had no respect. (I, VII, p. 64)

Never will he be free from the complications arising from these forces; never will he be able to integrate them satisfactorily with his spiritual quest.

In Jude's walk with Arabella, Hardy projects into the environment Jude's misgivings, increasing tension and suspense, and increasing our sense of the seriousness of the situation. He has 'no will to thwart' Arabella's 'inclination' to pursue a fire which takes him much further than he had intended. That fire suggests the nature and likely consequence of his passion, for it had been extinguished by the time they reached it and was represented by nothing but 'melancholy ruins' (p. 66). This image is recalled repeatedly: by the 'picture of Samson and Delilah' within the 'depressing', 'uncongenial atmosphere' of the inn (p. 66); by the gloomy darkness as they ascend 'the white highway' which suggests their future path together; by the sudden dream-like appearance of two anonymous men who associated 'lovers' with 'homeless dogs' and then 'vanished' (p. 67). As soon as he leaves her, a temporary 'sense of relief' suggests the reassertion of his own will. Yet the precariousness of the relationship only emphasizes that prevailing tension. It is re-emphasized through the Greek New Testament, which seemed to regard 'him with fixed reproach in the grey starlight, like the unclosed eyes of a dead man' (p. 68). Nonetheless, passion predominates.

Jude's burning of the framed photograph marks more than the end of this temporary passion which had diverted him from his true quest. He is actually consuming his own image— symbolically, an image of those disturbing sexual forces within him which had once thrust him towards Arabella. It seems that he fails, as yet, to perceive that they are an integral part of himself. He believes that he can put back the clock (I, XI, p. 93). He fails to acknowledge the sexual implications of the fact that he is now a man (p. 96). 'He remembered . . . that he was standing not far from the spot at which the parting from his father and mother was said to have occurred' (p. 94). Yet he fails to acknowledge the implication—that the problems aroused by his recently found awareness of sexual desire may not be dismissed as easily as his union with Arabella seems to have been. They concern, too, other members of the family, other generations. Indeed, his 'ultimate impulse' to go to Christminster is the haunting photograph of his cousin Sue (II, I, pp. 96–7), and his newly acknowledged need for someone to love (II, IV, p. 117). Admirably, he resolves 'to move onward through good and ill—to avoid morbid sorrow even though he did see uglinesses in the world', to 'battle with his evil star'. However, he is, unlike Oak at the hiring-fair, failing to take full account of changed circumstances. His desire to study is as strong as ever before; but he seems not to consider that, whether or not he divorces Arabella, his sexual aspirations contradict the clerical aspects of his resolve to 'follow out his original intention' (p. 94).

In effect, it is only frustrating for Jude to grow aware of his true aspirations. As a child he found alienation painful. Hence, inspired by his one friend, he strove towards society's highest honours. It is difficult for him to face the temperamental impossibility of forcing his aspirations into existing 'social moulds'.[23] Moreover, the more he realizes his alienation from society, the more he realizes that he remains acutely susceptible to its rules. Although his class and comparative poverty bar him from participation in college life, his respect for Christminster, while it lasts, endorses society's value-systems. Even when he changes his attitude, he remains powerless to change society. As Jude enters Christminster alone, without friend or guide, Hardy intensifies our perception of that powerlessness. His comment that 'save his own soul he hath no star' (II, titlepage, p. 95) prompts us to recall that the only aspect of that 'battle with his evil star' over which Jude can have any control is that battle to comprehend and develop his own character. Hardy's reference to Jude as 'a species of Dick Whittington whose spirit was touched to finer issues than mere material gain' (II, I, p. 97) further encourages us to recognize those efforts of Jude's 'unconscious' to be 'the great guide, friend, and adviser of' his 'conscious' will.[24] The raising of Jude's consciousness is crucial; he has to learn to comprehend himself. Yet unless, like Sue, he chooses to deny himself, it will not enable him to divert tragedy: rather, it will make it seem 'inevitable'. Either way, his Christminster aspirations remain unattainable.

The succession of 'dream-country' perspectives upon Christminster during Jude's first evening there suggests a tension out of which this realization grows. Here Jude begins to question his instinctive response to 'those lamps which had sent into the sky the gleam and glory that caught his strained gaze in the days of his dreaming': now they wink 'their yellow eyes at him dubiously . . . as if, though they had been awaiting him all these years in disappointment at his tarrying, they did not much want him now' (p. 97). The 'windy, whispering, moonless' night seems to suggest his awakening unconscious (p. 97). Wind and darkness seem to suggest flickerings of the unconscious which confuse Jude's sense of 'the direction he should take to reach the heart of the place' (p. 98). The curfew bell seems to warn him to go home to bed (p. 98). (See also Note on p. 431.) He finds that the gates are shut. Yet, only when he is 'at Christminster again' returning to die (VI, IX, p. 411), do the personal implications appear to reach Jude's consciousness; by that time they can only have an ominous, rather than a warning, function, for it is too late for Jude to change his course.

At first, 'when he passed objects out of harmony with its general expression he had allowed his eyes to slip over them as if he did not see them' (p. 98); as night draws on, his mind becomes focused upon those negative aspects of the environment which he had previously ignored. Even as this process begins,

> he began to be impressed with the isolation of his own personality, as with a self-spectre, the sensation being that of one who walked but could not make himself seen or heard . . . seeming almost his own ghost. (p. 98)

Thus Hardy suggests the raising of a deep, unconscious, instinctive recognition that Jude will die rather than enter here. The sombre atmosphere suggests that Jude is striving to suppress that feeling as 'he gave his thoughts to the other ghostly presence with which the nooks were haunted (p. 98):

> the brushings of the wind against the angles, buttresses, and door-jambs were as the passing of these only other inhabitants, the tappings of each ivy leaf on its neighbour were as the mutterings of their mournful souls, the shadows as their thin shapes in nervous movement, making him comrades in his solitude. In the gloom it was as if he ran against them without feeling their bodily frames. (p. 99)

In the first part of the novel, Hardy showed Jude being forced into consciousness of his sexual nature. In this part of the novel,

Hardy suggests a more gradual development towards spiritual self-knowledge. Jude's progress 'down obscure alleys, apparently never trodden now by the foot of man, and whose very existence seemed to be forgotten' seems to suggest a journey into the labyrinth of the unconscious.

A new stage in his awareness is suggested when Jude suddenly finds that he is 'speaking out loud, holding conversations with' these spirits 'as it were, like an actor in a melodrama who apostrophizes the audience on the other side of the footlights' (p. 100). Hardy seems to be dramatizing Jude's potential for contributing to the life of the university. At the same time, the image suggests his aloneness, his distance, his apartness from life. Hardy also emphasizes society's rôle in encouraging that distance; for the 'voice' which 'reached him out of the shade' proves to be, not one of those resurrected spirits, but the 'real and local voice' of a suspicious policeman, who sends Jude away from the seat of learning, now as later, when he is ill and dying, to his bed. The destructive consequences are suggested through Jude's growing awareness of the approach of disease, albeit it only 'that he seemed to be catching a cold'—a condition he is later to incite deliberately as he returns to Christminster to his death.

Jude's alienation from these 'spirits' seems also to reflect his spiritual dis-ease: not only his conflict with Christminster, but also that between conscious and unconscious awareness. For, 'as he drew towards sleep' the spirits are raised again, this time from his unconscious rather than from the colleges (p. 100). Their words, like messages in a dream, are sometimes 'audible', sometimes 'unintelligible to him'. Nevertheless, they are inspired from his own memory and reflect his own unconscious spiritual development (p. 100). Christminster may well suggest to Jude ideas which may fuel his spiritual development; but here, as in that initial scene at the well in Marygreen, the prime source of Jude's spiritual development is within his own psyche.

Jude's ability to perceive this is still limited, as is his spiritual development. He listens to Arnold's call to Christminster as 'the true goal of all of us, to the ideal, to perfection'; but he forgets that this same 'spectre' 'afterwards mourned Christminster as "the home of lost causes" ' (p. 100). Presumably, he interprets in terms of mental and spiritual sustenance Peel's ideal that in

'a country threatened with famine . . . there should be free
access to the food of man from whatever quarter it may come'
(pp. 100–1); but he seems not to be warned by that archetypal
antagonism suggested by Gibbon's reference to 'the sages' who
'turned aside' from the progress inspired by new and honour-
able Christian ideals, apparently 'unconscious of any altera-
tions in the moral or physical government of the world' outside
their walls. Rather, Jude attunes to Browning's belief that it is
possible for 'the world' to be 'made for each of us'—for Jude,
with his personal quest, to be one of 'each of the Many' who
'helps to recruit/ The life of the race by a general plan'.

Thus, Jude clings to those ideas which encourage him to
sustain his ideals; but that persistent 'stress of his old idea' (II,
II, p. 104) prejudices his ability to become fully conscious of
conflicting ideas. He recognizes Browning as 'the last of the
optimists'. Yet he does not proceed to acknowledge the unlikeliness of literal success within Christminster, where it was
assumed, at that time, that the process of spiritual seeking had
been completed, that the 'absolute certitude' of its dogma was
unassailable. Jude seems to be encouraged by Keble's exhortation that he should not fear the loneliness necessitated by his
quest; yet the ominous tone of the idea which prompts the
exhortation—that we have to die alone—somewhat subdues its
encouraging intent.

Despite Jude's contrary efforts, the perspective of death
gathers momentum. This is suggested by the words of the
following, and final, two phantoms; upon these memories and
realizations Jude falls asleep. First, the levelling function of death
is acknowledged. Yet the consoling tone is counteracted by a
tragic sorrow at how 'quickly' Jude must 'follow' (p. 101). Then
follows the sad childhood rhyme which suggests the positive
value of living so that neither death nor judgement need inspire
fear; yet it can hardly fail to depress in its present context as Jude
falls asleep on the line, 'Teach me to die' (p. 102). Thus, despite
the constructive vein in this experience, Jude's first night in
Christminster seems to culminate in a series of phantoms which
cast an 'adumbratio' (an anticipatory shadow) of his 'unknown
approach of death' over Jude's 'life and dreams'.[25]

These shadows seem to be dispelled when, after the disappearance of 'the spirits of the great men' (II, II, p. 103) and a

night-time of unconscious assimilation of these ideas, Jude sees Christminster more clearly. The 'treacherous' change in the 'countenances' of the colleges by light of day almost inspires rejection of those 'perfect and ideal' (*Arnold*, p. 103) notions about the city which were founded upon illusions. Its present 'wounded, broken' (p. 103) appearance suggests, rather, that Jude's attention has turned towards the idea of Christminster as 'the home of lost causes' (*Arnold*, p. 100). Jude's observations reflect a change in his attitude towards Christminster—from blind adoration to sympathy for its 'maimed' (p. 103) condition. Hence, the perspective of death emphasized by Jude's final three 'spectres'—Keble, Addison and Ken—might now seem to suggest the 'deadly struggle' of Christminster against the archetypal forces of 'years, weather, and man' (p. 103), rather than a kind of premonition of Jude's early death. For a while, it seems as if a changed attitude towards Christminster may allow him to avert that spiritual and physical fate.

Hence, Peel's democratic ideals (the second phantom) can be regarded now less from the point of view of persuading Christminster to allow Jude 'free access to the food of man' (p. 101) than from that of an awareness of Christminster's need for 'renovation' (p. 103) and 'regeneration' (p. 104) by those outside her walls. Thus,

> there fell on Jude a true illumination: that here in the stone yard was a centre of effort as worthy as that dignified by the name of scholarly study within the noblest of colleges. (p. 104)

His later reservations about the products of this effort does not invalidate this illumination regarding the effort itself. It is as if his unconscious is communicating the relative insignificance of the social goal—a bishopric—upon which Jude's mind had been focused at the time of his sexual awakening. The scene reflects perceptions that such social goals have little to do with his true quest.

Possibly, too, the scene communicates a more general— almost political—idea, in advance of his time: that revolution in social attitudes to be precipitated, apparently, by the Great War, but with psychic roots in the 'fin de siécle' pessimism of Jude's times. The ugliness of modern Marygreen did not only suggest the misery of an unwanted boy; it also illuminated destructive aspects of contemporary forms of change. Later, the doctor who attends the dead children—described by Jude as 'an advanced man', 'says there are such boys' as Father Time

> springing up amongst us—boys of a sort unknown in the last generation—the outcome of new views of life. They seem to see all its terrors before they are old enough to have staying powers to resist them. He says it is the beginning of the coming universal wish not to live. (VI, II, p. 356)

I know of no evidence that Hardy's view coincided with this. However, in the context—perhaps the emotional climax of the novel—it is difficult to dismiss the idea.

If the doctor assesses the trend correctly, the wider context of the novel would suggest that an impossibly intense struggle against a destructive current in society causes this despair. In retrospect, the Great War might, indeed, be perceived as the culmination of 'this universal wish not to live'—the attendant destruction of the social fabric a manifest symptom of the psychic devastation signified by that war. Looking back, we may perceive what Hardy cannot consciously have known— that Jude's ultimate tragedy is a kind of small-scale model of the tragic outcome of a tide of thought which is approaching universal consciousness. Jude's present 'illumination' regarding the dignity of labour also suggests a sense of an attendant development in modern thought not yet fully conscious in Jude's time. It suggests, too, how Jude might be a 'worthy' touchstone for this constructive development. Instead, that development is to come about only as an indirect consequence of a war which devastates a too rigid society.

Yet, at this perhaps most supreme of those moments where Hardy shows how 'worthy' Jude is (and, by implication, how tragic is his failure) to attend Christminster, Jude loses sight of that 'true illumination' 'under stress of his old idea'. His old unqualified respect for Christminster reasserts itself. He no longer recalls Gibbon and Newman (the third and fifth phantoms, p. 101). Now he fails to qualify his 'illumination' by bringing to consciousness an earlier suggestion that the obstinate dogmatism of 'the sages' and their refusal to recognize the changing nature of the modern world, has led to Christminster's complementary spiritual fossilization. Jude recognizes the limitations and irrelevance of the retrograde Gothic forms to which the stonemasons direct their regenerative effort. Yet he cannot, at this time, perceive that this work in stone reflects a misdirected kind of spiritual regeneration both within the colleges and within himself.

Eventually, however, his 'growing impatience of faith' leads to a conscious decision to follow his feelings at the expense of that 'old idea' (III, X, p. 216). By the time of his death he appreciates fully the irrelevance of discussing 'the eastward position' with 'all creation groaning' (III, II, p. 357), and the irony of Christminster's performance of that anthem, 'Truly God is loving unto Israel'. As Jude's awareness strengthens, Hardy emphasizes more and more the opposing strength of society. Eventually it breaks both Jude and Sue.

Unconsciously, at least, Jude always seems to have recognized how oppressive society might prove. His quest for even one like mind seems doomed from his first meeting with Sue 'at the cross in the pavement which marked the spot of the Martyrdoms' (II, IV, p. 119)—a place 'gloomy and inauspicious in its associations'. Soon 'the trees overhead deepened the gloom of the hour, and they dripped sadly upon him, impressing him with forebodings' (II, V, p. 129). In this context, Hardy imbues with symbolic significance that image of those 'two figures under one umbrella coming out of the vicarage gate'. Hence, Jude suffers, as in a dream, an awakening into ' "the hell of conscious failure", both in ambition and in love' (II, VII, p. 144). Jude responds by abandoning his 'University hopes' (p. 145). He tries to be financially realistic. However, his new desire to become a licentiate of the Church shows limited self-comprehension. The only resolution of his sexual needs which the Church will sanction is reunion with Arabella. However, in the first part of the novel Hardy has revealed enough for us to foresee what a grotesque affront to his spiritual sensitivities such a reunion would be. Alternatively, perhaps, he could accept the limitations of lifelong sexual abstinence. However, full adherence to the spirit of the Church would not allow him to be true to himself. In the second part of the novel Hardy shows that the religious ideals of the contemporary Church would provide no less grotesque a form for his sensitivities than would remarriage to Arabella. His decision to become a licentiate ignores even

Jude's earliest perceptions of the perversity of this Church and of those who 'subscribed' to it (I, II, pp. 35–6).

Yet, even now, unconsciously, Jude recognizes an affinity between the 'mournful wind' which 'blew through the trees' and 'the deep murmurs' of the curate 'praying with his aunt in the adjoining room' (p. 144). That same 'mournful wind' sounds 'in the chimney' of his room 'like the pedal notes' of the church organ. The ivy leaves which peck their 'neighbours smartly' are 'overgrowing the wall of the churchless' and 'now abandoned' churchyard. The creaking weather-vane belongs to that same 'new Victorian-Gothic church' which, from the beginning of the novel, symbolized values antipathetic to Jude's nature. As before, his instincts recognize that his misery is partly a product of that incompatibility between his own nature and the sterile, perverse spirit of that church; but so eager is he for 'any kind of hope to support' (p. 145) him that he debars himself from growing conscious of these symbolic expressions of that awareness.

Thus, Hardy exposes the dangers of suppressing Jude's questioning spirit. That spirit encourages the search for constructive paths through the inevitable complexities of human experience. Jude's second attempt at sexual fulfilment does incorporate an alternative attempt at spiritual fulfilment. But society will not condone their failure to marry. Hence, it involves subjecting Sue and his children, as well as himself, to a dreadful life-style, culminating in illness and death. In the character of Sue, Hardy dramatizes the destructive potential of society's limitations when imbibed into the human character. One could argue that Jude and Sue might go further towards resolving the resultant conflict within Sue by taking more account of society as it is. However, Hardy partly forestalls this criticism by showing, through Jude's bitter experience, how society limits the freedom of the human spirit to seek out constructive alternatives, and thence to reintegrate with society (V, VI). By remarrying Arabella, Jude abandons hope at a point when, had he had the strength, he might have begun a new quest to fulfil himself in the light of experience. It was at just such a point that Oak began to reconstruct his life after the ruin of his hopes, both in work and in love, with the attendant emotional exhaustion. However, Jude has striven to overcome this pressure. In *Jude*, Hardy offers a far more complex illustration of society's exacerbation of the destructive forces which inhibit such a reconstruction, and of the hopelessness underlying Jude's emotional exhaustion.

As Jude enters Christminster for the last time, Hardy recalls and intensifies aspects of his first visit there and of his first walk with Arabella. Thus he recalls Jude's earlier sexual and spiritual confusion and society's thwarting of Jude's reconstructive efforts. Hardy seems to be relating these factors to Jude's present physical and spiritual condition. That focal point of Jude's early experiences 'by the Brown House, where the road to Alfredston crosses the old Ridgeway' (VI, VIII, p. 410) is now acknowledged to be the 'coldest [spot] of all' in Wessex. Now, in 'the teeth of' its 'wind and rain' Jude begins to experience that 'deadly chill' which both prefigures his death and recalls his warning experience of catching cold on his first 'pilgrimage'. The milestone upon which he once carved his quest, already obscured by stinging nettles after his first setback, is now 'nearly obliterated by' the more permanent moss. The spot where the gibbet of his ancestor and Sue's had stood—the associations of which were then unknown to Jude— is now imbued with intense emotional significance on account of his associations with Sue. Once he fulfilled his 'fancy' to arrive in Christminster on foot; now he is physically unfit to do so. He has to depend on surprisingly indirect and tedious modern means of transport. He is no longer able to control the direction of his life.

Christminster is again peopled with those 'spirits' that Jude 'saw when I first walked here' (VI, IX, p. 411); but their significance as 'spirits of the dead' has now fulfilled its ultimate threat in representing the condition of Jude's spirit. He believes that, when he is dead, 'you'll see my spirit gliding up and down here among these' (p. 413); thus he half recognizes that the affinity between himself and these spirits is already complete. When 'he seemed to hear voices' he repeats them 'as if to gather their meaning' and concludes that they 'seem' to be 'laughing at' him. And yet, in acknowledging that he was talking to himself, he half recognizes them as projections into the environment of his own spiritual condition.

The symbols which he projected into the environment clarify

the roots of his failure and despair. The 'chilly fog ... as if death-claws were grabbing me through and through' comes 'from the meadows of Cardinal', whose 'windows with lifted eyebrows' are 'representing the polite surprise of the University at the efforts of such as I' (p. 412). No amount of clamouring on Arabella's part can convince us that the physical reality is a greater reality than that projected by Jude into the 'dream-country' environment. Even the physically 'real' policeman, in recalling to mind the policeman who unconsciously sided with Cardinal by sending Jude away on his first pilgrimage, is unable to convince us that Arabella's perspective is a greater reality. Thus, as Jude approaches death, his ability to relate to his environment more closely than he has ever done before results in the creation of a 'dream-country' more 'real', more significant, than the physical world which inspires its outline.

The significance of the 'series of seemings' expressed through this 'dream-country' may be clarified further by comparison with those 'seemings' experienced by Hardy the man. Creighton argues that, upon marriage to Emma, Hardy acted as, and believed himself to be, a 'pious Anglican', despite contradictory 'seemings' experienced in another 'part of his consciousness'.[26] His use of such 'seemings' 'for artistic purposes', as in *Jude*, seems to illuminate a retrospective recognition of the folly of dismissing contradictory insights. Like Jude, Hardy's religious background inhibits his search for God; Hardy separates that search from the impulse towards self-discovery, for fear of creating a god in his own image, rather than as an 'external personality'.[27] Hence, while 'appalled at the feebleness of the arguments for infant christening', the young Hardy had 'incontinently determined to "stick to his own side"', as he considered the Church to be, at some costs of conscience'.[28] The early Jude reacts similarly, as does the later Sue. Fowles shows the importance of considering literature in terms of the 'benign psychosis of the writing experience', involving a 'deeply exhausting' 'loss of secret self'.[29] Perhaps Hardy's dual struggle to discover God and to discover the nature and significance of his 'secret self' inspired the creative force which fashioned Jude's life and character.

The struggle to discover and to fulfil one's spiritual identity is part of a general struggle for survival, and has long been expressed in 'dream' form. (See Chapter 1.) This novel shows how Jude's society suppresses that spiritual search. His society tolerates only orthodox patterns of behaviour; thus it inhibits the freedom of the human spirit to regenerate itself, according to situations which arise. Now, as then, the complexities and confusions of the social environment can exacerbate that struggle. Every age evolves new variations upon old evils, new forms of injustice. It is precisely because the forms of evil change that it is so difficult to fight it, or even to be conscious of it. In *The Woodlanders*, Hardy suggested the archetypal nature of this problem in terms of the evolution of the Loki myth. (See Chapter 1.) In *Jude*, he emphasizes the specifically modern aspects of this problem—those insensitive, destructive changes which counteract constructive social reform, and which exacerbate Jude's crippling sense of alienation.

Now, the problem of spiritual alienation has grown increasingly acute, its consequences increasingly destructive. Material change was a crucial aspect of progress in Hardy's time; but the material changes which devastate Jude's environment show the importance of attendant spiritual reform. In this nuclear age it no longer needs a genius to perceive the dangers of spiritual disharmony. With the advantage of hindsight, we may perceive within *Jude* the 'fin de siècle' pessimism which seems to have precipitated the Great War. Now, amid the tension of an apparently precipitate nuclear holocaust, the contemporary reader might, I suggest, be especially sensitive to the need to respond to this instinct for survival. In unconsciously striving to express his struggles with his 'secret self' in terms of Jude's relationship with a 'dream-country' environment, Hardy has, I suggest, foreshadowed the psychic development of humankind in the century after his own.

In conclusion, then, this 'dream-country' environment is more than a means of reflecting, and conveying, Jude's unspoken impressions; Jude's developing relationship with this 'dream-country' shows a desperate striving to tap the regenerative potential of the human spirit. Hardy shows the importance of this striving by suggesting the destructive consequences of following a succession of false tracks. He emphasizes it by showing how society exacerbates those destructive consequences. Hence, Jude's confusion and despair deepen, although experience brings him closer towards self-comprehension.

Hardy's use of a 'dream-country' to help evoke social criticism is important. His use of the 'dream-country' to show the striving of the unconscious towards consciousness is also important. This fictional technique is especially relevant to our day, for spiritual alienation has become an important subject of fiction. In expressing that striving in terms of Jude's relationship with a 'dream-country' environment, Hardy simultaneously projects onto the reader a privileged point of view towards his character. Thus Hardy relates to us at an unconscious level, as if communicating within that otherwise solitary world of the dream. Hardy's use of a 'dream-country' is more than a new way of perceiving well-trodden landscape; it is an effective way of breaking down spiritual barriers.

3. Jocelyn Pierston

> There is, of course, underlying the fantasy followed by the visionary artist, the truth that all men are pursuing a shadow, the unattainable, and I venture to hope that this may redeem the tragicomedy from the charge of frivolity.[30]

Hardy's subtitle for *The Well-Beloved*, 'A Sketch Of A Temperament', suggests a light treatment of the artist's fantasy. Nonetheless, Pierston's temperament expresses acutely what Hardy perceives as a universal experience of pursuing an unattainable ideal. Hardy shows how this pursuit relates to Pierston's art and to his experiences. Hardy seems to regard his own art as the refining of experience. Yet, through Pierston's experiences with the second and third Avices, Pierston begins to perceive how his artistic temperament has led him to limit his all-round development. On the other hand, when he loses interest in the ideal altogether, he becomes a broken, sterile old man. Others have discussed the artistic and romantic aspects of Pierston's ideal.[31] Sumner has discussed the psychological implications of its affinities to Jung's concept of the 'anima'.[32] Here I consider how far the environment illuminates this paradoxical relationship between art and experience.

Pierston's name draws attention to the significance of the island of stone. In striving to objectify this pursuit of the

Well-Beloved through his art, Pierston carves sculptures in stone from his native island. Comparison with Jude the stone-mason is pertinent. (Hardy wrote *Jude* during the years between his two versions of *The Well-Beloved*; in his autobiography, he discussed the latter in his chapter on *Jude*.) Jude is not creating original art. He sustains the physical fabric of institutions such as Christminster. Thus he sustains his own physical fabric. Thus he saves for a chance to pursue his ideals within those walls. He is thwarted. Nonetheless, Hardy suggests Jude's spiritual development through that work. Comparison with Jude's plight intensifies our awareness of Pierston's conde-scension towards the father who provides the financial support and security necessary for him to pursue his art (I, I, p. 30). The relationship seems imbalanced; the quarrier gives and the sculptor takes. Pierston the quarrier is described indirectly—as if he were important only as an aspect of the sculptor's back-ground consciousness. Hardy's primary concern is to explore the course and consequences of pursuing a spiritual ideal when free to do so. Yet he seems also to suggest that Pierston's freedom is unusual and artificial; and it encourages him to neglect important aspects of human experience.

Hardy keeps us aware of these neglected aspects through oblique references to the father's work in stone. Although his father was 'not at home', his work is imbued with archetypal significance through the

> eternal saws . . . going to and fro upon eternal blocks of stone—the very same saws and the very same blocks that he had seen there when last in the island, so it seemed to him [Pierston the artist]. (I, I, p. 30)

Even when the father is long dead, his psychological significance is preserved:

> the silent ships came and went, the chisels clinked in the quarries; file after file of whitey-brown horses, in strings of eight or ten, painfully dragged down the hill the square blocks of stone on the antediluvian wooden wheels just as usual. (III, I, p. 146)

Huge blocks of stone are continually being taken from the island and transported to London—the practical parallel of the movements of Pierston the sculptor. The second Avice—the practical one—travels on a boat engaged upon similar work.

Only at this time, and on her account, is Pierston concerned about the precariousness of the boats and the dangers of the work. Until now, Pierston seems able to ignore physical practicalities. Thus Pierston's attitude to his father is suggested by these reflections upon the environment. Thereby Hardy shows Pierston gradually recognizing how his artistic pursuits have been limiting his psychological development.

Nonetheless, Hardy encourages us to respect Pierston's 'solid artistic reputation' (I, IX, p. 68). Physical practicalities are important. But so are artistic instincts. Indeed, finally, Hardy reasserts their importance by showing what are regarded as improvements by those whose artistic sensitivities are dead. In this he criticizes the trend of the age. Thus it is important to perceive how Hardy uses the same stone island to suggest the roots of Pierston's artistic pursuits. In his Preface (p. 25), Hardy emphasizes that this 'peninsula carved by Time out of a single stone, whereon most of the following scenes are laid' has been Pierston's family home 'for centuries immemorial'. 'Fancies . . . seem to grow up naturally here, in particular amongst those natives who', like Pierston, 'have no active concern with the labours of the "Isle" '; hence, 'it is a spot apt to generate a type of personage like the character imperfectly sketched' here. Pierston 'never much' considers that the ideal might be 'a subjective phenomenon vividified by the weird influences of his descent and birthplace' (I, II, p. 34). Yet, despite separation from his father and despite 'kimberlin' influence, there are times when Pierston perceives that 'the spot seemed what it was said once to have been, the ancient Vindilia Island, and the Home of the Slingers' (I, I, p. 28). Even after Pierston's long absence abroad, 'the quarries of ruins in the Eternal City reminded him of the quarries of maiden rock at home' (III, I, p. 147). Without Pierston's presence, the island seems primarily a place of work; with the expectation of Pierston's presence, Hardy draws our attention towards its symbolic significance as the 'rock' which 'instigated' his 'first use of the chisel'—the beginning of his artistic pursuit (III, I, p. 146).

As Pierston's thoughts of that 'maiden rock' develop into thoughts of Marcia and Ann Avice, that rock suggests, too, the roots of his romantic pursuits. Near the end of the novel, Pierston suggests to Marcia that 'the island ruled our destinies,

though we were not on it' (III, VIII, p. 203). He has long
associated his romantic tendencies with descent from a 'strange,
visionary race' (I, VII, p. 54). Yet, until Avice's death, he does
not begin to perceive how this association is reflected in that
'unity' between the 'towering rock' and the stone houses (I, I,
pp. 28–9) in which his family, and Avice's, had always lived.
Gradually the association becomes clear. The first Avice merely
adjoined his at a corner (I, II, p. 31). The second Avice lives in
his very house. The third Avice sleeps in his very room.
Increasingly, too, Pierston perceives that his romantic pursuits
have encouraged that dangerous dissociation from more prosaic
'influences of his descent and birthplace'. Through the second
and third Avices Pierston strives in vain to reintegrate his
artistic and romantic pursuits with his island roots—presumably
in the interests of psychological unity. Pierston's tone is
lighthearted when he suggests that his strange experience may
follow a universal pattern (I, VII, p. 54), but Hardy invites the
reader to take the idea seriously. Through suggesting that
Pierston's 'fantasy' may be reflected in the people, as well as in
the substance, of this awesome island of stone, Hardy uni-
versalizes that fantasy into what he refers to as the pursuit of the
'shadow'. The suggestion that Ann Avice and Pierston may
have inherited this tendency from an unknown ancestor, the
ancient history of the island and its temple to a love-goddess,
combine to suggest that this 'shadow' bears comparison with
Jung's concept of the 'anima'— an archetype of the collective
unconscious, latent in the individual unconscious.[33]

In this respect, it is interesting that a 'visionary artist' who
undervalues the significance of the practical 'father', perceives
his shadow, by contrast, as feminine. The idea has affinities
with Jung's theory that the 'anima' might represent female
elements in a man. It is also interesting to consider that, when
dreaming, the physical work of the body functions at a low ebb
and seems relatively unimportant, compared with the more
active mind or human spirit. By relating Pierston's experience
to the environment in this way, Hardy encourages the reader to
perceive Pierston's experience as an adventure into a kind of
'dream-country'.

Hence, too, as in *Jude*, Hardy illuminates through contrasts.
He projects antithetical male/female characteristics into

Pierston's experience in order to communicate with the reader's conscious mind. In this, he parallels a process which, Jung suggests, has always characterized Man's striving towards consciousness in his dream-life. Theories derived from Jung's studies of dreams seem to be illustrated, before Jung's time, by the 'dream-country' figures born out of Hardy's creative unconscious to inhabit Pierston's island home. Both Hardy and Jung may have been misled; but the parallels may, on the other hand, help explain the sense of authenticity which seems to derive from Hardy's attempt to emphasize universal aspects of Pierston's experience. More important is this: Jung's theories help us to comprehend how, and to what effect, Hardy creates those 'dream-country' figures.

Initially, the male/female antithesis helps to convey a sense of flux and reflux in Pierston's state of mind. That polarity fades in significance as he perceives more closely the physical working life of humankind. More noticeable then is the growing tension between opposing aspects of the 'anima' itself. In rejecting Avice, Pierston seems to reject that aspect of his 'anima' which works to the good, as 'guide, friend and adviser',[34] in favour of more erotic and less dependable aspects. Recognizing that 'his affection for her now was rather that of a friend than of a lover' (I, II, p. 31), that 'his feeling for her now was rather of comradeship than love' (I, II, p. 34), Pierston's artistic temperament encourages him to pursue a 'subjective phenomenon' whose 'ghostliness' and 'independence of physical laws and feelings, had occasionally given him a sense of fear' (I, I, p. 34).

'The wile-weaving Daughter of High Zeus' is a symbolic expression of an instinctive archetypal fear, brought to consciousness in his dreams, that his blind pursuit might possibly be an abandonment to some frightening, dangerous spirit. Although he shuns the more prosaic aspects of his 'anima', he cannot forget it—hence the recurring 'Avice' motif. Thus Hardy suggests a prevailing tension within Pierston. His idea that this 'creature' is 'masquerading'[35] seems to derive from his 'presentiment that', despite the apparently advantageous artistic consequences of leaving Avice for this pursuit,[36] he 'should ache for it some day' (III, III, p. 165). Thus, even during the first part of the novel, when Pierston's uppermost perception of the 'Well-Beloved' was as 'the essence and epitome of all that is desirable in this existence' (II, IX, p. 118), that 'seeming' is undermined by contradictory 'seemings'.

The action of the novel shows the course of the artist's pursuit of the Well-Beloved. Yet the 'dream-country' seems to reflect aspects of that action which relate to those suppressed contradictory 'seemings'. Hardy describes, directly, Pierston's initially confused state of mind regarding marriage to Avice. He then emphasizes his reluctance in the slow homeward climb 'by the Old Road, Pierston dragging himself up the steep by the wayside hand-rail and pulling Avice after him upon his arm' (I, II, p. 35). Pierston has been encouraged by a fresh awareness that Avice is 'one of the class with whom the risks of matrimony approximate most nearly to zero', 'that of all the girls he had known he had never met one with more charming and solid qualities', that 'this was not a mere conjecture—he had known her long and thoroughly, her every mood and temper'. Yet his appreciation of these qualities is less powerful than his more dangerous instincts. Hence, he is still reluctant. On that account, so is she. (She also serves the 'dream-country' rôle of representing aspects of Pierston's character which he prefers to dismiss.) The consequent tension between and within them seems to be reflected in that 'deep, hollow stroke like the single beat of a drum' so reminiscent of a powerfully beating heart—a heart stimulated by physical exertion and by that associated emotional strain.

'The intervals being filled with a long-drawn rattling, as of bones between huge canine jaws', his attention is drawn towards the source of the sound—'the vast concave of Deadman's Bay' before them. As he considers his course, Pierston seems to be disturbed by the complexity of the image.[37] As it relates to his proposed marriage to Avice it seems possible that it may hint at a further, otherwise unexpressed, reason for his reluctance: sexual fear and shame. His reaction to Avice's first kiss provokes her to feel ashamed of her sexuality. Yet he proposes that they walk together by moonlight, engaged but unwed—a proposition of doubtful propriety by 'kimberlin' custom, and yet of overt significance by island custom. It is astonishing that a fastidious character such as his could disregard both at once; rather, the incident suggests his confusion— a product of conflicting moral codes. His failure to acknowledge

80

island custom is not simply a concession to his reading public: Hardy need not have mentioned the custom; some other reason could have been found for her non-appearance. Rather, Hardy suggests Pierston's dawning consciousness of the sexual fear and confusion prevalent among Hardy's reading public. Perhaps, for censorship reasons, no more direct method was open to Hardy.

Paradoxically, the 'vagina dentata' image is generally associated with that destructive aspect of the 'anima' which Pierston pursues. This pursuit of an ideal Well-Beloved who vanishes before consummation would enable him to avoid facing this fear. With Marcia he takes the plunge. Yet, almost immediately, he reverts to his former state of fear and confusion. His unconscious assistance of Leverre and alternative marriage to the aged Marcia support this supposition. And yet, Pierston seems to sense that it is more dangerous to use his pursuit of the Well-Beloved for this evasive purpose rather than to face, and determine to overcome, that fear. Those 'intervals' seem to suggest that a frightening kind of death awaits Pierston if he succumbs to that emotional pull away from Avice, towards an unknown Well-Beloved. Thus, these images of sexual fear and confusion intensify the complexity of Pierston's 'presentiment' about the consequences of rejecting Avice.

A further expression of the dangers latent in his alternative pursuit is suggested by 'the evening and night winds' here, which

> were to Pierston's mind, charged with a something that did not burden them elsewhere. They brought it up from that sinister Bay to the west, whose movement she and he were hearing now. It was a presence—an imaginary shape or essence from the human multitude lying below: those who had gone down in vessels of war, East Indiamen, barges, brigs, and ships of the Armada—select people, common and debased, whose interests and hopes had been as wide asunder as the poles, but who had rolled each other to oneness on that restless sea bed. There could almost be felt the brush of their huge composite ghost as it ran a shapeless figure over the isle, shrieking for some good god who would disunite it again. (I, II, pp. 35–6)

His kiss in the 'solemn spot' of 'the old Hope Churchyard' is like an appeal to that 'good god' to 'disunite' him from that spirit. But 'in this last stronghold of the Pagan divinities, where Pagan customs lingered yet, Christianity had established itself precariously at best' (I, II, p. 36). The image of the fallen, ruined church serves as a focus for Pierston's fear that there may be no resurrection, no escape from death, no second chance, if he succumbs to the dangers inherent in his alternative pursuit. Thoughts of Death's levelling function seem to provoke a warning: that social and financial advantage may prove futile—that, in accordance with natural, archetypal laws, he will be bound to accept the consequences of his actions.

Deep beneath the overt action of the novel lies this sub-structure of Pierston's suppressed, unconscious fears and expectations, reflected through this complementary 'dream-country' perspective, Hardy even uses the other characters as images through which to express those fears and expectations. In the next, short chapter, an islander interrupts his own expression of surprise that Pierston should care for Avice, 'nice maid as she is notwithstanding', to predict 'a change in the weather' (I, III, p. 39). The islander seems to voice Avice's own unease—'something more than the natural sadness of a parting which was not to be long'.[38] Her excuse might even be perceived as a cover for an unexpressed, perhaps even unconscious, precaution against the possibility that Pierston might not return (I, IV, p. 40). Certainly Hardy has prepared the reader to expect the precipitate development of Pierston's hitherto suppressed unconscious expectations.

After reading Avice's letter, Pierston finds 'that the evening seemed louring': that precipitate development seems to be beginning. Already 'the sea behind the pebble barrier kicked and flounced in complex rhythms, which', presumably because they seem to reflect Pierston's state of mind, 'could be trans-lated equally well as shocks of battle or shouts of thanksgiving.' Presently, 'for a moment', he still hopes that Avice may have changed her mind; the next moment, his pursuit of his so-called 'Juno'—that queen of Roman goddesses—has begun (I, IV, p. 41).

Hardy's subsequent use of a 'dream-country' perspective suggests developments of which Pierston is not yet consciously aware. 'While overtaking and conversing with her he had not yet observed' in 'the rising wind' a reflection of his trepidation.

As it 'proceeded from puffing to growling and from growling to screeching, with the accustomed suddenness of its changes here', he did not recognize a reflection of this initial stage in the pursuit of a form of the Well-Beloved. As it 'at length brought what it promised by these vagaries'—a rain described in terms of the accelerating action of 'pellets of a popgun'—it seems certain that the consequences will be destructive. Soon the onslaught 'assumed the character of a raking fusillade from the bank adjoining, one shot of which was sufficiently smart to go through Jocelyn's sleeve' (I, IV, p. 42). 'The roar of the storm' (I, V, p. 46) reflects their rising anger as they quarrel, but it is not until they are in danger of drowning that they 'realized the force of the elements'. Only as Pierston grows conscious of this does he become 'conscious of a sensation which, in its incipient and unrecognized form, had lurked within him from some unnoticed moment when he was sitting close to his new friend under the lerret' (p. 47).

Pierston is 'alarmed—even dismayed' at this sign of 'a possible migration of the Well-Beloved'. But he does not appear to perceive the danger inherent in the situation. Hardy conveys this impression by showing Pierston as unaware of that gathering 'force of the elements'. Pierston forgets the implications of their quarrel as he muses upon the sensation of holding her 'so tightly'. Yet Hardy seems anxious to suggest the danger inherent in this negligence. He seems to compare their reunion with that 'sudden breach in the bank' which, while often causing pedestrians to be 'blown into the sea hereabout, and drowned', would then 'close up and join itself together again after such disruption, like Satan's form when, cut in two by the sword of Michael, "The ethereal substance closed,/ Not long divisible" '.[39] The reference to Satan and his spiritual nature suggests the dangerous temptation inherent in Pierston's quest. The possibility of sudden drowning—of becoming part of that ghastly essence of the dead which haunted the scene with Avice—heightens our awareness of that danger. The whole passage serves as a series of images, functioning, as in a dream, to alert us to the depth of the dangers.

Of course, Hardy has already conditioned the reader's response to these 'dream-country' aspects of Pierston's environment by acquainting the reader with Avice. When, after falling 'into a reverie' over a bundle of clothes, Pierston breaks faith with Avice, the reader's sympathy is likely to remain with Avice—all the more so when Avice's character is compared with that of the petulant Marcia. However, Hardy's use of 'dream-country' elements also draws attention to the limits of Pierston's awareness. This encourages the reader to sympathize with him to a far greater extent than a straight account of his desertion would allow.

That sympathy is further encouraged by hints of a 'supernatural power' (p. 46) beyond Pierston's comprehension or control. Whether or not this power originates from within his own psyche, it suggests Pierston's extreme confusion—a product of his dangerous dilemma. It relates, too, to that image of the Well-Beloved which he projects upon the wearer of those empty clothes. He and Marcia are 'old friends' (I, VI, p. 50) only in a deceptive sense—because she seems to house the returned spirit of the Well-Beloved; 'hereditarily' they are 'mortal enemies' (p. 51). Marcia is only temporarily angry with her father. However, she is a bitter enemy of Pierston's father. That enmity is the root of their incompatibility. Archetypally, the single-minded pursuit of this aspect seems to increase one's vulnerability, for it necessitates the neglect and disintegration of sounder instincts (symbolized by Avice). Here, Hardy seems to suggest how it may entail conflict with the 'father'—or conscious self. Thus, the 'sardonic voices and laughter in the wind' which 'he seemed to hear' 'in the night' (I, VIII, p. 65) after the departure of the Well-Beloved leave him feeling temporarily empty and depressed. Those voices do not simply recall an episode past and nearly forgotten. They even suggest more than his sense of foolishness over his mistake. They seem to testify to mysterious, dangerous, self-destructive elements within Pierston. Ultimately, it seems that the essence of his quest for his Well-Beloved is his attempt to comprehend and control these elements.

Thus, while the 'dream-country' reflects and illuminates aspects of the artist's pursuit, it can also relate them to the development of his life and character. The second part of this novel opens with 'news of his father's death' while he is far from home. Thereupon his 'artistic emotions were abruptly suspended' (II, I, p. 72). His life assumes a new direction. The shock seems

to encourage Pierston to recognize his neglect of the 'father'
aspect as he pursued his Well-Beloved. Indeed, he is so
unemotional about his father that his death seems, almost
entirely, to be a dream-like symbolic expression of that crisis in
his art—that recognition of his vulnerability as 'a one-part
man—a presenter of her only' (II, I, p. 79).

This crisis is also expressed in terms of his contrastingly
dramatic reaction to news of Avice's death, in the subsequent
chapter. Hillis Miller has shown how an apparently straightforward pattern of repetition can embrace an apparently contradictory pattern of differences.[40] Until now, Pierston has
perceived the simpler pattern. Here, however, he reacts to the
novel aspects of the phenomenon. The object of his desire is dead.
Perhaps her death qualifies her to take the form of the Well-
Beloved by rendering her 'inaccessible' (II, III, p. 88). However,
with this transition of the Well-Beloved from a society lady to his
native Avice comes a new stage in Pierston's understanding. For
the first time there is no conflict between the image of his
Well-Beloved and his appreciation of Avice's more 'solid qualities'
(I, II, p. 35); at the same time, his love becomes 'rarefied and
refined to its highest attar' (II, III, p. 88). Developing the
archetypal aspects of Part I, Hardy has Pierston perceive 'in her
nature, as in his . . . some mysterious ingredient sucked from the
isle; otherwise a racial instinct necessary to the absolute unison of
a pair' (II, III, p. 89). He even imagines it to be rooted in
prehistoric associations with a 'love-goddess of the Slingers'
(p. 89) supposedly worshipped by their common ancestors. This
attempt to recreate a myth through which to express the intensity
of his feeling culminates in an assumption that she is 'the true
star of his soul' (p. 89). Acknowledging now their common roots,
recognizing her point of view, he no longer dismisses as 'a bygone
barbarism' (I, IV, p. 40) that crucial island custom. He now
believes that 'had she appeared, the primitive betrothal, with its
natural result, would probably have taken place' (p. 91); moreover, as 'no islander had ever been known to break that contract'
she would inevitably 'have become his wife' had that probable
event occurred (p. 91). This appreciation has come to him too
late. His alternative pursuit of the Well-Beloved distracted him.
It led, instead, to art and 'Academy interests'. Hence his
dramatic denial of them now (p. 90).

This dramatic and, for Pierston, exceptionally emotional change in attitude is emphasized through Hardy's use of 'dream-country' elements. Chapter I ends with news of Avice's death. Chapter II begins with a deliberate shift of focus into a 'dream-country' environment which illustrates the new direction in Pierston's thought and feeling. 'By imperceptible and slow degrees' a 'dream-country' perspective upon 'Avice Caro, and the old, old scenes on Isle Vindilia' (II, III, p. 86) gradually displaces the reality of the dining-room. 'Nothing could less express the meaning his recent news had for him than a statement of facts' (II, III, p. 87); the 'dream-country' perspective into which Hardy draws us suggests that complex 'meaning' more powerfully than can Pierston's words or actions alone.

In this context, the scene in Pierston's room may also have meaning as a scene in a dream, the room representing Pierston himself. He withdraws 'a small box tightly nailed down' from a lower drawer of an escritoire 'at one side of this room'. He has to force the cover with a poker before he can withdraw, 'from the melancholy mass of . . . odds and ends, which Pierston had thrown into it from time to time in past years for future sorting', his image of Avice, taken 'in the primitive days of photography' (II, III, p. 87). Thus his recollection of Avice is described as if in the language of a dream. This has the effect of suggesting that Pierston is discovering, as if in a kind of hypnotic trance, hidden depths of his being.

While in this state of mind, his attention becomes focused anew upon that 'vivid presentiment of Avice Caro, and the old, old scenes on Isle Vindilia' (II, III, p. 86)—this time as inspired by the sight of the moon from out of the window of his room. As if in a dream, 'the young pale moon' which overhangs the isle seems to be a 'symbol' which

> signified well. The divinity of the silver bow was not more excellently pure than she, the lost, had been. Under that moon was the island of Ancient Slingers, and on the island a house, framed from mullions to chimney-top like the isle itself, of stone. Inside the window, the moonlight irradiating her winding-sheet, lay Avice, reached only by the faint noises inherent in the isle; the tink-tink of the chisels in the quarries, the surging of the tides in the Bay, and the muffled grumbling of the currents in the never-pacified Race. (II, III, p. 89)

All those aspects of the island which were imbued with 'dream-country' significance in Part I of the novel are brought together here. And under the influence of this consummate image, Pierston 'began to divine' that perception of 'the truth' which is to inculcate a new and profound variation upon the theme of an old pattern of behaviour.

Pierston has long been striving to comprehend and hence to control that dangerous pursuit of the Well-Beloved. Now he seems to recognize that his father and Avice illustrated neglected inner resources which might have helped him to control destructive aspects of his pursuit. Now he feels that, by 'grafting' his pursuit of the 'love-goddess' upon that 'groundwork of character' long appreciated by his sounder instincts, he may be capable of 'fixed and full-rounded constancy to a woman'. Hardy has used 'dream-country' perspectives upon the environment to convey a complex body of shifting and apparently paradoxical experiences which culminate in this acknowledgement. The effect is like that of a dream from which one might awaken to cite some well-known platitude which seems to summarize the dream, knowing, however, that the dream expressed far greater profundities.

Hence, Hardy continues to suggest 'dream-country' perspectives more complex than Pierston can express or comprehend. There is a striking disparity between the 'dream-country' image of Avice, rooted in certain aspects of his own character and ideals, and her daughter and grand-daughter, who conform less and less closely to that image. When he first sees Ann Avice, on her mother's grave, he finds himself capable of 'fixed and full-rounded constancy' towards her. Yet he thinks of her in the context of 'the haunted atmosphere of Roman Venus about and around the site of her perished temple there' (II, V, p. 97). Ann Avice's perspective upon herself and upon her relationship with her mother is strikingly different. Ironically, it is when he discovers that she shares his problem regarding the Well-Beloved—as her mother did not—that he realizes how independent she is of his 'dream-country' image of her (II, VIII; II, IX, p. 118). Thus, the 'dream-country' perspective still focuses upon Pierston's experience, illuminating the limits of his— nonetheless developing—awareness. At the same time, it becomes increasingly clear, even to Pierston, that the characters within the 'dream-country' have perspectives of their own. Indeed, through the contrast between Ann Avice and her mother, Hardy emphasizes the change in Pierston.

The 'abstracted literalness' of his response to Somers' indignation—that 'it was *only* nineteen and three quarters' years since he last saw Avice (emphasis mine)—shows how close Pierston now feels to that aspect of his psyche symbolized by the first Avice and her island home. Somers' reference to Pierston as a Praxiteles suggests his sculpture of images of his Well-Beloved. His correction suggests Pierston's newly developed awareness that an artist must take account of the 'real' world. However, 'embittered by regret beyond words' (II, III, p. 88), he is distracted from his art by his need to exorcise guilt through a form of restitution. His interest in his art continues to decline (II, IV, p. 96). He is apathetic to the change in public feeling suggested by 'a spiteful criticism of a late work of his' (II, VI, p. 102). His desire to 'make amends for his infidelity to her family forty years back in the past' is to overcome his 'bodement that it would be folly to press on' with his pursuit of the third Avice (p. 165). It is the basis of his insistence that no one 'blame her' for deserting him: 'she didn't make the circumstances. I did. . . . It was how I served her grandmother' (III, VI, p. 187). (See too III, VII, p. 195.) Thus, while obsession with guilt encourages the withering of artistic and physical potencies, he develops that capacity for 'loving-kindness' in which Hardy perceives hope for humankind.

After all, then, like Jude, Pierston learns through experience, and through the failure of his quest. His 'aimless' revisiting of 'spots he had formerly visited with' Avice suggests his painful reluctance to learn in this way. His consciousness that, 'as if tethered to the churchyard by a cord' he is 'at the end of a radius whose pivot was the grave of Avice Caro', suggests that his compulsion to proceed is balanced by an equal reluctance. The image also suggests a sense that he is only just beginning to grow aware of this paradox: the first emanations from the unconscious seem to be crystallizing on a course towards conscious awareness. Yet 'as the dusk thickened he closed upon his centre' as if drawn towards meditation upon the significance of the image. Avice's grave now seems to symbolize a crucial experience for Pierston. As he 'entered the churchyard gate', drawing close to that experience, he seems almost to be falling asleep and entering into a dream (II, III, p. 92). The ambiguity between dream and waking experience grows as intense as at the beginning of the chapter as he loses 'count of time and consciousness of incident' (II, IV, 93).

Hardy uses the movement of light upon the environment to help suggest the strangely romantic aspects of the awakening. 'The same young moon' which prompted those imaginings 'the previous evening from his window in London' illuminates the grave. The calming of the breeze 'with the setting of the sun' seems in tune with Pierston's meditative frame of mind as he reaches his destination at last. 'The lighthouse' which 'had opened its glaring eye' seems to suggest Pierston's unconscious expectation of precipitate adventure; that image of the 'glaring eye' of the lighthouse or lightship frequently accompanies romantic scenes in this novel (II, III, p. 92). 'The lispings of the sea beneath the cliffs' contrast with that deadly sea which once helped to illustrate his confusion and passion. Yet this is also a reminder of the old ardour of his response to feminine sexuality, temporarily forgotten. Having 'lost count of time and consciousness of incident . . . he seemed to see Avice Caro herself, bending over and then withdrawing from her grave in the light of the moon'; thus the scene culminates in an ultimate expression of that ambiguity between dream and waking experience. That ambiguity seems to express Pierston's projection of this new stage in his psychic development upon 'the phantom of Avice, now grown to be warm flesh and blood' (II, V, p. 97). Because this stage in Pierston's perception of the Well-Beloved seems to signify an increase in wisdom, he perceives a 'Minerva cast' in her 'profile' (II, VI, p. 101). She does nothing to inspire either that 'sudden Sapphic terror of love' or that dream where 'he saw dimly masking behind that young countenance "the Weaver of Wiles" herself "with all her subtle face laughing aloud" ' (II, VI, p. 105). It is occasions such as the writing in stone (II, VI, p. 104), the three occasions when he unwittingly overhears her arguing with Isaac (II, VII, p. 108; II, VIII, p. 115; II, IX, p. 119) in three consecutive chapters, his realization that he is 'one of the corpses from which the ideal inhabitant had departed' (II, VIII, p. 114), which bring him to recognize a distinction between Ann Avice and the image he projects upon her. Just before that exposure, Hardy emphasizes the extent of that delusion:

> how incomparably the immaterial dream dwarfed the grandest of substantial things, when here, between those three sublimities— the sky, the rock, and the ocean—the minute personality of this washergirl filled his consciousness to its extremest boundary, and the stupendous inanimate scene shrank to a corner therein. (II, VIII, p. 113)

Thus, the 'dream-country' perspective suggests how the 'sprite, witch, troll' (II, IX, p. 121) she seems to be is an emanation of his own 'Psyche' (II, X, p. 123).

Although he has developed a capacity for 'constancy' and a desire for restitution so strong that it distracts him from his art, that 'Psyche' finds means to torment him still. The revelation is a development of the Lokian principle discussed in the first part of this thesis, with reference to *The Woodlanders*: not only does the principle of evil change into different, unpredictable forms; but as Pierston strives to humanize his behaviour towards others, that principle of evil changes its manner of tormenting him, causing him to harm himself rather than others. In the third part of the novel it encourages him to attempt suicide (in the original version); in both versions, it abandons the artist to a sterile old age.

Hardy suggests the archetypal inevitability of this final stage by the 'dream-country' context of the third Avice's birth. An unconscious travail at the birth of this final stage seems to be suggested by the association between the sea and the mother:

> the sea moaned—more than moaned—among the boulders below the ruins . . . accompanied by an equally periodic moan from the interior of the cottage chamber; so that the articulate heave of water and the inarticulate heave of life seemed but differing utterances of the selfsame troubled terrestrial Being— which in one sense they were. (II, XIII, p. 141)

As Pierston waits 'Between the travail of the sea without, and the travail of the woman within', 'the incipient being whom he was to meet again under very altered conditions' is born; in the ending of 'that dream' is the germ of another—of that final stage (II, XIII, pp. 143–44).

In the third part of the novel, those aspects of Pierston's

character suggested by his father and by the first Avice are
developed considerably, despite the continuing 'curse' of the
Well-Beloved. In the first part of the novel, Pierston's con-
descending acceptance of financial support from his father and
his callous desertion of Avice suggest an unpleasant or, at least,
thoughtless character. That impression is muted a little when
his artistic potential and psychological aberration are revealed.
His capacity for feeling is awakened by his consciousness of the
death of the 'father' and of Avice; and, 'ever since this jade of an
ideal learnt the unconscionable trick of inhabiting one image
only' he has 'ached' for his desertion of Avice (III, III, p. 165).
By now, however, gradually,

> a change had come over his regard of womankind. Once the
> individual had been nothing more than the temporary abiding-
> place of the typical or ideal; now his heart showed its bent to be a
> growing fidelity to the specimen, with all her pathetic flaws of
> detail; which flaws, so far from sending him further, increased his
> tenderness. (III, I, p. 150)

Now, the wealth of the 'father' is used to offer practical help to
Avice's daughter and grand-daughter, while his capacity for
'friendship', symbolized by the first Avice and experienced by
the second, develops into 'the further sentiment'—a 'cordial
loving-kindness' (III, VII, p. 193).

Pierston's physical and artistic decline, his developing
humanity, and the reader's developing sympathy, inspire a
strikingly new mood to this final part of the novel. Hardy draws
attention to the reasons why Pierston restricts his courting of
the third Avice to moonlight hours. In this, Hardy seems to
focus attention upon an aspect of the 'dream-country' environment which is developed dramatically in this final part of the
novel. Of 'those three sublimities' (II, VIII, p. 113), 'the rock'
and then 'the ocean' had dominated the scene. In the second
part, Hardy shifts attention towards the higher plane of the sky.
Now Hardy emphasizes how Pierston has come to feel that the
moon symbolizes his compulsive pursuit of the Well-Beloved.
His adulatory attitude is suggested by his worship of 'this
sisterly divinity on the first appearance monthly'. The form this
worship takes—bowing 'the knee three times' and directing 'a
kiss towards her shining shape'—symbolizes his submission to

his compulsion, to his Well-Beloved, every time she reappears. The monthly reappearance of the moon reflects what has become a seemingly regular pattern of behaviour. His perception that 'the sight of the new moon . . . made him feel as if his wraith in a changed sex had suddenly looked over the horizon at him' seems to suggest an awareness that the Well-Beloved is a projection of his own psyche—a psyche still dominated by this potentially dangerous aspect, despite his development of the contrary aspect symbolized by the first Avice (III, II, p. 156).

His memory of the second Avice clearly influences his perception of the moon. She housed that Well-Beloved. She also inspired friendship—a product of that development of the contrary aspect of his 'anima'. She also inspired the unprecedented longevity of the passion which Pierston experienced as a result. At the same time, her own parallel pursuit seems to inspire that image of 'his wraith in a changed sex', as does her consequent 'inconstancy'. As she is later to strive so desperately to establish, they are, in a sense, 'one people' (III, IV, p. 173).

However, the significance of that moon shifts considerably. Formerly, it had signified to Pierston the seemingly pure goodness of the first Avice; to him 'the symbol' of 'the young pale moon' 'signified well' how

> the divinity of the silver bow was not more excellently pure than she, the lost, had been. Under that moon was the island of Ancient Slingers, and on the island a house, framed from mullions to chimney-top like the isle itself, of stone. Inside the window, the moonlight irradiating her winding-sheet, lay Avice, reached only by the faint noises inherent in the isle; the tink-tink of the chisels in the quarries, the surging of the tides in the Bay, and the muffled grumbling of the currents in the never-pacified Race. (III, III, p. 89)

Avice had been educated out of island ways to a considerable extent, as had Pierston. Even so, to Pierston's mind she is defined in terms of their island—the 'dream-country' island as it is used by Hardy to reflect Pierston's unconscious psyche. Here, the moonlight illuminates how her death stimulates him to focus upon that aspect of his psyche which he deserted in deserting her—that capacity for friendship and 'loving-kindness' without which his actions seem those of 'a wicked, cruel man' (II, VII, p. 110).

Throughout the novel, the moon is also associated with an expectation of sexual passion. Pierston seems certain that, had Avice come to 'watch the moon rise over the sea' (I, III, p. 38), he would have married her. This implies that he would have awakened to that aspect of his psyche represented by her. At the time, he is amazed and amused at her reason for refusing; later, he acknowledges that the 'primitive betrothal' might well have taken place. Hardy seems to suggest that, unconsciously, the rising of the moon over the sea signifies to Pierston the awakening and consummation of his response to feminine sexuality.

With the appearance of the second Avice, Hardy integrates these two kinds of symbolic meanings. 'The same young moon' which seemed to signify the first Avice and that capacity for friendship and 'loving-kindness' illuminates the second Avice. Thus Hardy seems to suggest that new development in Pierston's character which is to stabilize this migration of the Well-Beloved. Yet it is his subsequent image of the second Avice as 'his wraith in a changed sex' which is to change his perception of the moon so that it seems to reflect that 'inconstancy', this time on her behalf, which prevents the consummation of sexual passion between them.

A 'new moon' helps suggest the changed atmosphere of the third part of the novel. It inspires Pierston's 'gigantic' fantasy as he pauses in passing 'the cottage in which the new Avice was born, from whose precincts he had heard her first infantile cry' (II, II, p. 156). He had already met her, fallen for her, and commented upon the strange coincidence of her occupying the room which 'had been his own' (III, II, p. 155). But that new moon 'near the west behind him . . . growing distinct upon the glow' (p. 156) illuminates the paradox of a passion which is 'far from having spent itself yet' despite the setting of his individual sun, the evetide of his physical life. The voice of his Well-Beloved calls, but it calls anyone's name but his. She is happy to see him, but only so that he may release her from the rock. Despite her friendliness, he is gloomy; only 'the dusk of evening' enables him to hide behind an illusion of youth; only while he meets her by moonlight can he sustain that crucial illusion. With the first Avice the moon signified purity; with the second, inconstancy; with the third, this gloomy, tense, unstable atmosphere suggests his consciousness of the precariousness of the third Avice's interest in him even while he can hide behind a youthful mask.

Yet this is not the first time in this novel when the moon illuminates perilous secrets. Once, in 'the faint moonrays he found a pair of names which, as a boy, he himself had cut. They were "Avice" and "Jocelyn" '. These are 'now nearly worn away by the weather and the brine'. Yet 'close by, in quite fresh letters, stood "Ann Avice", coupled with the name "Isaac" ' (II, VI, p. 104). The moon seems to illuminate an unconscious impression of which Pierston is growing aware—one which inspires 'a sudden, Sapphic terror of love'. It inspires a dream expressive of the perilous potential of his Well-Beloved (p. 105), and which points to that result of her inconstancy which is to prevent their union. Similarly, in the third part of the novel, the moon illuminates a potential cause of his failure to unite with the third Avice—the disparity in age. This time, it heralds the failure of his final opportunity. Most of all, it heralds the death of the artistic sensibilities associated with the Well-Beloved. The gloomy atmosphere is therefore more sustained than before, reflecting the overall mood of this final part.

While the moon continues to suggest this pervasive gloom, the strength of moonlight seems to reflect the intensity of Pierston's emotions. Despite his 'dread of encountering her in full light' he 'fancied he had won the younger Avice's interest, at least' and knew he had her mother's full approval. Hence his precarious optimism seems to be reflected in 'the now strong moonlight' (III, III, p. 162). 'Such evening promenades' became 'frequent'. Pierston believed 'it was impossible that' she 'should not have guessed the ultimate reason of these rambles'; but her assumption that he desires her mother confirms the precariousness of that increasing optimism which seems to be reflected in 'the waxing of the Summer moon' (p. 163). Thus, the tension mounts as he meets her at the 'very spot that he was to have met' her grandmother 'had she chosen to keep the appointment, a meeting which might—nay, must—have changed the whole current of his life'. Hardy suggests the intensity with which the environment reflects Pierston's complex emotions by suggesting how 'the whole present reality faded from Pierston's mind under the press of memories' (p. 163). As Pierston's love becomes 'permeated' with 'the tenderest, most anxious, most protective instinct he had ever known', Hardy takes care to suggest, too, how 'he was not without a bodement that it would be folly to press on' (p. 165). Both his fervour and his gloom seem to be reflected, thus, in that 'full moon' which 'streamed down upon them' (p. 163).

Soon, moon and moonlight are to develop a new kind of significance. Before this, the optimism signified by the waxing of this moon culminates in Avice's agreement to marry. Pierston's optimism reaches its peak when he awakens, the following dawn, to express a fairy-tale ideal of possessing the aptly named Sylvania Castle and living there with Avice until the end of his days. Even so, the idea provokes a suspicion that his optimism is unrealistic.

As soon as she agreed to marry, a dream-like description of a noise 'upon the window-panes, as of fine sand thrown' revived apparently gloomy aspects of the moon. Symbolically, 'lifting the blind, Pierston saw that the distant lightship' which Hardy uses frequently to reflect the characters' perception of the imminent sexual situation, now 'winked with a bleared and indistinct eye'. The 'drizzling rain' which 'had come on with the dark' and which 'was striking the window in handfuls' seemed to suggest that Pierston's unconscious was prompting him to acknowledge the likely outcome of the agreement just made. That gloom which had been signified, formerly, by the moon, returns again, immediately after his idealistic perception of their life together. As the dawn gives way to a 'cold grey morning light', he perceives 'a movement of something ghostly' and sees his 'spectre' reflected in the looking glass (III, IV, p. 170). The dispelling of the illusion shocks Avice as much as it shocked him when she sees him, subsequently, 'in the full stroke of day' (p. 171). The optimism once signified by the waxing of the moon no longer recurs, but the gloom signified by that same moon persists, presiding over what seems now to be his 'ghost story'(III, VII, p. 193).

At the same time, Hardy suggests certain parallels between Pierston and Leverre, implying his imminent displacement by the latter. Thus, 'in the gloom of the . . . evening' before their proposed wedding, Hardy describes Pierston as 'a creature sullen with a sense that he was about to withdraw from its keeping the rarest object it had ever owned'. His perception of himself seems to be reflected in 'the ruins of the Tudor castle and the long, featureless rib of grinding pebbles that screened off the outer sea'. His sense of Avice's unapproachable sexuality seems to be reflected in that 'outer sea, which could be heard lifting and dipping rhythmically in the wide vagueness of the Bay' (III, V, p. 177). His assistance of Leverre (p. 177), the offering of 'his walking stick and his arm' (p. 178), Avice's obvious expectation of Leverre rather than Pierston as she waits at the door of her house (pp. 178–79), Leverre's use of the best bedroom linen prepared for Pierston and conveniently left unused by him (III, VI) and Pierston's ultimate financial provision for them (III, VII), all suggest his growing recognition and encouragement—if unconsciously at first—of Avice's and Leverre's desire that Leverre should displace him.

Once Pierston has allowed Leverre to displace him, the subsequent renewal of moon imagery relates to Leverre and Avice, leaving Pierston in the shade, as, symbolically, at the funeral of the second Avice. As early as that first meeting with the third Avice, she had been looking 'at something out to sea just discernible in the evening light as assisted by the moon' (III, II, p. 157); already Hardy is using moon imagery to communicate a sense of what is to come. Now, 'standing at the front door as she had been doing when he came, looking into the light of the full moon, which had risen since his arrival' (p. 180), she is looking out for the man who is to displace Pierston. Until Pierston's footsteps cease, she approaches the entrance to Sylvania Castle; turning back, she meets Leverre in the castle of the Red King. As it stands against the background of 'the moonlit, indefinite sea', the moon seems now to suggest her own sexual feelings. After this, the moon no longer signifies Pierston's emotions; its rising reflects, now, the renewal of Avice's feelings for Leverre.

By transferring the symbolic significance of the moon, to reflect the feelings of Avice rather than of Pierston for Avice, Hardy seems, in a way, to be writing Pierston out of the story. Not only is he an artist no more; he is no longer a man, but a 'ghost'. Subsequently, Hardy describes the house and island of Pierston's birth to similar effect. In that house, Leverre has displaced Pierston, Avice has deserted him, and her mother—with all she symbolized for Pierston—has died. Even while Pierston is, as yet, unconscious of these things, its 'vacant, dazed look' suggests to him 'a person gaping in sudden stultification'. This 'dream-country' image of the house seems to suggest a bringing to consciousness of his own condition (III, VI, p. 185). Meanwhile, Avice and Leverre 'beheld . . . the grim wrinkled forehead of the isle above, sliding away northwards' (III, VI, p. 190)—a personification which suggests their perception of him 'as a strange, fossilized relic in human form' (III, V, p. 172). The churchyard, where the new moon once revealed the second Avice, now seems 'the bleakest churchyard in Wessex' (III, VIII, p. 198); it houses her grave as well as that of the first Avice, and Pierston's knowledge that the third Avice will never appear as her mother did seems to provoke that illness from which Pierston awakens to find his artistic sensibilities dead. Of all the women he has loved, only Marcia remains—an 'image and superscription of Age' which reflects himself (III, VIII, p. 201). All he has left is a capacity for friendship (p. 202).

This subtle development of Hardy's use of a 'dream-country' perspective does, I suggest, encourage the reader to perceive Pierston's quest as an archetypal pursuit of 'a shadow, the unattainable'. In particular, this final perspective seems to suggest a kind of re-integration into the stone island from which Pierston's life sprang, as he declines as an artist and as a man. At the same time, Hardy's use of the 'dream-country' perspective is far from impersonal. It moves towards an objectification of Pierston's subjective experience. It suggests aspects of the unconscious as well as of the conscious workings of his mind. It suggests his character and its development. Paradoxically, too, it shows the value of the artistic sensibilities with which he loses touch.

As Hardy suggests, this novel differs 'from all or most others of the series in that the interest aimed at is of an ideal or subjective nature'; 'frankly imaginative verisimilitude in the sequence of events has been subordinated to the said aim'.[41] As a result, Pierston seems almost immune from the complex practical situations such as Tess and Jude, and even Oak, endured. Hence, it may, at first, seem difficult to relate to Pierston, or to perceive his problems as other than faintly absurd. This limitation can, therefore, work against the reader's perception of Hardy's powerful and subtle use of the 'dream-country' environment to suggest universal aspects of the course and consequences of Pierston's pursuit of a 'shadow'.

A related limitation of this approach to the novel is its extreme seriousness. As it fails to take account of the comic aspects of Pierston's quest, it emphasizes unduly the tragic aspects of the 'tragicomedy'. Some might feel that Pierston's character development is at least more interesting than the static condition of Somers and Mrs. Pine-Avon. Yet the 'dream-country' perspective emphasizes the impetus towards death (despite indicating character development); in this way, it may limit our perception of some important contradictions inherent in the novel.

Nor does the 'dream-country' perspective take much account of the pleasure and excitement which Pierston's artistic and romantic pursuits afford, for much of his life. His 'susceptibilities' are 'not only innate but cultivated'—because they are enjoyable and because they provide crucial inspiration for his sculpture and, consequently, gain him fame and fortune. Yet the 'dream-country' perspective seems to support Pierston's simplistic view that 'it was in his weaknesses as a citizen and a national-unit that his strength lay as an artist' (II, VII, p. 110). This is an important paradox in the novel. However, both his character development and his art are more active—and hence more interesting—than a single-minded 'dream-country' perspective will allow.

The 'dream-country' approach does show the danger of losing sight of artistic sensibilities. It shows, too, how his pursuit of the Well-Beloved is subtly destroying him through his art as well as through his romances. But it does not comment upon Hardy's criticism of society's taste for bad art, suggested by that 'danger of drifting away from a solid artistic reputation to a popularity which might possibly be as brief as it would be brilliant and exciting' (I, IX, p. 68). Pierston's pursuit is clearly not entirely an unchanging, archetypal, universal pursuit, characteristic of all artists in all times, or all art would, to Hardy's mind, be bad art.

Nonetheless, the 'dream-country' does draw attention to some important aspects of the novel. It shows Hardy's art as a refining of experience. It shows the limits of Pierston's ability to relate art and experience. It illuminates areas where Hardy implies criticism of Pierston—as an artist as well as, initially at least—as a man. Clearly Hardy is criticizing single-minded, impossible ideals which he perceives in society, and which society desires to see reflected in its art. Out of Pierston's art and experience Hardy finally draws out the importance of humane values. Despite his early promise, Pierston fails, finally, to express these through art. Yet his artistic and physical deterioration throws into relief all the more vividly the value of his belated capacity for friendship and 'loving-kindness'.

Hardy is not recommending a marriage of friendship only. Nonetheless, this final emphasis is vital. Had Alec truly perceived Tess as a 'friend' he could not have abused her through thinking of her solely as a sexual object.[42] Had Angel perceived her as a friend, he might not have abused her through perceiving her solely as a projection of his own ideals. It seems that Alec's and Angel's attitudes were both so common that Hardy's readers failed to comprehend the criticism implied. In *The Well-Beloved*, Hardy seems to be expressing his criticism in a different form, through suggesting Pierston's development of a capacity for friendship and 'loving-kindness', despite his pursuit of an impossible ideal; it is as if such a capacity must be brought to consciousness before society can recognize what is wrong with the attitudes of both Alec and Angel.

'Dream-country' elements are also part of the technical equipment through which Hardy creates the fascination, power and suspense necessary to the success of a novel. Hardy uses the cliff path, the churchyard and ruined church, the sea and its currents, to render layer upon layer of meaning upon the island of stone, with its stone houses and their inhabitants. The actions of the characters serve important functions within the 'dream-country' environment. So does the weather. Wind, rain and storm frequently illustrate the 'force of the elements'. Strange natural occurrences such as that 'sudden breach in the bank' play a crucial rôle. The language used by Hardy to describe these occurrences hints at supernatural powers. By drawing together all these 'devices' at Hardy's disposal, we can appreciate that Hardy's use of them can be extraordinarily subtle; in these circumstances, the extent to which he avoids overbalancing into melodrama is a mark of his genius.

Hardy's artistic sensibilities enable him to use the environment thus to effect a level of tension appropriate to the moment, and reflective of significant flux and reflux in the development of Pierston's character. Early in the novel it becomes clear, too, that Hardy's use of 'dream-country' elements encourages the reader to sympathize with Pierston to a far greater extent than a straight account of his desertion would allow. By the end of the novel, Hardy has developed this so far that the reader is highly conscious of what 'nobody would ever know' regarding Pierston—the nature of his quest and the crucial development of that 'further sentiment—the cordial loving-kindness' (III, VII, p. 193). Thus the 'dream-country' also illustrates that archetypal habit of the human mind—the attempt to trace a pattern through, and elucidate meaning from, the environment. By evoking the landscape of dreams, Hardy brings that archetypal habit to consciousness; for nowhere is that habit so clearly evident as in the language and imagery of dreams. In this way, Hardy uses 'dream-country' elements to represent the universal struggle of the human spirit to comprehend itself.

Hardy's use of a 'dream-country' to suggest Oak's character development showed how archetypal heroic fable could be an important element in fiction. Hardy made Jude's heroic qualities purposefully ambivalent; Jude's experience, in a time of transition into modern society, showed the continuing importance of this element in fiction, even to the present day. Hardy's use of a 'dream-country' here suggests a prototypal resolution of the particularly modern problem of alienation: he works towards breaking down the spiritual barriers between author and reader; he also works towards encouraging a more intimate sympathy with fictional characters, allowing the reader to relate to the character's unconscious more directly than to the character's conscious self. In this way he creates a sense of spiritual adventure. Indeed, he deliberately stresses the archetypal aspects of Pierston's spiritual adventure. And in no other novel is the spiritual life of the protagonist more comprehensively reflected in the environment. Yet the environment also incorporates a strong sense of a 'real' and 'solid' Wessex. Hardy's genius is demonstrated in his ability finely to attune his images of it in order to convey a complex, and ultimately more significant, world of 'impressions'.

That old struggle to elucidate a 'real' Wessex from Hardy's fiction shows how much readers need to feel able to fix a novel into a discernible 'real' world—a world they can believe in, even if they cannot literally see it. The island which provides the setting for *The Well-Beloved* is outside the normal boundaries of Hardy's Wessex. This helps us to remember that the peculiarly subjective nature of this novel renders the non-'real', 'dream-country' elements more dominant here than in the main body of Hardy's fiction. The 'dream-country' perspective is particularly apparent in this novel because the nature of the quest requires that one character must serve as the centre of consciousness for the novel. Now we consider how relationships between characters illustrate further aspects of the 'dream-country' of Hardy's fiction.

NOTES

1. C. G. Jung, *Man and his Symbols* (Picador, Pan Books, 1980), p. 75.
2. W. Archer, 'Real Conversations', *The Critic* XXXVIII (April, 1901), quoting Thomas Hardy.
3. C. G. Jung, *Archetypes of the Collective Unconscious* (Princeton/Bollingen Series, XX, 1980), Vol. 9, i, p. 18. Oak's vision invites comparison with Jung's comment upon a Protestant minister's dream (ibid., p. 17): 'The dreamer descends into his own depths, and the way leads him to the mysterious water. And now there occurs the miracle of the pool of Bethesda: an angel comes down and touches the water, endowing it with healing power. In the dream it is the wind, the pneuma, which bloweth where it listeth. Man's descent to the water is needed in order to evoke the miracle of its coming to life. . . .'
4. C. G. Jung, *Modern Man in Search of a Soul* (Routledge and Kegan Paul, 1966), pp. 277–78.
5. C. G. Jung, *Man and his Symbols*, p. 75.
6. C. G. Jung, *Archetypes of the Collective Unconscious*, p. 38.
7. Ibid., p. 110.
8. The lone magpie seems to relate to Fanny's lonely and outcast state. The many established superstitions associated with a lone magpie help to

endue her situation with archetypal significance. See, for example, E. and M. A. Radford, *Superstitions of the Countryside* (Arrow Books, 1978), ed. & revised by Christina Hole, p. 76. See too, p. 75: with reference to Fanny, it could be considered a 'friendly . . . warning of danger'. Its more frequent interpretation as 'a creature of ill-omen' also applies.

9. E. Maple, *Superstitions and the Superstitious* (W. H. Allen, 1971), p. 112. 'Should more lambs be born than usual . . . it is taken as a warning by the countryman of some holocaust to come.'

10. E. Neumann, *The Great Mother: An Analysis of the Archetype* (Bollingen/ Princeton/Routledge and Kegan Paul, 1974), translated by Ralph Manheim, Ch. V, especially p. 55.

11. Consider, too, Chapter XVIII, p. 129, where Bathsheba begins to realize, 'what a great flame a little wildfire was likely to kindle'. The difficulty of arresting destructive forces, once unleashed, is also noted: 'a resolution to avoid an evil is seldom framed till the evil is so far advanced as to make avoidance impossible' (p. 130). Bathsheba's behaviour is also, of course, relevant; it leads to the frame of mind which drives Boldwood to effect Troy's destruction.

12. C. G. Jung, *Dreams* (Princeton/Bollingen, 1974), translated by R. F. C. Hull, pp. 296 and 122.

13. *Jude*, p. 23, Preface, 1st edn. (August, 1895).

14. See Part I, Note 29.

15. 'A Defence of Jude the Obscure: Three Letters from Thomas Hardy to Sir Edmund Gosse', Letter I, in, for example, Purdy and Millgate (eds.), *Collected Letters*, Vol. II (1980), p. 99.

16. Ibid., Letter I: '. . . the characters necessitated (the plot), and I simply let it come.'

17. David Lodge, 'Jude the Obscure: Pessimism and Fictional Form', Dale Kramer (ed.), *Critical Approaches to the Fiction of Thomas Hardy* (Macmillan, 1979), pp. 193–94. It is arguable whether the Open University and the Permissive Society have completely solved the social problems which thwarted Jude.

18. See Postscript to *Jude*, p. 24 of text. See, too, Note 3: Letter III.

19. F. E. Hardy, *Life* (Macmillan, 1975) Ch. XX. p. 251, 24 October 1892, i.e. while writing *Jude*.

20. D. R. Schwarz, 'Beginnings and Endings in Hardy's Major Fiction', Dale Kramer (ed.), p. 33.

21. Erich Neumann, *The Great Mother* (Bollingen/Princeton/Routledge and Kegan Paul, 1974), Part Two: Section I, Note 10, Ch. 4, p. 48. '. . . in fairy tales a well is often the gate to the underworld and, specifically to the domain of the earth mother—in the spring the rising, erupting motif of "being born".'

22. That possibility is reflected through Jude's observations upon the 'phantoms' of Christminster (II, I, pp. 98–102), followed by his recognition of the regenerative potential in the stonework of Christminster (II, II, p. 103ff). The 'modern Gothic design' (I, I, p. 31) of Marygreen's new church reminds us that attempts at renovation or rebuilding might be misguided. At Christminster, Jude 'perceived that at best only copying,

patching and imitating went on here' (p. 104). But Hardy's suggestion that '*he did not at that time see* . . . . that other developments were shaping in the world around him, in which Gothic architecture and its associations had no place', and that 'the deadly animosity of contemporary logic and vision towards so much of what he held in reverence *was not yet revealed* to him' (p. 104, emphasis mine) seems to imply that Jude was to perceive these things in time.

23. See F. E. Hardy, Ch. XX, p. 258, and Sue's complaint, *Jude*, IV, I, p. 226.
24. C. G. Jung, *Man and his Symbols* (Picador, Pan Books, 1980), p. viii.
25. Ibid., p. 63.
26. T. R. M. Creighton, 'Some Thoughts on Hardy and Religion', Lance St. John Butler (ed.), *Thomas Hardy After Fifty Years* (Macmillan, 1977), p. 72.
27. F. E. Hardy, Ch. XVIII, p. 224.
28. Ibid., Ch. II, p. 29.
29. John Fowles, 'Hardy and the Hag', *Thomas Hardy After Fifty Years*, p. 29.
30. F. E. Hardy, *Life* (Macmillan, 1975), Ch. XXIII, p. 286, 1 March 1897.
31. See, for example, John Fowles, 'Hardy and the Hag', from Lance St. John Butler (ed.), *Thomas Hardy After Fifty Years* (Macmillan, 1977), pp. 28–42. See too, Michael Ryan, 'One Name of Many Shapes: The Well-Beloved', from Dale Kramer (ed.), *Critical Approaches to the Fiction of Thomas Hardy* (Macmillan, 1979), pp. 172–92.
32. R. Sumner, *Thomas Hardy: Psychological Novelist* (Macmillan, 1981), Ch. 3, pp. 32–45.
33. C. G. Jung, *Integration of the Personality* (Routledge and Kegan Paul, 1940), Ch. 1.
34. C. G. Jung, *Man and his Symbols* (Picador, Pan Books, 1980), p. viii.
35. C. G. Jung suggests that an emanation of the 'anima' can change 'into all sorts of shapes like a witch'. *Archetypes of the Collective Unconscious* (Princeton/Bollingen Series, XX, 1980), Vol. 9, i, p. 25. Pierston's 'masquerading creature' is also like that Lokian principle of evil, embodied in Norse mythology, which contributes to the mythic substructure of *The Woodlanders*. See Chapter 1 for discussion of how the changing face of evil seems to be its most important survival mechanism; human victims are duped into following a course, the evil aspects of which they are kept in ignorance until it is too late.
36. I, IX, p. 67: 'He prospered without effort. He was A.R.A.'
37. Regarding the 'vagina dentata' image associated with the 'Terrible' aspect of the 'anima' see, for example, Erich Neumann, *The Great Mother* (Bollingen/Princeton/Routledge and Kegan Paul, 1974), Ch. 11, p. 147ff, especially p. 168ff.
38. I, III, p. 38. See also her distress in the garden (I, I, p. 31) and her reserve when he kisses her (I, II, p. 36).
39. I, V, p. 46. From Milton, *Paradise Lost*, Book VI, ll. 330–31.
40. J. Hillis Miller, *Fiction and Repetition* (Oxford: Basil Blackwell, 1982), Ch. 1, p. 6. In Chapter VI, the author shows how *The Well-Beloved* reveals Pierston's efforts to break away from what seems to him to be a cyclical pattern of repetition.
41. Preface, 1912. Originally dated 1887, p. 26.

42. Alec only poses as a friend in order to persuade Tess to accept his sexual attentions. A true friend could not have been so insensitive to her disinclination to sleep with him; nor could a true friend have been so insensitive to her feelings for her husband.

3

Man and Woman

'The immortal puzzle—given the man and woman, how to find a
basis for their sexual relation.'[1]

While Hardy's 'dream-country' environment illuminates the
development of individual characters, it illuminates, too,
developments in relationships between men and women. A
particularly subtle instance was detailed in II, III: having used
the moon to suggest Pierston's feelings for Avice, Hardy transforms the image so that it suggests Avice's feelings for Leverre.
Hardy also offers direct and indirect comments upon 'the
immortal puzzle'. Some are unnecessarily destructive—for
example, *Jude* I, IX, p. 78 and VI, VIII, p. 404. However, some
are provisional conclusions drawn from a web of 'impressions'.
He uses the 'dream-country' to help suggest those 'impressions'
and the ideas which develop from them.

For example, Hardy frequently and explicitly sympathizes
with Tess. He argues that 'most of her misery had been
generated by her conventional aspect' (II, XIV, p. 127). When
the issue becomes especially delicate, he dissociates himself
from such commentary: 'some might risk the odd paradox that
with more animalism [Angel] would have been the nobler man'
but 'we do not say it'. Nonetheless, he proceeds to assess the
situation in the strongest terms he dare (V, XXXVI, p. 287).
Of course, he also uses more subtle means of generating
audience sympathy, as by emphasizing Tess's beauty so that 'it
was impossible for even an enemy' not to pity her (p. 126). Yet
more subtle still, he dramatizes his 'impressions' of that
'immortal puzzle' with especial reference to his own times. An
analogous process is a dream where a story develops out of a set

of ideas, thereby intensifying and developing those ideas. Alec and Angel are, in part, personifications of two common attitudes to women which Hardy has observed. Through their relationships with Tess, he illustrates their effect upon a 'pure woman'.[2] Presumably, he knows from the beginning that those attitudes will prove destructive. Even so, his novel suggests a developing consciousness of how hypocritical and destructive those attitudes can be.

When Alec boasts, in effect, of how well he knows women, Hardy has that 'pure woman' accuse Alec of perceiving 'every woman' as uniform in words and behaviour (II, XII, p. 112). We identify with her point of view; we see that Alec does not perceive Tess as an individual, while Hardy has taken pains to ensure that we do. Rather, Alec expects Tess to correspond with a projected image of his own sexual desires. He cannot comprehend Tess's disinclination to play the rôle in which he sees her, after she has overcome the initial thrust of his seductive power. Nor can he ever comprehend that money cannot heal the injury to Tess.

His conversion experience inspires no more 'regard for' her 'feelings' (VI, XLVIII, p. 383). He insists that Tess tempts him. We know she does not. Thus Hardy suggests an intensification of his initial attitude. Alec attempts to deceive and confuse Tess by his hypocritical pretence that humane considerations prompt him now. In so doing, he deceives and confuses himself. Once the libertine, now the reformed rake, Alec continues to reflect the socially acceptable attitudes to women which suit him. Thus Hardy shows how inadequate a solution to the first problem is the so-called 'reform' of a rake.

As before (I, XI, p. 106), Alec touches Tess's most vulnerable point—concern for her 'little brothers and sisters' (VI, XLVIII, p. 383). His help is conditional upon her sexual acquiescence. Thus, he is indeed 'an Enemy in the shape of a Friend' (VI, LII, p. 414). Through this abuse of Tess's good nature, together with that antithesis between Tess's desires and the desires which Alec projects upon her, Hardy suggests that attitudes for which society would barely condemn Alec may offend neglected principles of friendship and 'loving-kindness' (VI, XLVII, p. 377).

Tess exemplifies those neglected principles. Walking with her in the early morning 'as if they were Adam and Eve' (III, XX, p. 169), Angel seems to reciprocate her capacity for love. Hardy has already told us that Angel has a similar secret (III, XVIII, p. 155). Indeed 'he seemed to be her double' (IV, XXXIV, p. 266). Tess might well expect a loving friend with a comparable secret to 'forgive' her (V, XXXV, p. 271). Although Hardy warns us of Angel's 'heterodoxy, faults, and weaknesses', he emphasizes that 'Clare was a man with a conscience. Tess was no insignificant creature to toy with and dismiss; but a woman living her precious life . . .' (IV, XXV, p. 195). Even on their wedding night Angel ponders,

> Do I realize solemnly enough how utterly and irretrievably this little womanly thing is the creature of my good or bad faith and fortune? . . . shall I ever neglect her, or hurt her, or even forget to consider her? God forbid such a crime! (IV, XXXIV, p. 261)

Now he claims that 'the woman I have been loving is not you' (V, XXXV, p. 271), while, unknown to Tess, 'he was smothering his affection for her' (p. 273). 'This was what their Agape had come to' (p. 273). A social principle inspires Angel's hypocritical, deliberate, and unnecessary destruction of their love and friendship, drawing out that 'hard and logical deposit' 'within the remote depths of his constitution', generally 'so gentle and affectionate' (V, XXXVI, p. 284).

To emphasize the sorrow of this, Hardy draws towards consciousness that which Angel strives to suppress. The 'tear' which Tess 'hardly observed' objectifies—and its magnifying effect draws us closer towards perceiving—that suppressed affection. Even while behaving as a man of 'principle' (V, XXXVI, p. 284), he yet 'wished for a moment that he had responded yet more kindly, and kissed her once at least' (p. 285). Hardy shows that suppressed instinct being forced into consciousness by having Angel enact his dream, uttering 'the words of endearment, withheld so severely in his waking hours': 'he really recognized her now as his wife Tess, and did not cast her off' (V, XXXVII, p. 291).

Hardy also uses Angel's idealization of Tess to intensify this sorrow. While Angel remains unaware that 'principle' conflicts with his love for Tess, his idealization of her seems to be a product of a normal yearning to express their intense spiritual and sexual compatibility. It is a beautiful thing. It is sincerely felt. It seems to signify Angel's potential as a loving friend. When Angel shatters that illusion on account of society's opinion, Hardy is, in effect, inviting us to consider how far society misuses an instinctive tendency to idealize the Beloved. Instead of simply recognizing its place in the course of a romantic relationship, Hardy's society expects real women to correspond with the ideal to an unreasonable extent. Through developing Tess's story, Hardy shows that his projected image of a 'pure woman' corresponds with that projected by the natural Angel—as Hardy would like Angel to be; but Hardy has Angel misinterpret that image in a manner typical of his day, thus perverting his own judgement until 'he hardly knew' that 'he loved her still' (V, XXXVII, p. 298).

Hardy also suggests that the 'principle' in which Victorians took such pride copies, and emphasizes, the archetypal mistakes of generations. Angel's idealization of Tess in terms of classical mythology (III, XX, p. 170) suggests that he may be perpetuating an archetypal illusion; for poets of former societies and former generations have imagined their human lovers to be goddesses, despite the plain fact that they are not. As if to emphasize the illusion, Hardy intensifies the experience of the 'real' Tess through alluding to a rather different, folk tradition—recalling tales and ballads which echo her secret (I, III, p. 46; II, XIV, p. 128; III, XXI, p. 174; IV, XXIX, p. 221; IV, XXXII, p. 248). Although Angel fails to comprehend the danger of deifying Tess, he is, in a sense, able to relate to the 'horrid fancies' which are a product of the latter experience (III, XIX, p. 163). Because of that experience, Tess would rather not be reminded that her 'nature' and past 'doings' are 'like thousands' and thousands' ' (p. 165). To Angel, her consciously expressed feelings seem almost 'those of the age', suggesting 'the ache of modernism'. Yet, at once,

> he reflected that what are called advanced ideas are really in great part but the latest fashion in definition—a more accurate impression, by words in 'logy' and 'ism', of sensations which men and woman have grapsed for centuries. (p. 163)

Hence, even apparently explicit philosophical comments such as these do not simply indicate Hardy's ultimate conclusions.

Nor do they point to any coherent 'scientific system of philosophy'.[3] Rather, they draw attention to the blurred outlines of issues such as the extent and limitations of that relationship between Tess and Angel. At the same time, they serve to culminate a process whereby 'impressions' derived from Hardy's 'dream-country' are drawn towards consciousness. At the same time, they can create bridges towards other developing threads of consciousness, creating new patterns of 'impressions' at the very moment when they seem to be providing final conclusions.

Having established this kind of temporary platform in understanding, Hardy continues to emphasize these and other aspects of their developing relationship. For instance, he uses ballads and traditional tales to suggest further perspectives upon that basic reflection that it has all happened before. He prompts us to consider why these sorrows recur, why people intensify those sorrows, how those sorrows might be alleviated.

In *Tess*, he develops this skill to an extent which can hardly be appreciated without first considering instances of its former use. For instance, in *The Woodlanders*, Hardy used a complex mythic substructure to express archetypal aspects of the novel; but he also showed that traditional ballads could serve a similar purpose. Mr. Melbury is offended by the ballad which, more constructively interpreted, might have reminded him that he would value high moral standards in his daughter's prospective husband (X, p. 83). The allusion is peculiarly appropriate considering Giles's associations with apple-trees and cider-making; his integration with his environment contrasts with Fitzpiers' failure to adapt—an idea like that of an orange-tree being expected to grow apples. It suggests, too, perhaps, that Grace may not be successfully grafted onto Fitzpiers. Hardy's use of the ballad is extremely subtle. On a first reading, it generates no more than vague promptings of such ideas, like the flickerings of latent, previously unconscious, thoughts and imaginings. Yet the essence of those promptings is a sense of warning. Paradoxically, there is also a sense in which the emotions generated are directed with peculiar accuracy; the question of Grace's loss of maidenhood is clearly subordinate to the need to explore questions of character.

In *Far from the Madding Crowd*, too, he uses traditional ballads to suggest archetypal themes; again, considering the early archetypal scene with Fanny by 'the oldest of the old' trees in the churchyard (VII, p. 60), and considering Fanny's tragic fate, it is significant that Hardy does not use those ballads to emphasize that particular warning.[4] Rather, Hardy draws attention to that failure of 'loving-kindness' in the 'sexual relation' which leads to trouble for the community in general:

> I've lost my love and I care not,
> I've lost my love and I care not,
> I shall soon have another
> That's better than t'other;
> I've lost my love and I care not. (XXIII, p. 159)

In retrospect, the audience recognizes the affinity between the subject of the ballad and the character of its singer. Bathsheba becomes entangled with Troy that very night.

In the second ballad, Hardy directs our attention towards the destructive consequences of callous attitudes in the 'sexual relation'. It is hardly surprising that 'the seeds of love' sown 'in the spring' cause 'the willow tree' to 'twist' and 'twine' (pp. 160–61), if they are sown in the manner of the first ballad. The audience does not appear to be consciously aware of these implications. However, through the humorous background, Hardy seems to prompt the reader to recall that laughter inside the barracks in the context of Fanny's sorrow (XI, p. 96), and that humorous attitude which disguises the danger in Troy's perverse morality (XXV, p. 171)—an attitude readily recognizable as prevalent in society.

Hardy draws these promptings towards consciousness through the third ballad and its context. Bathsheba sings. Gabriel and Boldwood accompany her in their distinctive manners, forming 'a rich unexplored shadow, which threw her tones into relief'. The community is 'silent and absorbed'. They listen 'as at suppers in the early ages of the world' (p. 162). Thus Hardy focuses our attention upon the archetypal significance of that old tale which Bathsheba sings. As his narrative shows her re-enacting that ballad, he also draws towards consciousness its crucial elements— how the failure of consideration and 'loving-kindness' in the 'sexual relation' can, but for the extraordinarily intense regenerative efforts of Oak, destroy the community of Weatherbury.

In *Tess*, Hardy develops further this ability to express archetypal aspects of the novel through ballads and traditional tales. In the first phase, while Tess remains a maiden, he illustrates how girls are brought up with the fear of succumbing to seduction. The singing of 'a vigorous gallopade, the favourite ditty of "The Spotted Cow" ' may stimulate excitement and interest in its dangerous subject—in those who cannot imagine themselves succumbing to the danger and suffering its consequences. At the same time, Hardy uses the ballad to suggest that Tess has been warned all her life against the chain experience expressed therein: 'I saw her lie down in yonder green grove;/ Come love! and I'll tell you where' (I, III, p. 46). The deepness of the fear instilled, even from babyhood, is emphasized retrospectively, just before Tess's wedding-day, when

> there came into her head her mother's ballad of the mystic robe—'That never would become that wife/ That had once done amiss' which Mrs. Durbeyfield had used to sing to her as a child, so blithely and so archly, her foot on the cradle, while she rocked to the tune. (IV, XXXII, p. 248)

While evoking this, to Tess, familiar archetypal scene, Hardy invites us to consider why, generation upon generation, girls succumb, despite this deeply instilled fear.

It may seem incredible that Tess, with her clearly defined intellect and integrity, could make such a mistake. Even the excited company at 'The Pure Drop' does not take the danger lightly. It has evolved a 'local phrase' (I, IV, p. 56) to express that danger, so well acknowledged is it. (Even the name of the public house acknowledges it.) A meaningful silence suggests a general recognition of Joan's foolishness in toying with that danger. Through describing as a 'fast-perishing lumber' Joan's stock 'of superstitions, folk-lore, dialect, and orally-transmitted ballads' (I, III, p. 50), Hardy shows that Joan is oblivious to any warning aspect. This point may seem particularly relevant to his day, but it also helps to define Joan's character. One of the reasons why girls succumb, generation upon generation, is that, in any age, there are characters like Joan. As before, Hardy uses the ballad to evoke traditional, expected themes, and to emphasize questions of character. Yet he also shows, as never before, how deeply society instils the fear of seduction and how human nature continues to work against that fear.

Once Tess has fallen, he develops as never before his use of the ballad to emphasize the sorrow underlying the humour of the situation. Friends 'mischievously' remind Tess 'of the ballad about the maid who went to the merry green wood and came back in a changed state' (II, XIV, p. 128). The very vagueness of the reference draws attention to the multiplicity of such ballads. Thus Hardy suggests that Tess's situation is no exception to be dismissed as statistically insignificant. The consequent intense episode surrounding the baptism and death of Sorrow emphasizes the suffering caused to Tess and her siblings, who, as 'passengers in the Durbeyfield ship', are powerless to control their fate (I, III, p. 51).

A certain sympathy is demonstrated by those who believe that 'a little more than persuading had to do wi' the coming o't' (II, XIV, p. 126). Hardy emphasizes their response that ' 'twas a thousand pities that it should have happened to she, of all others' by focusing upon her beauty. He then shows the contrasting limitations of their sympathy:

> she was not an existence, an experience, a passion, a structure of sensations, to anybody but herself. To all humankind besides Tess was only a passing thought. Even to friends she was no more than a frequently passing thought. . . . (p. 127)

Despite their sympathy, she is 'interesting', above all, as 'a social warning' (p. 128), and 'most of her misery had been generated by [this] her conventional aspect' (p. 127). Thus, while intensifying our perception of Tess's sorrow, Hardy also shows how society's principles cause her to suffer despite the 'friendliness' of her fellows (p. 128).

Thus Hardy uses the ballad to intensify our response to Tess's story. He also uses Tess's story to provide a context for the ballad. Juxtaposed thus, Hardy uses them to develop our consciousness of archetypal themes within the novel. Tess's fellows disapprove of Alec's behaviour. Yet Alec, like Troy, remains free to wreak further havoc. He is, at this time, unaffected, unconscious of Tess's sorrow. Tess, like Fanny, feels obliged to hide from society, striving to survive alone when most in need of support, so that society need not face her sorrow either. It is the inevitable consequence of threatening from birth the maidens rather than the men. Through his use of the ballad, Hardy suggests that this has always been so. Victorian society exacerbates an age-old problem by intensifying those pressures with its harsh and hypocritical definitions of virtue and exhortations for maidens to conform.

Later, he develops his use of ballads and traditional tales to show how society's 'principle' is so destructive as to allow no possibility of regeneration; it rejects basic Christian principles of forgiveness and 'loving-kindness' in the tradition of that arrogant Pharisee who assumed himself sinless. At haymaking time 'some spirit had induced her to dress herself neatly as she had formerly done, and come out into the fields' (p. 127). A 'year or two' later, Hardy shows her unable to believe that 'the recuperative power which pervaded organic nature was . . . denied to maidenhood alone' (II, XV, p. 135).

> Some spirit within her rose automatically as the sap in the twigs. It was unexpended youth, surging up anew after its temporary check, and bringing with it hope, and the invincible instinct towards self-delight. (p. 136)

As she sets out for a fresh start, 'the irresistible, universal, automatic tendency to find sweet pleasure somewhere, which pervades all life, from the meanest to the highest, had at length mastered Tess' (III, XVI, p. 140). She finds 'at least approximate expression for her feelings in the old Benedicite that she had lisped from infancy' (p. 141) as 'her spirits, and her thankfulness, and her hopes, rose higher and higher' (p. 140). But the 'half-conscious rhapsody' relates more to 'Pagan fantasy' than to the systematized religion (p. 141) upon which her society is founded. While Hardy warns against 'such high contentment with such a slight initial performance' (p. 141), his first hint that society will crush Tess's regenerative hopes is her inability to find a ballad adequate to the occasion, although 'she tried several' (p. 140).

As soon as she returns to human society, at the dairy, Hardy uses ballads and traditional tales to re-establish her real relationship with society; he shows that she cannot escape that relationship by escaping from those who knew her history. Her simple reconstructive hopes begin to be crushed into a jumble of complex psychological tensions as the dairyfolk sing 'a cheerful ballad about a murderer who was afraid to go to bed in the dark because he saw certain brimstone flames around him' (III, XVII, p. 147). Tess's sorrow arose initially from her guilt regarding Prince—from seeing 'herself in the light of a murderess' (I, IV, p. 63) and, hence, responsible for reversing family fortunes. Compounded with that idea of 'the recuperative power' being 'denied to maidenhood alone' and her hopes of forgetting the past, Hardy conjures up vague, as yet, associations between Tess and the ballad evoked.

As on these other occasions, a ballad is sung without conscious awareness of the sorrow it describes (I, III, p. 46; II, XIV, p. 128; and, indirectly, in IV, XXXII, p. 248). The singing is not only 'cheerful' but 'in purely business-like tones' (p. 147). The conversation, too, is markedly humorous. Similarly, when 'the butter would not come' (III, XXI, p. 172) the conversation turns to 'a humorous narration' of superstitious and traditional tales. 'None of them but [Tess] herself seemed to see the sorrow of it; to a certainty, not one knew how cruelly it touched the tender place in her experience' (p. 174), as they relate a tale similar to hers. As Angel presses Tess to marry him, the dairy folk relate its even more appropriate sequel. Even more than before,

> what was comedy to them was tragedy to her; and she could hardly bear their mirth. . . . This question of a woman telling her story—the heaviest of crosses to herself—seemed but amusement to others. (IV, XXIX, p. 221)

As Hardy recalls that association between the maiden Tess and the ballads 'archly' and 'blithely' sung to her as a child (IV, XXXII, p. 248), we realize how far he has developed our consciousness of the archetypal implications of this ballad, how far he has released a latent awareness of the painful and destructive consequence of breaking the social code, how unlikely it is that Tess may escape those destructive consequences.

From this point, a totally fatalistic atmosphere pervades the novel. Immediately, there follows the obscured revelation of Tess's secret by the Trantridge man (IV, XXXIII, p. 250), and Angel's consequent dream. Hardy uses fatalistic superstitions regarding the d'Urberville coach (p. 256) and the 'afternoon crow' (p. 257) to provide commentary upon the wedding (IV, XXXIII). The atmosphere they generate is sustained by succeeding death-threatening disturbances at the dairy which Jonathan specifically relates to that 'afternoon crow' (IV, XXXIV, p. 264). Hence, Tess sees her recuperative hopes as unrealistic (V, XXXVI, p. 286). She sees death as the only solution. Her offer to drown herself, after hearing of Retty's attempt to do so (V, XXXV, p. 276), hints, perhaps, at that old tradition that a river deprived of a drowning body will claim another victim; both suggest the idea that Tess's regenerative hopes are doomed. Even more ominously, thoughts of drowning turn to thoughts of hanging, suggesting the apparent irrevocability of her ultimate fate (XXXVI, p. 282). Tess's suicidal thoughts are echoed by Angel's dramatic and dangerous sleep-walking, during which she accepts, and half expects, that he may drown her. Meanwhile, Angel emphasizes her death horribly; while expressing his affection for her, he also enacts his sense of being responsible for destroying her by rolling 'her in the sheet as in a shroud' and delivering her into 'the empty stone coffin' (III, XXXVII, pp. 290–93).

Hardy emphasizes this sense that her fate is sealed by a sudden change in the point of view, just before Tess's idea of drowning herself. Suddenly he seems to be relating one of those archetypal traditional tales, but with Tess as the subject:

> It was said afterwards that a cottager of Wellbridge, who went out late for a doctor, met two lovers in the pastures, walking very slowly, without converse, one behind the other, as in a funeral procession, and the glimpse that he obtained of their faces seemed to denote that they were anxious and sad. Returning later, he passed them again in the same field, progressing just as slowly, and as regardless of the hour and of the cheerless night as before. It was only on account of his preoccupation with his own affairs, and the illness in his house, that he did not bear in mind the curious incident, which, however, he recalled a long while after. (XXXV, p. 276)

The narration occupies a significant space of time. While it lasts, it seems as if Tess has jumped from the pages of fiction and become a historical personage—a real person, now dead.

Hardy has used this point of view before in this novel, though significantly more briefly, and yet with gradually intensifying significance. First, he simply described her in the title-page as being 'Faithfully presented by Thomas Hardy'—as if she had really lived. At that crucial moment at the archetypal May Day dance when Angel failed to dance with Tess, Hardy adds that 'the name of the eclipsing girl, whatever it was, has not been handed down' (I, II, p. 44)—as if reciting a true traditional tale. Similarly, at that traumatic baptism he notes 'the stopt-diapason note which her voice acquired when her heart was in her speech, and which will never be forgotten by those who knew her' (II, XIV, p. 131). We seem to be hearing flashes of vital, intense moments in her life, recalled as equally intense memories by those who share an empathy, if not a sympathy, with her tragedy. None of these incidents has the effect of the longer narration (V, XXXV). However, recalled now, they add to the sense of Tess as one of those archetypal maidens of ballads and traditional tales. Indeed, she seems transformed into the specific subject of her own traditional tale.

Hardy even suggests that Tess may regard herself in this rôle. When her initial trouble seems almost forgotten, Tess muses upon her regenerative hopes. Yet, at the same time, she imagines the unknowable anniversary date of her death alongside those dates associated with her trouble and with her birth (II, XV, p. 134). In imagining the time when people 'would say: "It is the -th, the day that poor Tess Durbeyfield died"' she is imagining that her tale will be well known. In thinking of that day as 'doomed to be her terminus in time through all ages' she acknowledges the archetypal significance of her tale. The ballads sung to her over her cradle seem to influence her view of herself as well as her view of history (III, XIX, p. 165). At Talbothays, she is painfully aware of her relationship to the Jack Dollop tales. Before her wedding she strives to suppress that awareness; nonetheless, it unexpectedly 'came into her head' in the form of 'her mother's ballad of the mystic robe' (IV, XXXII, p. 248). Thus, through having Tess regard herself in this rôle, Hardy shows how she has learnt, from society, to see her situation fatalistically. Despite her regenerative hopes, the fatalism of 'Tess's own people'—'It was to be' (I, XI, p. 108)—proves the stronger force.

Through Tess's ambiguous perspective upon her tale, Hardy seems to be questioning the wisdom of that fatalistic tone.

When he suggests that her tale is a historical one, he, in effect, acknowledges that a fatalistic attitude is a practical one when the sufferer is now dead, for it is too late to resolve the trouble. The fatalistic tone is also valid insofar as it acknowledges the unlikelihood of change as overwhelming as that for which he hopes. Yet, through using archetypal tales to suggest the crushing of her regenerative hopes, Hardy provokes anger and profound sympathy for the fictional Tess. In this sense, the response he hopes for is far from fatalistic. He aspires to provoke his readers to question their attitudes, and to make them wonder why society responds so destructively, making Tess's trials so much worse than they need be that her tremendous potential is utterly unappreciated and destroyed.

Thus, Hardy refers to latent archetypal aspects of traditional ballads and tales to deepen 'impressions' of that 'immortal puzzle'. He also makes special use of their forms to create patterns out of those 'impressions'. He also uses aspects of the 'dream-country' environment to symbolize 'impressions' of that 'puzzle', and so to draw them towards consciousness. Thus he creates an illusion of a living, immediate Tess, alongside that dead historical one.

For instance, her seduction dissociates 'the original Tess' from 'her living will' (VII, LV, p. 429). Years of striving to reassert herself cannot heal the breach. (Society allows no second chance.) This dissociation, and its effect on Tess, are both suggested by projections of her unconscious on to the environment. In her innocence, her intuitive response to these projections is still sound, suggesting her innate common sense. She recognizes a 'thorn of the rose remaining in her breast' which 'accidentally pricked her chin' (I, VI, p. 73) as a warning or 'ill-omen'. Because of the pressure of Alec's seductive personality, it is only 'the first she had noticed that day'. Even so, that one warning is enough for her to respond 'thoughtfully' (pp. 74, 76) and to discourage her from returning to his home, even though she does not 'quite know why' (p. 74) she does not 'quite like Mr. d'Urberville being there' (p. 76).

Yet, against her better judgement, she is sent to him, bedecked in white, like a virgin sacrifice. Her excessive sense of responsibility towards her siblings, stimulated by the cruel chance of Prince's death, but instigated by parental irresponsibility

(I, IV), makes her vulnerable. Hence, her mother's pleadings crush her into submission: 'with calm abandonment' she invites her mother to 'do what you like with me' (I, VII, p. 78). The gently contemptuous humour of Hardy's parting reference to her father as 'Sir John' (p. 79) reminds us that Tess is a scapegoat for his sins. His sleep-inspired recognition that he is saying 'Goodbye' to his 'maid' suggests the sacrifice to which she will be called on that account. The 'slight misgiving' which prompts her mother to walk with her grows into conscious recognition that she should have first 'found out whether the gentleman is really a good-hearted young man' (p. 81), before leaving her to mount that unnecessarily 'steep ascent to the outer world' alone (p. 79). Thus Hardy shows the destructive pressures which suppress Tess's innate integrity. Moreover, he encourages sympathy for Tess by prompting indignation that her own mother should so intensify them.

It is in the context of this pressure that Tess chooses to deny her intuitive response—to mount Alec's gig despite her 'misgiving' (p. 81). Her subsequent journey seems to parallel her unconscious anticipation of powerful forces driving her to act against her 'living will'. By suggesting that 'the accident with her father's horse' (I, VIII, p. 83) has prompted her exceptional sensitivity to 'the least irregularity of motion' (p. 83), Hardy traces Tess's vulnerability back once more to that scene which illuminated parental irresponsibility and cruel chance (I, IV). At the same time, the present 'irregularity of motion' is a product of Alec's deliberately reckless driving. Thus Hardy suggests how Alec forces his powerfully seductive personality on to the sensitive and vulnerable Tess.

Alec seems unable to recognize Tess's right to refuse him. Certainly he tries to persuade her that she has no such right. A peasant girl's training in submission helps him here. Yet he meets resistance. Thus, his driving of the horse also signifies his development of strategies to break down that resistance. It makes Tess both physically and emotionally unable to escape his at present nominal, and yet masterful, sexual encroachments (p. 85). He intensifies her terror with anecdotes about the horse's supposedly 'grim' look, 'queer temper', and dangerous behaviour (p. 83). Nonetheless, Tess retains integrity enough to reassert herself 'in defiant triumph' (p. 86). As 'her hat was in place and tied' (p. 86) again, it seems to signify the triumph of her independent personality, as Bathsheba's symbolized hers (*FFMC*, II and III). Yet her triumph is less complete than she realizes. That 'kiss of mastery' (p. 85) is not fully 'undone' (p. 86), for she rejects as unsound her instinct to return home; instead she continues on the path towards Alec's home, alongside him and his horse.

Clearly, Alec's relationship with his horse symbolizes, and encourages us to recognize, aspects of his relationship with Tess. It provokes in us complex and ominous emotions, as it might in a dream; in this, Hardy develops further his use of such a horse in *The Woodlanders*. Alec's emphasis upon the horse's ability to kill people recalls again that crucial scene with her father's horse which left Tess so vulnerable, but now from the perspective of how it left Tess regarding 'herself in the light of a murderess' (p. 63). Together with the image of Alec risking his life in the struggle to master her, the relationship with the horse suggests the intensity of Tess's ultimate determination to kill, and to be killed, rather than be mastered by him. Thus it illuminates her inner determination to retain the integrity of the 'original Tess'.

At the same time, Alec's comments upon his relationship with the horse illuminate discrepancies between 'the original Tess' and the attitudes he projects on to her. By not confirming the truth of Alec's allegations about the horse's nature, Hardy leaves us in doubt as to Alec's truthfulness. Of course, a seducer might use those anecdotes in his strategy whether or not they were true. However, Hardy does suggest that the horse 'knew so well the reckless performance expected of her' that her own will in the matter was immaterial (p. 84). By leading straight into the dizzy, dangerous, and yet exhilarating descent (p. 84), Hardy illuminates how the seductive power of Alec's personality makes the journey what it is. When he tries to brainwash Tess into thanking him afterwards for deliverance from danger—as if it were not his fault (p. 84)—this becomes clearer still. The extent to which he is prepared to warp Tess's will and judgement is symbolized in his determination to 'manage' his horse, even though he doubts if 'any living man' but he 'has the power' to do so. As Alec 'nipped his cigar with the tips of his large white centre-teeth, and allowed his lips to smile slowly of themselves' (p. 83), Hardy draws attention to the sexual motivation underlying the words from those lips. In this context, the banks on either side of the straight road which, naturally enough, appear to divide like 'a splitting stick' (p. 84), seem also to symbolize the force with which Alec tears Tess's body apart from her innermost convictions in seducing her.

Just before her seduction, Hardy re-emphasizes Tess's integrity. She stands alone outside an apparently universal abandonment to 'the ecstasy and the dream . . . in which emotion was the matter of the universe, and matter but an adventitious intrusion likely to hinder you from spinning where you wanted to spin' (I, X, p. 97). By refusing to 'have a turn' she avoids injury in the subsequent fall (p. 97). Although she walks 'in the flock' she remains immune to that illusion

> that they were soaring along in a supporting medium, possessed of original and profound thoughts, themselves and surrounding nature forming an organism of which all the parts harmoniously and joyously interpenetrated each other . . . sublime as the moon and stars above them. (p. 98)

It is precisely because of 'painful experiences of this kind in her father's house' (p. 99) that Tess is determined to retain her integrity.

Thus Hardy reminds us again of the significance of that crucial scene (I, IV), this time drawing to a head those pressures outside herself to which she falls victim. The 'black stream' which 'glistened like a slimy snake in the cold still rays of the moon' (p. 99) symbolizes the danger from within that company for which Tess has waited so patiently for the sake of safety. Tess's culpability lies simply in adding her 'soberer richer note' to a 'chorus of laughter'. Thereby she inflames 'to madness' the Queen of Spades' 'long-smouldering sense of rivalry' (p. 100). (This is fitting comment upon Alec's assumption that Tess's sensitivity is unusual in a woman (I, VIII, p. 85; II, XII, p. 112).) The symbol also points forward to Tess's seduction, where 'the serpent hisses where the sweet birds sing' (II, XII, p. 110). It suggests, too, the ghastly consequences of breaking the treasured vessel. Terror-struck, Tess is far from perceiving these things. Rather, she makes her second mistake. Through voicing her inner awareness of higher integrity, she is forced to back away, 'out of the frying-pan into the fire' (p. 101).

While the workfolk resume their walk and their former illusions of a harmonious relationship with the universe, Tess's relationship with the environment suggests quite different things. 'A faint luminous fog, which had hung in the hollows all the evening' seems to represent all those pressures upon her which intensify her inexpressible weariness. The confusion they generate is intensified by Alec's proximity. Hence, the fog 'became general and enveloped them'. Her disorientation and its sexual consequences are suggested by the moonlight which seems 'more pervasive than in clear air':

> whether on this account, or from absent-mindedness, or from sleepiness, she did not perceive that they had long ago passed the point at which the lane to Trantridge branched from the highway, and that her conductor had not taken the Trantridge track. (I, XI, p. 103)

Even so, she remained alert enough to perceive that 'the horse was not the spirited one' and yet to remain 'dubious' on other scores. Nonetheless, as the fog closes in, she grows more confused by Alec's present pacifying manner—so much more subtle than formerly; symbolically as well as physically, 'the quietest' horse Alec rode is still 'powerful' (p. 104). Tess plays further into his hands than before when she insists on getting down from the horse, for, unlike on that earlier journey, she is unable to find her way, on account of that 'growing fog' 'which so disguises everything' (p. 105) both literally and symbolically.

As tired as 'the jaded animal' (p. 107), she is disarmed by Alec's apparent complicity, by 'the painful sense of the awkwardness of having to thank him just then', by his increasingly tender speech, and by the gesture—apparently tender and yet symbolically otherwise—of putting his overcoat around her. Hardy emphasizes her helplessness: that 'white muslin figure' once sent to him like a virgin sacrifice, now 'sleeping soundly' with tears lingering 'upon her eyelashes' (p. 107). 'Tess's moonlit person' (p. 107) suggests the sexual charms which distracted Alec from following the way. The 'setting of the moon' seems to relate to the setting of her fate through her sexual surrender (p. 106). The 'gentle roosting birds' and 'the hopping rabbits and hares' perceive no anomaly. Yet the 'darkness and silence' and 'the primeval yews and oaks' have dark archetypal significance for Tess: 'an immeasurable social chasm was to divide our heroine's personality thereafter from that previous self of hers' (p. 108).

Now it is even harder to undo that 'kiss of mastery'. Soon the 'original Tess' is at peace with herself for leaving Alec (II, XII, p. 113) despite all the contrary pressures. Yet, through her projections upon the environment, Hardy shows how far those pressures are the product of conventional attitudes which she has imbibed, although they are 'antipathetic to her' (II, XIII, p. 120). Thus Hardy makes us aware of the destructive potential of her imposed sense of guilt.

By contrast, when Sorrow is dead and Tess's tale almost forgotten, Hardy has her project her regenerative hopes upon the environment. He shows how, even with this attitude, she is powerless. Her 'pilgrimage' proves 'more troublesome . . . than she had imagined . . . owing to sundry wrong turnings' before she reaches 'the long-sought-for vale' (III, XVI, p. 139). She is of no more consequence to the surroundings than a fly. The call which indicates her direction is coincidental: 'not the expression of the valley's consciousness that beautiful Tess had arrived, but the ordinary announcement of milking-time' (p. 142). Thus Hardy harshly undercuts Tess's 'hopes' as they 'mingled with the sunshine in an ideal photosphere which surrounded her' (p. 140). And yet, independently of Tess's perceptions, Hardy describes a beautiful and fertile valley where 'the milk oozed forth and fell in drops to the ground', and where 'the Froom waters were clear as the River of Life shown to the Evangelist' (p. 140). Thus Hardy suggests the healing and recuperative power of Nature which will be denied to Tess by society.

Simultaneously, Hardy uses the scene to suggest the dominant aspects of her subsequent relationship with Angel: the fulfilment of the highest dreams of the 'pink and flawless' Tess, undercut by the fulfilment of the worst fears of the 'pale and tragical' Tess (p. 140); the too-perfect sensuous and spiritual attunement, undercut by Angel's callousness on account of society's opinion. When Angel first notices Tess, she is describing that voluntary dissociation from her body 'which you don't seem to want at all', suggestive of her desire to pursue her dreams regardless of physical and social realities. Unaware of this, Angel responds to the sensuousness of her renewed 'vitality' of which 'she little divined the strength' (III, XIX, p. 164). Hardy shows that Angel is not deceived in this. That 'something that was familiar, something which carried him back to a joyous and unforeseeing past before the necessity of taking thought had made the heavens gray' (p. 159) suggests a response to the 'original Tess'. Yet his failure to dance with her then prefigures, as she rightly perceives (IV, XXX, p. 232), his ultimate rejection of her. As Dairyman Crick plants 'his great knife and fork . . . erect on the table, like the beginning of a gallows' (p. 158), Hardy draws attention to that ominous 'series of seemings' relating to murder and its consequences, which counteracts Tess's dreams. In this context, the act she describes also suggests death. 'The fire of logs, with its one flame pirouetting on the top' seems 'to jig to his inward tune' (p. 157). That striking 'fluty voice' in his 'phantasmal orchestra' belongs to the milkmaid whom he is to 'select . . . in preference to the' others 'when he wished to contemplate contiguous womankind' (p. 159). He does not perceive the ominous aspects of its 'dying dance'.

Hardy uses the 'dream-country' to show how the balance between these conflicts shifts as their relationship develops. In the garden, Tess begins to believe that Angel 'can raise up dreams with' his music, and 'drive away' the 'horrid fancies' which she sometimes projects on to her environment (III, XIX, p. 163). His music renders her 'conscious of neither time nor space. The exaltation which she had described as being producible at will by gazing at a star, came now without any determination of hers' (p. !62). Thus Angel seems to suggest to her the hoped-for fulfilment of her dreams. Consequently, 'the floating pollen seemed to be his notes made visible, and the dampness of the garden the weeping of the garden's sensibility'. The sensuous aspect of her feeling is illuminated by that 'stark quality like that of nudity' with which she imbues 'those notes' as 'they wandered in the still air'. Yes—Angel could fulfil her dreams. However, he is not as perfect as she imagines. The music is only 'a very simple performance, demanding no great skill' (p. 162). 'To speak absolutely, both instrument and execution were poor; but the relative is all, and as she listened, Tess, like a fascinated bird, could not leave the spot' (p. 161).

Her growing interest colours her judgement, the 'typical summer evening . . . atmosphere being in such delicate equilibrium and so transmissive that inanimate objects seemed endowed with two or three senses, if not five'. As she loses sight of her 'horrid fancies' 'she drew quite near to Clare' (p. 162). Then Hardy draws attention to those 'offensive smells', 'dazzling' weeds, cuckoo-spittle, the cracking of snails underfoot, the stains of thistle-milk and slug-slime, and 'upon her naked arms sticky blights which, though snow-white on the apple-tree trunks, made madder stains on her skin' (p. 161–62). Thus, Hardy recalls those pressures which counteract her 'exaltation'.

Hardy uses the shifting qualities of light to draw attention to that changing balance of conflicts as the relationship develops. Hardy interrupts his description of their apparent compatibility to suggest that, although in 'the gray half-tones of daybreak . . . the morning light seems active, darkness passive', yet 'in the twilight of evening it is the darkness which is active and crescent' (III, XX, p. 169). Thus he hints that the apparently fading aspect of Tess's dilemma will reassert itself in time. Just as 'the degree of . . . shade may be the same', the difference between Tess now, and on her wedding day, lies not in what she is, but in the attendant course of events and Angel's changing perspectives. Hardy suggests Angel's idealization of the 'original Tess' through 'the spectral, half-compounded, aqueous light' in which she 'looked ghostly, as if she were merely a soul at large'. As Tess reminds him that she is simply Tess, 'it would grow lighter, and her features would become simply feminine; they had changed from those of a divinity who could confer bliss to those of a being who craved it' (p. 170). In the 'strong and commonplace' light of day she 'lost her strange and ethereal beauty'. However, she remains a 'dazzlingly fair dairymaid' (p. 171). Yet once he knows her 'Magdalen' (p. 170) aspect, a candlelight view of the d'Urberville portrait over her bedroom door is enough to convince him of sinister aspects he wants to perceive in her.[5] The light of the subsequent 'dawn' seems 'ashy and furtive, as though associated with crime' (V, XXXVI, p. 279). The ominous aspects of Angel's initial 'dying flame' have become fully conscious.

Hardy suggests that Angel's gradually dawning consciousness

of these aspects gradually transforms the atmosphere of their wedding evening. Angel recognizes that draughts are responsible for 'the grease guttering down the sides' of the candles (IV, XXXIV, p. 261); still in a sound frame of mind, he does not consider superstitious explanations. However, when 'he looked into the fire' to muse upon the diamonds, they seemed to gleam 'somewhat ironically' (p. 262). When he dismisses the doubt as social 'vanity' and 'turned from the fire to help her' (p. 263), he is rewarded with an unprecedented vision of her beauty. 'A jerk in the fire-smoke' (p. 264) signifies the entrance of Jonathan with disturbing news. It signifies, too, the disturbance it causes the pair. The 'steady glare from the now flameless embers' (p. 266) illuminates the intensity of their response and their mutual concentration upon their secrets. As Tess tells her secret, the fire suggests the shattering of the unity of feeling between them. Angel's soundness of mind and consequent attitude towards her is warped by the 'intelligence' (V, XXXV, p. 270). The 'Last Day luridness in this red-coaled glow' suggests his judgemental attitude and its destructive consequences. 'The large shadow' produced by this light serves as a projection of his distorted perspective upon Tess. The 'sinister wink' of 'each diamond' similarly undercuts his former vision of her (IV, XXXIV, p. 268). As 'the fire in the grate looked impish—demoniacally funny, as if it did not care in the least about his strait' (V, XXXV, p. 270), Hardy hints at her sense of the dawning callousness of her lover. Thus 'the complexion even of external things seemed to suffer transmutation as her announcement progressed', suggesting the dramatic change in Angel's attitude to Tess, and the shattering of their relationship.

While nuances in light and fire suggest Angel's changing attitude towards Tess, changes in the wider environment suggest an increasingly oppressive emotional intensity. The change in the weather creates suspense. It seems significant. We await its counterpart in the action. Perhaps this is because Hardy also draws attention to Tess's attendant suffering. The 'noises as of silk smartly rubbed' suggest her slighting by Angel. 'The restful dead leaves', like Tess's past, 'stirred to irritated resurrection, and whirled about unwillingly' and 'tapped against the shutters' as if threatening to undercut Angel's idealization of Tess (III, XX, p. 170). The sun shining upon her 'amid the oozy fatness and warm ferments of the Froom Vale' in midsummer once inspired the unveiling of their reciprocated passion (III, XXIV, p. 189ff). Now the sun 'made a spot like a paint-mark set upon her' skirt (IV, XXXIV, p. 260). Soon her worst fears are fulfilled. Thereafter, 'the gold of the summer picture was now gray, the colours mean, the rich soil mud, and the river cold' (V, XXXVII, p. 295). The whole environment seems to reflect and draw attention to the intense emotional changes in their relationship.

In the summer at Talbothays, the environment seemed to reflect a compatible relationship: as 'the season developed and matured' they had converged 'under an irresistible law, as surely as two streams in one vale' (III, XX, p. 168). 'The aesthetic, sensuous, pagan pleasure in natural life' seemed to reflect the nature of Angel's love for Tess (IV, XXV, p. 199). Even the once 'insignificant' house seemed to breathe 'forth "Stay!" The windows smiled, the door coaxed and beckoned, the creeper blushed confederacy' on account of 'a personality within . . . so far-reaching in her influence as to spread into and make the bricks, mortar, and whole overhanging sky throb with a burning sensibility' (IV, XXV, p. 195). Tess, for her part, was 'physically and mentally suited to these new surroundings'. Hence, 'the sapling which had rooted down to a poisonous stratum on the spot of its sowing had been transplanted to a deeper soil' (III, XX, p. 168). That 'appetite for joy which pervades all creation' (IV, XXX, p. 232) developed until it pervaded 'every seesaw of her breath, every wave of her blood, every pulse singing in her ears' (IV, XXVIII, p. 218).

However, Tess's fears frequently reassert themselves. They are catalysed by those apparently supernatural interventions and the subsequent relation of increasingly relevant tales. These incidents accompany high points in their relationship, including his attempts to propose to her. Hence the shift in tone is marked—as is the consequent emotional tension. Yet while Tess's circumstances force her to suppress her innermost feelings, Hardy illuminates those feelings through reflections upon the environment. Thereby he intensifies our sympathy for her. Thus, in the very next chapter after Angel's idealization of Tess in an Edenic setting, 'the evening sun' seemed 'ugly to her, like a great inflamed wound in the sky. Only a solitary cracked-voiced reed-sparrow greeted her from the bushes by the river, in a sad, machine-made tone' reminding her of Alec (III, XXI, pp. 174–75). That day, 'the butter would not come' until she left the dairy. Next day it was found to have been contaminated. The search for the offending garlic in the noonday sun, while Tess tries to redirect Angel's interest, draws attention once more to the hidden source of her trouble and to Tess's fears of exposure. The 'old pointed knives' (p. 178) and keen 'eyes fixed upon the ground' determined not to miss 'a single inch of the pasture' (p. 179) are like a 'dream' projection of her fear.

When Tess promises to reveal all, the tension between Tess's nightmarish fear and 'sublime trustfulness' (IV, XXXI, p. 234) in Angel is epitomized in the contrast between 'palpitating misery' and 'momentary shoots of joy' (IV, XXVIII, p. 218). The impact of that tension is intensified to cosmic proportions by the apparently reciprocal behaviour of sun and moon: the sun 'settled down upon the levels, with the aspect of a great forge in the heavens'; 'a monstrous pumpkin-like moon arose on the other hand' (IV, XXVIII, p. 219). The earlier, ugly evening sun seemed to reflect her experience with Alec. That subsequent noonday sun, reflected in the buttercups, suggested 'an elfish moonlit aspect' to that search for the offending 'shoots of garlic' (p. 179), suggestive of Tess's fears. Even when the sun seems to illuminate 'the ardour of' Angel's love—'so palpable that she seemed to flinch under it like a plant in too burning a sun' (IV, XXVII, p. 211)—that reaction also implies her hidden fear. The sun which came 'slanting in by the window upon his back' (p. 210) as he embraces her in preparation for his proposal, suggests that fear which he cannot see, now so vivid to Tess.

The complex effects of sunlight upon the environment suggest the colder season to come. Thus Hardy suggests the likely consequences. While the horizontal sun 'formed a pollen of radiance over the landscape', they see 'tiny blue fogs in the shadows of trees and hedges' despite the 'bright sunshine elsewhere'. That same sun creates shadows of the pair, 'like long fingers pointing afar' towards 'the sloping sides of the vale' which they must soon ascend, literally and metaphorically (IV, XXXI, p. 235). Here 'the sound of the same purling weir' seemed attuned with their passion. Yet soon 'the reflected sun glared up from the river', dazzling them, while the sun is 'hidden by the bridge' and those fogs begin to close in on them. Thus Hardy refers back to those treacherous fogs on The Chase. And he looks ahead to Angel's suppression of his affection, and its revelation, as he sleepwalks, carrying Tess across that other bridge, in the light of the old moon (V, XXXVII).

While setting out on her 'pilgrimage' 'her hopes had' once 'mingled with the sunshine in an ideal photosphere' (III, XVI, p. 140); now 'her affection for him . . . enveloped her in a photosphere' irradiating her 'into forgetfulness of her past sorrows'. Yet she is only

> keeping back the gloomy spectres that would persist in their attempt to touch her . . . waiting like wolves just outside the circumscribing light. . . . A spiritual forgetfulness co-existed with intellectual remembrance. She walked in brightness, but she knew that in the background those shapes of darkness were always spread.

Through the effects of shifting sunlight, Hardy suggests Tess's feelings as those shapes seem to 'be receding, or approaching, one or the other, a little every day' (IV, XXXI, pp. 236–37).

The consequences seem to be suggested by those 'changing' meads. 'Gnats, knowing nothing of their brief glorification' cross that track of gossamer webs, illuminated by the sun to appear 'like the track of moonlight on the sea'. As Angel presses her to suggest a wedding-day 'in the presence of these things', it seems that Tess's own time of 'glorification' will be as brief (IV, XXXII, p. 242). At Stonehenge, the moon 'sunk, the clouds seemed to settle almost on their heads, and the night grew as dark as a cave' (VII, LVIII, p. 444). As during that Edenic summer scene, there seems to be 'no folk in the world but we two' (p. 445). Now Tess's sexual feelings and 'living will' have been fulfilled. However, with the sunrise comes the fulfilment of that nightmare aspect of the moon (p. 447).

Thus, through the action of fire, light, sun and moon upon other aspects of the environment, Hardy intensifies the inner feelings of individuals and suggests the development of relationships between Man and Woman. Thus Hardy creates provisional patterns out of his 'impressions' of that 'immortal puzzle' at certain stages in the development of the relationships. Yet out of these provisional patterns, he also abstracts greater patterns. For instance, through the changing perspectives upon the tensions which torture Tess, the novel incorporates a tension between 'tragedy' and 'comedy' (IV, XXIX, p. 221). As in a drama, the Jack Dollop scenes provide comic relief from the tragic tension. Yet, paradoxically, they also alienate Tess and intensify her pain. In dramatic terms, 'tragedy' suggests that troubles are resolved in death; 'comedy' suggests that they are resolved in marriage. Tess's fulfilment incorporates both.

The final comment upon the Jack Dollop tales suggests the apparent inevitability of battle between the sexes for the sake of survival (p. 221). Tess's insuppressible search for higher ideals in the relationship between Man and Woman makes her incapable of that battle mentality. Even so, she is driven to murder by force of circumstances in a far from ideal world. Her original vulnerability is encouraged by Angel's manner—'so much that of one who would love and cherish and defend her under any conditions, changes, charges, or revelations' (p. 223). She intensifies her vulnerability by refusing to allow herself to influence his judgement when he plans to leave her. She will not embarrass him by revealing how 'his inclination had compromised his dignity when reason slept' (V, XXXVII, p. 294). Besides her pride, 'her mood of long suffering made his way easy for him' as he leaves (p. 297). Yet in neither case was he as certain of his course as he appeared. Upon this kind of misunderstanding hangs the tragedy.

Thus Hardy shows Tess's tremendous potential as Angel's wife. He shows, too, the vulnerability of a woman passionately in love. He shows Angel's limitations in dealing with that vulnerability. He shows too how destructive social conditioning can be. Through drawing attention to these patterns of 'impressions', Hardy suggests areas where reform is possible. Angel's attitudes seem to change. But Alec's change little. The deaths of Sorrow, Alec and Tess remain unchangeable. The world remains resistant. Such are the limits of a novel.

Bearing in mind those limits, *Tess* may be regarded as the culmination of Hardy's power to intensify the 'inner expression' of that 'immortal puzzle', and to draw us into sympathy and understanding with a character. Just as he refines his use of the forms and archetypal significance of traditional tales and ballads to this end, so too are the nuances of feeling brought closely into focus through his use of the 'dream-country' environment. Nonetheless, his other fiction offers a further range of insights. The movements of fire, light, sun and moon often seem to interact to illuminate aspects of the 'sexual relation'. Often they are compounded with extremes in the weather or unusual events. Thus they frequently draw attention to the dangers, and to the destructive consequences which can ensue.

There are fewer shadows in *Under the Greenwood Tree*. Hence, Hardy's use of light is comparatively unequivocal. For instance, moonlight helps to set the scene for Dick to fall in love (I, IV, p. 50). The tranter's 'smile of miserable satire at the setting new moon' emphasizes his reaction to Dick's lovesick state (II, III, p. 93). The wedding is illuminated by a moon 'just over the full, rendering any light from lamps or their own beauties quite unnecessary to the pair' (IV, II, p. 208). Such effects enhance the atmosphere of the idyll; Hardy seems to immortalize the very ordinariness of the sexual relation by hinting that it is part of the pattern of the universe for all time, disturbed but little by Fancy's secret.

In *Far from the Madding Crowd*, Hardy is more equivocal. Oak's confident stride, Bathsheba's 'rejuvenated appearance' (p. 397), and the community's musical tribute on their wedding day suggest that the central relationship, like that of *Under the Greenwood Tree*, is ultimately resolved. However, there are reasons for Poorgrass's final comments (LVII). Whatever the implications for the future, that 'damp, disagreeable morning' (p. 396) is certainly a comment upon the past. The whole community has been shaken. Even Oak's increasingly heroic regenerative efforts have been unable to prevent irrevocable destruction. The demonic images associated with the initial fire (VI, p. 55) suggest the beginning of those efforts. They suggest, too, the beginning of a developing consciousness of destruction which culminates in the fight 'against water' (XXXVIII, p. 258).

The 'dream-country' environment suggests the true sense in which the Harvest Supper is 'also a Wedding Feast' (XXXVI,

p. 245). The storm is a random act of Nature. However, the trouble it causes is attributable to this ill-founded 'sexual relation'. While the 'weather was yet dry and sultry', 'the night had a sinister aspect' (XXXVI, p. 243). Oak perceives that sheep show 'terror of something greater than their terror of man' (p. 246) and that toad, spider and slug prepare for 'the later rain' (p. 246). Thus Hardy intensifies our perception of Troy's foolishness in insisting that 'it will not rain' (p. 245). By contrast, Oak knows that 'this complication of weathers being uncommon, was all the more to be feared' (p. 247).

As Bathsheba speaks 'warmly to him', confessing her story and joining him in the struggle, Hardy suggests the first sign that she recognizes the destructive potential of her marriage. That lightning which 'was the colour of silver, and gleamed in the heavens like a mailed army' (p. 251, suggestive of Troy's bedazzling of Bathsheba, now suggests 'a perfect dance of death', with 'skeletons' 'intertwined' with 'undulating snakes of green' (p. 253). Together, Oak and Bathsheba perceive the 'inexpressibly dangerous nature' of the lightning, concealed at first by 'the magnificence of its beauty' (XXXVII, p. 253). 'Love, life, everything human, seemed small and trifling in such close juxtaposition with an infuriated universe' (p. 253); nonetheless, the value of that 'golden legend' (XXXVI, p. 247) is enhanced by this illustration of the destructive potential of that contrasting relationship.

Bathsheba's regenerative efforts may be less effective than Oak's, but they do moderate that sense that her 'vanity' (I, p. 19) and 'coquetries' (XLIII, p. 301) make her culpable. Fancy Day was vain too, the consequences no more than ripples upon a stream. Bathsheba, however, has learnt 'what a great flame a little wildfire was likely to kindle'. Unfortunately, her 'resolution to avoid an evil' is framed when 'the evil is so far advanced as to make avoidance impossible' (XVIII, pp. 129–30). Troy's powerful personality, 'unfathomable lies' (XXXI, p. 211) and destructive use of truth intensify that evil. Through the demonic fire imagery, Hardy draws attention to Troy's destructive sexual behaviour before he even appears. The 'gigantic shadows of both man and woman' projected by Troy's lantern are 'distorted and mangled upon the tree-trunk till' the fused shadow is 'wasted to nothing'. Thus Hardy suggests the

131

destructive consequences of his bedazzling Bathsheba (XXIV, p. 167). In that 'uncultivated tract of land' suggestive of Bathsheba's state of mind, where ferns are 'plump and diaphanous from recent rapid growth, and radiant in hues of clear and untainted green', every detail shows her being drawn towards a feeling that she is understandably 'powerless to withstand or deny him' (XXVIII, p. 192), despite the danger. Hence Hardy shows how Troy has led her to the pit, where the 'sharp hisses, resembling a sky full of meteors close at hand' (p. 190) suggest a disturbed atmosphere with destructive implications.

Fanny Robin is a 'steady girl' (X, p. 90) without Bathsheba's faults. Yet she is even more vulnerable because of her servant status, of her gentle nature, of her 'slight and fragile' constitution, and of her having no 'friends or relations alive' (VIII, p. 79). (Boldwood's offer of financial help comes too late to help Fanny. Oak's efforts to help Bathsheba are rather more effective.) Fanny seems to serve as an archetypal shadow to more directly observed relationships, illustrating the ultimate impact of destructive sexual behaviour. Thus, Hardy introduces her in terms of Oak's impressions of her 'throb of tragic intensity' (VII, p. 61), and of 'feeling himself in the penumbra of a very deep sadness' (p. 62) by that 'oldest of the old' churchyard trees (p. 60). She is characterized by that deep sadness. On a dreary, dark, depressing wintry night over the moor Fanny seems crushed by the 'strangely low' 'vast arch of cloud above' like 'a large dark cavern, gradually sinking in upon the floor', as if 'the snow lining the heavens and that encrusting the earth would soon unite into one mass without any intervening stratum of air at all'. Even as she speaks she is no more than a 'blurred spot in the snow', 'like a mere shade upon the earth' (XI, pp. 92–4). Thus Hardy seems also to crush her individuality in order to emphasize that Nature is indifferent, and society unaware of, her archetypal human suffering. Thereby, he intensifies our horror that her suffering can count for so little.

Now he has raised our consciousness, Hardy projects her feelings into the environment as the destructive consequences unfold. He used fire imagery to introduce us to the nature of that original sadness which Oak sensed. He uses storm imagery to introduce us to Fanny's consequent 'poverty' and 'sadness' (XXXIX, p. 264). Her hopelessness is suggested by the 'moonless and starless night. A heavy unbroken crust of cloud . . . shutting out every speck of heaven' (XL, p. 266). Her sense of imminent death seems to be symbolized by that 'sublimation of all dismal sounds, the bark of a fox' suggestive 'of a funeral bell' (p. 268). She feels obliged to avoid human sounds. Yet her desperate yearning for help is suggested by that 'strange and mysterious' dog to whom 'she looked up . . . just as in earlier times she had, when standing, looked up to a man'. While, 'Night, in its sad, solemn, and benevolent aspect . . . was personified in this form' (p. 270), its 'stealthy and cruel side' proves the stronger—just as, for all Oak's regenerative efforts, much destruction remains irrevocable.

By the end of the novel, Fanny's fate is known. Bathsheba's faults are seen in perspective (LIII, p. 366). And it is generally acknowledged that 'nothing has prospered in Weatherbury since [Troy] came here' (p. 368). Hence, his reappearance is 'everybody's business' (p. 369). They wish him dead (p. 373). They are deeply moved by Boldwood's reprieve (p. 384). Yet earlier in the novel, the general attitude seems no less idle and unreflective than Bathsheba's is seen to be (XIII, p. 105). A comic background accompanies the Malthouse discussion of 'the origins of the fire' (VIII, p. 63). Though 'conscience-stricken' (XXXVIII, p. 259) after the Harvest Supper, the men do not at once perceive the full implications. Poorgrass seems to be depressed by Fanny's death. 'The hollow echo' of the drops falling from the fog-saturated trees remind him 'powerfully of the grim Leveller' (p. 285). To some extent he seems to identify with her sorrow. Like her, 'he wished he had the company even of a child or dog' (XLII, p. 284). Unlike her, he can distract himself from these feelings. However, through the accompanying 'dream-country' environment, Hardy emphasizes her painful story. 'The air was as an eye suddenly struck blind.' 'The trees stood in an attitude of intentness' (p. 284). The 'strange clouds' 'closing in upon the sky' suggest 'a sudden overgrowth of atmospheric fungi which had their roots in the neighbouring sea'. As with Tess, in the Chase, the pervasive fog emphasizes the widespread and arche-typal implications of destructive sexual behaviour. (Unlike with

Tess, Hardy does not emphasize that social law compounds that destruction.)

In *Tess*, Hardy uses the 'dream-country' to focus primarily upon the innermost feelings of individuals; here, however, the main focus seems to be upon the destructive potential of archetypal problems and their impact upon the community. Intertwining episodes of different relationships dramatize, and the 'dream-country' illuminates, aspects of that 'immortal puzzle'. For example, a detailed description of an unusual moonlight suggests how Boldwood's awakening sexual interest changes his perception of his environment, 'casting shadows in strange places, and putting lights where shadows had used to be' (XIV, p. 107), both within and without the house. The sun, 'half-visible', 'rayless, like a red and flameless fire shining over a white hearthstone', illuminates the 'frost-glazed surface of the snow' suggesting the initial impact of his newly aroused sexuality. It contrasts with that 'bristling ball of gold' which suggests Troy's impact. It contrasts too with the more benevolent sun with which Oak tends to be associated. (See, for example, I, p. 15.)

Thus, while dramatic episodes serve their purpose, so too do these changing, intertwining views of the environment. Even the initial long description of Norcombe Hill is as replete with inferences regarding the course of the novel as is the description of Egdon Heath at the beginning of *The Return of the Native*. At the same time it suggests, like Egdon, 'a shape approaching the indestructible ... which may remain undisturbed on some great day of confusion when far grander heights and dizzy granite precipices topple down' (*FFMC*, p. 20). Thus it suggests the timeless aspects of the situation; it seems that, although the subsequent 'pulls-all-together' of Spring (XVIII, p. 128) will pass, the pattern of events will recur.

Even so, Norcombe Hill and the wintry moor (XI) do not assume the sublime character of the heath which dominates *The Return of the Native*. Through its timeless aspects, Hardy expresses the insignificance of Man's problems, relationships and feelings— and Nature's indifference to them. Even the passionate and fated pair, Eustacia and Wildeve, are 'as two horns which the sluggish heath had put forth from its crown, like a mollusc, and had now drawn in' (I, IX, p. 94). While Eustacia cannot bear to see her hero shrunk into the form of a furzecutter, he yet 'seemed to be of no more account in life than an insect' (IV, V, p. 283)—'a brown spot in the midst of an olive-green gorse, and nothing more' (IV, III, p. 258)—in the context of the heath.

> The imperturbable countenance of the heath ... having defied the cataclysmic aspects of centuries, reduced to insignificance by its seamed and antique features the wildest turmoil of a single man. (V, II, p. 329)

On the other hand, Eustacia's form is its 'focal point'—its 'perfect, delicate and necessary finish ...' (I, II, p. 20). Increasingly, Hardy emphasizes the extent to which Egdon illuminates her character, until, at the last, 'harmony' was never 'more perfect than that between the chaos of her mind and the chaos of the world without' (VI, VII, p. 359). (See Chapter 1.)

At the same time, through the respective attitudes of individual characters towards the heath, Hardy shows how character differences affect relationships. 'Take all the varying hates felt by Eustacia Vye towards the heath and translate them into loves, and you have the heart of Clym' (III, II, p. 180). The attitude of his calmer, more prosaic, cousin, conflicts less dramatically with Eustacia's.

> To her there were not, as to Eustacia, demons in the air, and malice in every bush and bough. The drops which lashed her face were not scorpions, but prosy rain; Egdon in the mass was no monster whatever, but impersonal open ground. (V, VIII, p. 369)

While she regards Egdon as 'a nice wild place to walk in' her husband seems to regard it as 'somebody's gaol' (V, VI, p. 353).

Hardy's use of the moon illuminates how these differences in attitude affect the ability to find a basis for the 'sexual relation'. Clym meditates upon the moon, imagining there a world consistent with his ideals (III, IV, p. 202), Egdon having disappointed him in this respect. The enlarging 'shadow on the moon's disc' (p. 203) seems to suggest the thwarting of his ideals. (Perhaps it suggests his blindness, too.) That same ominous moonlight illuminates Eustacia's face, inspiring his avowal of love and passion (p. 203). That same moonlight upon

Clym's face inspires Eustacia's hope and vision of him 'doing better things' (p. 206). And the final stage of the eclipse inspires her desperate terror that their happiness will not last (pp. 206–7). At the gipsying, the going down of the sun seems to reflect her fading interest in Clym (IV, III, p. 266); the 'increasing moonlight' seems to reflect her growing interest in Wildeve. And that 'certain degree and tone of light which tends to disturb the equilibrium of the senses' (p. 267) drives her to her emotional abandonment. In this way, Hardy illuminates the heath to show that the sources of conflict and misunderstanding may be inherent within their own characters.

At the same time, these attitudes seem part of that timeless archetypal pattern suggested by that original powerful description of the heath. The 'chaos of the world without' may relate to that of Eustacia's mind. Yet it also inspires Everyman 'instinctively to dwell on nocturnal scenes of disaster in the chronicles of the world, and on all that is terrible and dark in history and legend' (V, VII, p. 359). Throughout, Hardy suggests a sombre sense of a 'time-worn drama' (III, III, p. 189) where relationships will develop according to an established archetypal pattern. For instance, the exhilarating proposal-scene is muted by Mrs. Yeobright's vivid recognition of the conflict between reason and passion, intensified by her deep attachment to her son. Thus Clym's 'nest of vivid green' negates the promise of newly awakened Spring. Rather, 'the scene seemed to belong to the carboniferous period . . . when there was neither bud nor blossom', and where 'no bird sang' (III, V, p. 212). This situation seems no less 'uncommon' than the subsequent wintry June days when 'trees, laden heavily with their new and humid leaves, were now suffering more damage than during the highest winds of winter . . .' (III, VI, p. 214). While Clym and Eustacia are temporarily blind to 'the heath and changes of weather', Hardy describes the heath as if in expectation of its 'winter period, representing night' (IV, I, p. 245). Even in the final storm this ominous sense of expectation persists in that 'little gate' to Clym's family home which 'continually opened and clicked together again—as if invisible shapes of the dead were passing in on their way to visit him' (V, VIII, p. 364). In this way Hardy seems to use Egdon to suggest the suppressed wisdom of a collective unconscious; at that level we know that relationships are often destructive as well as passionate.

In this way, Hardy uses Egdon to suggest that sexual relations are more complex and dangerous than society has led Thomasin to expect (I, V, p. 51). Hardy further disturbs the expectations of society by his subtle inversion of the part which society would expect of her as a 'lost woman' (II, II, p. 119). In Eustacia he dramatizes the foolishly romantic notions encouraged by current literature for young ladies. Because society would not acknowledge the dark complexities of sexual relationships, it could not advise on resolving them. Rather, these ideas intensify Eustacia's inherent emotional confusion. Thus she is dazzled by the 'brilliancy' of that dream which projects her ideal sexual relationship, although the implications are sober enough. Through her inability to see her partner's face Hardy suggests her frustrating inability to fall in love. He suggests, too, the impossibility of finding a man to correspond to her ideal. Hence she is never able to assess her feelings for Wildeve and Clym. The 'ecstatic' 'mazes of the dance' may seem to prefigure the dance at the house of her prospective husband. But it suggests more closely the dance with Wildeve, where the like-mindedness of her partner proves so dangerous:

> suddenly these two wheeled out from the mass of dancers, dived into one of the pools of the heath, and came out somewhere beneath into an iridescent hollow, arched with rainbows.

She seems to assume that the 'figure' which 'fell into fragments like a pack of cards' simply reflects her preference for a short, intense relationship rather than a long, cooler one. However, through this apparent death-omen and through her elation at being 'a woman in Paradise', Hardy shows her inability to recognize that the emotions which create and dissolve such a relationship can also destroy life. Thus, she is too elated by the dream to perceive its inherent dangers.

She sees but 'dimly' that heath beyond. Thus Hardy suggests her inability to assess the affinity between her personality and the heath or to perceive the archetypal implications. In this sense, then, Hardy uses the heath to suggest the expectation of tragedy. Thus, too, while Hardy frequently condemns Eustacia for blaming external factors for her own actions, he also uses an image of Egdon to show how the confused emotions of a vulnerable, guideless girl may be genuinely beyond her understanding.

Bonfire Night on Egdon celebrates that instinctive determination to enjoy life which causes Eustacia such trouble (I, III, p. 23). Like weddings and christeninngs, then—but not funerals (p. 29)—it culminates in dance (p. 37). Even this dance suggests danger. As Rainbarrow became a 'whirling of dark shapes amid a boiling confusion of sparks' 'the strumming of the wind upon the furze-bushes . . . formed a kind of tune to the demonic measure' and Christian feared that ' 'tis tempting the Wicked One' (p. 38). That danger has sexual connotations. Clym's dance inspires Eustacia to note that, by concentrating 'a twelvemonth's regulation fire' on a man 'in the fragment of an hour' a dance can prove 'that most subtle of lures' (II, V, pp. 138–39). The same dance inspires Christian to recall an ominous 'shadder last night [which] seemed just the shape of a coffin'. When 'a whole village full of sensuous emotion, scattered abroad all the year long, surged . . . in a focus for an hour' at the gipsying 'for the time Paganism was revived in their hearts, the pride of life was all in all, and they adored none other than themselves' (IV, III, p. 266). As Eustacia's emotions are driven 'to rankness' she hears 'her name whispered by a voice over her shoulder' (IV, III, pp. 266–67). As in her dream, the dance embraces equivocal instincts: the instinct for living seems inextricably bound to dangerous, even demonic impulses encouraging destruction, even death.

To a significant extent it is Eustacia's abandonment to such instincts which puts her outside society. Discussion of that 'immortal puzzle' leads to dance (I, III). Dance leads to fearful superstitions. The Egdon folk cannot name those fears; they see the devil in the reddleman (because he lives outside society) as well as a witch in Eustacia (I, V, p. 58; II, VIII, p. 172; III, II, p. 184, 186; V, VII, p. 359ff). In *Far from the Madding Crowd* Hardy showed how the survival of an agricultural community could depend, literally, upon responsible sexual behaviour. Small wonder then that the sexual emotions generated by the dance can arouse fear. Small wonder, too, that Eustacia's behaviour seems destructive. Her 'passions and instincts' encourage death though they seek life. They are common to humanity. They are liberated by dance. But a 'model woman' strives to control them (I, VI, p. 73). By contrast, Eustacia is inordinately proud of her 'power' to call up and triumph over Wildeve 'as the Witch of Endor called up Samuel' (I, VI, p. 72), regarding him as 'some wondrous thing she had created out of chaos' (p. 69).

Wildeve's reciprocal power makes hers even more dangerous (p. 72). Her fire proves the symbolic focus of the destruction latent in all the fires upon the heath. Through it she calls up powers which prove, ultimately, beyond her control—as illuminated by the fire lit by Charley in accordance with her will and yet without her consent (V, V, p. 342ff). In this, Hardy develops further the significance of demonic images in fire and storm in *Far from the Madding Crowd*. Behaviour which endangers individuals and their community is no worse than that of 'a model goddess':

> Had it been possible for the earth and mankind to be entirely in her grasp for a while . . . few in the world would have noticed the change of government. There would have been the same inequality of lot, the same heaping up of favours here, of contumely there, the same generosity before justice, the same perpetual dilemmas, the same captious alteration of caresses and blows that we endure now. (I, VII, pp. 73–4)

If there is a driving force ruling the world, its moral quality is, Hardy suggests, lower than that of common humanity.

Thus Hardy uses Eustacia's 'passions and instincts' to suggest a disenchanting illustration of the human condition. (See Chapter 1.) So, after the dance, the 'linguistic peculiarity of the heath' seems to echo Grandfer Cantle's 'ruins of human song' and to mingle with Eustacia's sighs (I, VI, p. 62). The 'boiling caldron' (V, VIII, p. 376) which kills Eustacia and Wildeve seems to be prefigured in those 'scalding caldrons' suggested by the communal impact of the bonfires. As they 'tinctured the silent bosom of the clouds above them and lit up their ephemeral caves' (I, III, p. 22), the bonfires seem to symbolize the effects of those instincts upon the human condition. Human consciousness seems like the heath beneath: 'a vast abyss', occasionally and partially illuminated by the flickering fire, but soon 'lost in darkness again' (p. 23). 'The muttered articulations of the wind in the hollows' seem to suggest 'complaints and petitions from the "souls of mighty worth" suspended therein' (p. 23). 'All was unstable; quivering as the leaves, evanescent as lightning' (p. 24). 'All was in extremity' (p. 24).

Thus, through Egdon, Hardy exposes, with astonishing depth, the complex nature of the sexual relation. He shows how, and to some extent why, passion can conflict with reason. He shows that the rules of an artificially ordered society can conflict with both. He shows how vulnerable the lonely and guideless can be. He shows how sexual entanglements can limit future potential. (Clym: see, for example, VI, I, p. 387.) At the same time, Hardy suggests that they need not. Desperate though Eustacia may have become, Clym was capable of forgiveness (V, VI). Already Charley's prudent 'loving-kindness' had forestalled her destruction (V, IV). From the beginning, the constructive regenerative potential of 'loving-kindness' is illustrated by Venn as he seems to arise from the heath alongside the 'old man', but demonstrating a protective rôle. Even so, with the best of motives, he frequently makes matters worse. He demonstrates, too, how cruelly class differences can exacerbate the inherent and destructive contrariness of sexual feelings. And he increases our sorrow that the constructive feelings of such a lover are so often not reciprocated (cf. Oak), while confused and unstable characters attract one another to appalling effect.

As we saw in Chapter 1, Hardy used Egdon Heath to suggest the opening up of a collective unconscious. Then, in *The Woodlanders*, he used mythic developments to suggest a complex web of sexual behaviour, highlighting contemporary issues. Moreover, symbols such as the tree and the horse, which seemed originally to relate to individual characters, gradually prove reflective of the condition of the community as a whole. However, we feel the significance of Giles's Niflheim experience in John South's tree, of the Jarnvid aspect of the woods, of the apparently universal sympathy of the woods at Giles's death, only because Hardy has translated mythic situations into immediate, identifiable experience. He does so by using the nuances of light, the changes in the weather, the seasonal cycles—all those manifestations of life and movement upon the landscape—to suggest the living experience of his characters.

Through these, he prefigures, reflects, dramatizes, and draws us into sympathy with their developing relationships.

These manifestations of life are ever-changing; they can, nonetheless, suggest important, if provisional, patterns. Recurring images of Giles's feelings are suggested by Hardy's use of fire (IV, p. 33; IX, p. 75; X, pp. 83–4; XXXI, pp. 235–36; XL, pp. 308–9). By contrast, Hardy shows Fitzpiers' feelings to be as unstable as the vagaries of light (VI, p. 51). The moon, as in Hardy's other novels, seems to be associated with feminine sexuality. When it illuminates the tombstone of Giles's father, it strengthens Mr. Melbury's resolve to surrender Grace to Giles (IX, p. 74). Later, the moon draws attention to Grace's own strong interest in the Midsummer Eve rites. It suggests Suke's as well. It also illuminates Fitzpiers' inconstancy, and his ability to forestall the girls' legitimate lovers (XX). Later still, Hardy uses it to suggest Grace's renewed interest in Fitzpiers— stronger than before, despite intervening events. That same moonlight illuminates the contrasting fate of the constant Marty (XLVII, p. 379), as once before (XV, p. 111). It illuminates, too, the ghastly web of circumstances surrounding that renewed association between Grace and Fitzpiers. Even more subtle and disturbing are those movements in the wind which, so often, reflect Melbury's equivocations. Even a 'fresh' and 'steady' breeze can make 'the point of each ivy leaf on the trunks scratch its underlying neighbour restlessly' (XII, p. 90). While the rudeness of the gentleman-farmer directs our sympathy towards the 'panting fox', it provokes Melbury to a perverse determination that Grace 'shall marry well'. When Melbury thus intensifies the original problem, instead of resolving it, 'the breeze . . . seemed to sigh a soft remonstrance' (p. 91). Through such patterns, Hardy suggests the complex nature of the intertwining relationships.

At the same time, movements and changes in the environment suggest the likely disturbance in those relationships. As so often in Hardy's novels, the casual conversation of the workfolk focuses upon hitches in relationships between men and women. From Giles's point of view, they discuss Mrs. Charmond's 'wanton' aspects to the 'accompaniment' of the 'regular dripping of the fog from the plantation boughs around' (IV, p. 29). Through 'the dark dawn' (p. 30), Hardy associates the scene

141

with the opening of the chapter and with the preceding depressing mythic developments. (The 'dark dawn' is also part of the reason for Melbury's late arising—the other reason being what Grammer Oliver perceives as typical parental concern for daughters (p. 30).)

Ominously, a third reference to Fitzpiers as being in league with the devil (I, p. 10; III, p. 18; IV, p. 33) accompanies Giles's mechanical 'stirring' of 'the embers with a spar-gad' (p. 33), as news of Grace's imminent return stirs up old feelings. Mr. Melbury's meditation upon 'the pair of dancing shadows . . . on the white-washed chimney corner—a yellow one from the window and a blue one from the fire' (p. 35) seems inexplicably significant here. Yet, as he calls Giles back, twice, from seeking Grace (p. 36), as he is to call him off twice from marrying her, and as Grace first becomes aware of Fitzpiers through that strange window-light (VI, p. 51), a sense of gradual revelation dawns. The light changes to blue, then violet, then red (p. 51), prompting Grace's awareness of 'something dissociated from . . . normal sequences' (p. 52). Her musings upon the man behind them prompts ominous 'kaleidoscopic dreams' which also involve 'the face of Giles Winterborne' (VII, p. 55). Her loss of interest by light of day seems to suggest that the fascination may not be backed by enduring affection. Thus Hardy creates the impression of a tale about to unfold according to a predictable, if unconscious, pattern of events. Thus Hardy prepares us to expect a sadly disturbed pattern of relationships.

More subtly now, signs of the 'ingress of the winter months' (VII, p. 56) and a robin's alarm at seeing snow (p. 58) suggest the Melburys' precipitate coldness towards Giles. That behaviour is reflected in Hardy's illustration of the 'Unfulfilled Intention which makes life what it is' (p. 56). It seems to accord with an inevitable pattern of human behaviour. Hardy's reference to 'the fabled Jarnvid wood' (Loki's home) recalls how Loki could pervert even the judgement of the gods, causing mischief, with endless repercussions. Thus Hardy hints at the possibility that 'the devil tempted' Melbury 'in the person of Fitzpiers'—that Melbury is not entirely responsible. However, it is Fitzpiers who has expressed the view that Man cannot control his fate (VI, p. 53). Perhaps, then, Hardy intends us to question that argument. Anyway, as they 'dived amid beeches under which nothing grew' (p. 56), Hardy seems to suggest that no good will come of their attitude.

This web of impressions weighs rather heavily against Giles's subsequent renewal of hope. The extent of these hopes is suggested by that 'western sky, which was now aglow like some vast foundry wherein new worlds were being cast'. It may seem to suggest that 'it will be fine to-morrow', but Giles has more than 'the weather . . . to think of'. His enthusiasm seems likely to render him vulnerable (IX, p. 73), despite Mr. Melbury's subsequent renewal of his vow (p. 74). The climax of his hope, during the heat and exertion necessary in preparation for the party, is suggested by 'the heat shining out upon his streaming face and making his eyes like furnaces', and by the 'great pot' which 'boiled on the fire' (p. 75). He acknowledges his failure when Grace is unable to dance because 'she had forgotten the old figures' (p. 81). As so often, his deepest feelings are reflected in fire imagery: he

> had abstractedly taken the poker, and with a wrinkled forehead was ploughing abroad the wood-embers on the wide hearth, till it was like a vast scorching Sahara, with red-hot boulders lying about everywhere. (p. 83)

Soon, he is 'shaking his head over the gloomy plain of embers, and lining his forehead more than ever' (p. 84). The veracity of those impressions is confirmed by Mr. Melbury's comments. And as the Melburys 'struck down the lane under boughs which formed a black filigree in which the stars seemed set' (p. 82), Hardy seems to remind us of that subtle web of impressions regarding Melbury's suppressed guilt about his failure to keep his vow.

That pattern of impressions culminates in the fog which finally 'inclosed him from her view' (XIII, p. 99). The 'increasing mist' seems to suggest the effect of Grace's behaviour upon Giles. She approaches only to ignore him. The consequent 'sudden fog' seems to suggest Giles's shocked dismay (p. 98). The Niflheim fogland seems to suggest the extent of his desolation as well as the sadness of his failure to fight for survival (p. 100). As the lingering fog causes a confrontation with Mrs. Charmond, so his lingering misery causes him to treat her tactlessly (pp. 101–2). As in *Tess* and *Far from the Madding Crowd*, Hardy uses the fog to suggest the scale of the destruction which can ensue when couples fail to work out a sound basis for their 'sexual relation'. The tree which 'seemed to shiver, then to heave a sigh' (p. 100) encourages us to sympathize with Giles's response. We regret the failure of their relationship. And we regret the Melburys' decision to despise Giles. Moreover, we recognize Hardy's hints that greater trouble will ensue.

'Under the black boughs which formed a tracery upon the stars' (XVI, p. 120) Hardy suggests the contrasting, superficial quality of Fitzpiers' affection. The image recalls that scene after Giles's party (IX, p. 82). The black boughs recall Melbury's behaviour then. The stars set between seem to recall those possible factors beyond his responsibility. The pheasants now roosting in those boughs, in danger of gunfire, seem to add a new perspective—of Grace's vulnerability. The 'accident of two large birds . . . tumbling . . . into the hot ashes at their feet, apparently engrossed in a desperate quarrel that prevented the use of their wings' (XIX, pp. 147–48) suggests 'the end of what is called love'. It seems the marriage will entrap Fitzpiers as well. The hot ashes remind us, too, of Giles's loss. Fitzpiers is unaware of her approach until what seems to him like a dream awakening (XVIII, p. 133). He is unconscious of how the weather seems to prefigure his imminent, mistaken, impulsive marriage:

> the weather now being the inevitable relapse which sooner or later succeeds a time too radiant for the season. . . . the strange mistakes that some of the sanguine trees had made in budding before their month, to be incontinently glued up by the frozen thawings now; the similarly sanguine errors of impulsive birds in framing nests that were swamped by snow-water. (XVII, p. 130)

For all Fitzpiers' faults, the Lokian factor, tempting Fitzpiers towards greater harm than he intends, is a pertinent aspect of his behaviour pattern which bears upon the behaviour of other characters too.

Indeed, his behaviour towards Grace reflects a common and natural pattern. Their 'mutual interest' grows 'as imperceptibly as the twigs budded on the trees'. Although 'Spring weather came on rather suddenly' there is nothing unnatural in 'the unsealing of buds' and 'the rush of sap in the veins of the trees' (XIX, p. 139). Yet she hardly seems more than that 'tree' upon which Fitzpiers' 'rainbow falls' (p. 123). Worse, she is 'disturbed rather than attracted by him' (XIX, p. 138), 'spell-bound' and 'powerless' (p. 132), even at her first interview. She feels 'not love, nor ambition, rather a fearful consciousness of hazard in the air' (XXII, p. 167), 'a premonition that she could not resist him if he came' (p. 164), an 'intoxication that . . . passed off somewhat with his withdrawal. She felt like a woman who did not know what she had been doing' (pp. 169–70). Her instincts are sound indeed (XXIX, p. 216). His influence is 'almost psychic'. 'She had never regarded him in the light of a destined husband' (p. 164). 'He seemed to be her ruler rather than her equal, protector, and dear familiar friend' (XXIV, p. 172). Yet she marries him. Not only is this 'domestic disaster' as 'thousands'. Not only is it as 'old as the hills' (XXXI, p. 231). It even seems part of Nature's perplexing pattern—of which social law fails to take sufficient account.

Hardy is also using Nature to suggest Grace's dawning consciousness of her feelings as she strives to comprehend them. Her awareness of Fitzpiers' displaced affection is suggested by his ride eastward, away from her. 'The evening sun which stood behind her back' seems to suggest his previous affection for her. 'As soon as he got out from the shade of the hill' it beams 'full upon him', suggesting that new passion (XXIII, p. 211). The 'deep violet' sky behind, 'white Darling in relief upon it—a mere speck now'—inspires her to muse 'on the vicissitudes of horses and wives' (p. 212). To her, 'the whole' seems 'intensified by the gilding of the declining sun' so that 'she wondered if there were one world in the universe where the fruit had no worm, and marriage no sorrow'. Soon, however,

> she discerned shapes moving up the valley towards her, quite near at hand, though till now hidden by the hedges. . . . Up, upward they crept, a stray beam of the sun alighting every now and then like a star on the blades of the pomace-shovels. (pp. 212–13)

They suggest her growing interest in Giles, which surfaces in that 'sudden impulse to be familiar with him' (p. 213). She emphasizes that she is 'returning' from her walk. She enjoys walking by Giles's side. She idolizes him as 'Autumn's very brother'. As 'her heart rose from its late sadness like a released bough, her senses revelled in the sudden lapse to Nature unadorned' and 'she became the crude country girl of her latent early instincts' (p. 213).

And yet, while using Nature to reflect this development in Grace's feelings, Hardy also uses it to suggest her consequent delusion. To her it seemed that 'Nature was bountiful. . . . No sooner had she been cast aside by Edred Fitzpiers than another being, impersonating chivalrous and undiluted manliness, had arisen out of the earth ready to her hand' (p. 213). Giles is infected by her delusion. Together,

> they passed so far round the hill that the whole west sky was revealed. Between the broken clouds they could see into the recesses of heaven as they mused and walked, the eye journeying on under a species of golden arcades, and past fiery obstructions, fancied cairns, logan-stones, stalactites of topaz. Deeper than this their gaze passed thin flakes of incandescence, till it plunged into a bottomless medium of soft green fire. (p. 214)

Thus Hardy suggests the potential of Giles's relationship with a hypothetical reformed Grace. Yet, while Giles's tiny, almost unconscious gesture shows that he reciprocates 'her revolt for the nonce against social law, her passionate desire for primitive life' (p. 214), her reaction shows how fragile is her delusion that they can escape social law. Hence, their usual condition of mind reasserts itself as they 'descended into the vale again to a place where their ways divided' (p. 218). Nonetheless, through those musings

> she had made a discovery. . . . She had looked into her heart, and found that her early interest in Giles Winterborne had become revitalized into growth by her widening perceptions of what was great and little in life.

She has discovered that she appreciates, above all else, 'honesty, goodness, manliness, tenderness, devotion' as 'manifested' by Giles 'from his youth up' (XXX, p. 227).

The 'wan' faces of the Woodlanders in the 'weird twilight of advancing day' (XXIX, p. 218) suggests the broad impact of her trouble upon the community. The depth of the trouble is

suggested by the 'chilly wind' which 'curled around' Grace and
her father as they halt beneath the 'half-dead oak'. Its
condition, 'hollow and disfigured with white tumours, its roots
spreading out like claws grasping the ground', seems to suggest
that their trouble exemplifies a long-standing human condition.
The breadth and depth of the trouble seems to be reflected, too,
in the 'dim atmosphere of unnaturalness' which envelopes the
whole vale. The 'livid curtain' in the east suggests the impact of
Fitzpiers' errant affections rather than hope of a new day—a
second chance. Thus Hardy shows that, while Fitzpiers'
behaviour may be part of a common pattern in Nature, it is still
unnatural in the sense that it causes disturbance throughout the
community (p. 219). It is precisely because it is so common that
humanity needs to strive to lessen its impact. Because society
fails to acknowledge this, its rules only exacerbate that pattern.
So too do individuals.

Hardy develops this impression by surprising us with para-
doxes. Nature seems to sympathize with human misery whilst
relentlessly intensifying it. Through striving to comprehend the
paradox, we realize that the woods which seem to weep for their
Balder-like hero only reflect the consciousness of the human
community. Their apparently demonic aspects during the
storm do suggest a destructive pattern in Nature. Yet humanity
has exacerbated it. Similarly, it is the sexual impact upon the
community of Mrs. Charmond's return which is conveyed as
'Autumn drew shiveringly to its end.' At first it just seems that
something is 'gone from the gardens'. Soon, however, the
consequences escalate.

> The forest leaves, which had been descending at leisure,
> descended in haste and in multitudes, and all the golden colours
> that had hung overhead were now crowded together in a
> degraded mass underfoot, where the fallen myriads got redder
> and hornier, and curled themselves up to rot. (XXX, p. 224)

Hardy relates his catalogue of evidence of how 'Winter had
come on' (p. 225) to Fitzpiers' state of mind. Here his use of
Nature seems to shrink the significance of human efforts by
implying that they simply follow this destructive pattern. Yet
elsewhere Hardy has suggested the possibility of more constructive alternatives. Even now, Giles would reclaim Grace if

social law would permit. Thus social law encourages Nature's destructive patterns but does not permit her regenerative ones. Clearly, Melbury thinks of that alternative pattern as he 'set out to look for Giles'. Hence his state of mind is both reflected in and dominated by 'a rimy evening when the woods seemed to be in a cold sweat; beads of perspiration hung from every bare twig; the sky had no colour'. The trees which 'rose before him as haggard, grey phantoms whose days of substantiality were passed' (XXXI, p. 232) suggest the dwarfing of his paternal power and authority—his lost confidence in society's values as well as in himself.

Yet he is not a better man for it. He does not consider whether he might still help Giles insofar as he is able. Indeed he cannot resist 'recklessly stirring up' fires in Giles. The extent to which he continues to intensify Giles's already profound sorrow is suggested by that 'darkness' which 'had closed in round them, and the monotonous drip of the fog from the branches' which 'quickened as it turned to fine rain' (p. 235) while 'they looked gloomily at the smoke that beat about the roof of hurdles, through whose weavings a large drop of rain fell at intervals and spat into the fire' (p. 236). Through that image Hardy relates Melbury's failure to redress a destructive behaviour pattern to Giles's ultimate sacrifice—under a roof of hurdles like this one, if not the very same.

Under the compound influence of father and social training, Grace finds that she has 'no ideas as to direction at all' in that 'wildest part of the wood' which recalls her childhood and her original affections. She cannot simply return to old ideas. The 'transformation' in her life, as in those woods, has been too great. Rather, her sense of imminent darkness seems to be reflected in the 'growing ... dark' of evening and in the 'night-moan' of the wind. She tries to resolve her dilemma, striking 'out hither and thither in random courses'. But 'denser grew the darkness, more developed the wind voices ...' (XXXIII, p. 248). Mrs. Charmond's experience is even worse. She is 'nearly dead with terror and misery and fatigue' (p. 249). Her mind, too, is on her failure to find a sound basis for the 'sexual relation'. That confusion is to lead to her death. 'The funereal trees' which 'rocked and chanted dirges unceasingly' seem to predict such a conclusion. Their efforts to comfort one another seem pathetically futile in comparison with the compound influence of destructive patterns in Nature and society. That 'nearly spent wind which, even in its enfeebled state, did not reach her shelter' (XXXIX, p. 296) suggests the consequent weakening of the rejuvenative power which Giles and Grace embrace. Yet the heaving of the saps 'with the force of hydraulic lifts inside all the trunks of the forest' (XXXIV, p. 253), followed by summer and Grace's idealization of Giles as 'fruit-god and wood-god in alternation' (XXXVII, p 286) combine to suggest the power in Nature which is denied them. Although she escapes to him, 'Summer was ending. . . . Creeping damps and twilight chills came up from the hollows' and the plantations are 'weird' and 'spectral' (XL, p. 307).

Not only does paternal and social influence deny them marriage. It even hinders her power to show Giles common humanity. Although Hardy describes the wood from Grace's point of view, she cannot recognize the significance of symbols which seem to derive from the human unconscious. Although 'weak, lidless eyes', 'strange faces and figures from expiring lights' (p. 307), 'sheeted shapes' and 'faint cloven tongues' (p. 308) seem to suggest an unconscious awareness of Giles's condition, she 'heeded these impressions but little' (p. 308). The increasingly human and supernatural imagery of the storm seems to symbolize those complex destructive forces for which Giles suffers and dies (XLI, p. 317). The disfigurations of personified trees seem to symbolize the consequent sufferings of humanity in general. Beneath the 'neighbours' whose 'struggle . . . she had heard in the night . . . were the rotting stumps of those of the group that had been vanquished long ago, rising from their mossy setting like black teeth from green grass' (XLII, p. 320). Thus Giles's situation seems to exemplify a long-standing human condition.

Yet Giles's character is identified with this condition less dramatically. His cough can be mistaken for a squirrel or a bird (XLI, p. 315; XLII, p. 321). His final 'endless monologue' is 'like that we sometimes hear from inanimate nature in deep secret places' (XLII, p. 322). Nothing could be more antithetical to the power of the storm.

Passive though this character may seem, he exemplifies important qualities. Contrary to impressions gained at the party, Grace recognizes now 'the purity of his nature, his freedom from the grosser passions, his scrupulous delicacy'. He whom she had rejected 'had loved her more than the mere lover would have loved' (XLIII, p. 328). 'He was pure and perfect in his heart' (p. 333). That crash of a tree, felled by Melbury 'in the depths of the nearest wood' (XLV, pp. 351, 353), reminds us of how deeply Melbury shares responsibility for Grace's situation when she deserts Giles after all. It reminds us too of Giles's wasted qualities. Yet in a sense his influence is not forgotten. Marty prolongs his memory. The young trees send 'out their roots in the direction that he had given them with his subtle hand' (XLIII, p. 336). The storm may suggest the potential power of those destructive patterns; but the quiet voice persists, suggesting those qualities which may triumph if that 'immortal puzzle' is ever resolved.

Thus, as in earlier novels, Hardy shows the attraction and danger of destructive personalities and how they relate to the human condition. But there is no Oak, not even a Venn, striving to counteract that destructive potential. Giles is too passive, Marty and Mrs. Melbury too unappreciated, to exert the influence they might otherwise have done. Rather, social law cruelly and vividly exacerbates that destructive potential. Fitzpiers, the most destructive personality, suffers least. Giles, the 'good man', suffers most. Besides this, Hardy develops further the humanizing potential of the 'dream-country' environment. Thus *The Woodlanders* shows a harsher, perhaps truer, picture of that 'immortal puzzle', accompanied by an increased intensity of feeling.

Both these aspects reach a summit in *Tess*. *Tess* shows the culmination of Hardy's power to use the 'dream-country' environment to suggest sensitive nuances of an individual's feelings, as well as to suggest the ultimate consequences of the destructive potential of human nature. The tragic waste of Tess's potential is emphasized by a superlatively beautiful vale. There is no such beauty in *Jude*. The initial ugly environment is a direct product of destructive attitudes. Thereafter the environment illuminates little more than the hopeless aspirations and struggles of a man who is alienated from society because he tries to transcend its debilitating and destructive tendencies. (See Chapter 2.) However, a ghastly intensity of emotion is generated through the resurgence of the 'dream-country' environment towards the end.

Sue's sufferings have driven her to love Jude as never before. But she also feels the need to construct an intelligent purpose behind such cruel sufferings. Moreover, she has little energy left for fighting old battles. Hence, she tears herself from Jude to embrace values which Hardy has, by now, discredited. As so often in Hardy's fiction, the destructive consequences of failing to resolve 'the immortal puzzle' are emphasized by fog. Thus, 'they proceeded ... like Acherontic shades for a long while, without sound or gesture' (VI, IV, p. 379) to part at the children's graves (p. 381). The 'funereal' implications of the 'familiar Christminster fog' 'persists' (VI, V, p. 382). Jude departs towards 'a dreary, strange, flat scene, where boughs dripped, and coughs and consumptions lurked, and where he had never been before'. Thereafter, wind, cold, and rain persistently interact, as if driving Jude towards his death. The fog travels up to Marygreen for Sue's remarriage, making the tower appear to loom 'large and solemn'. Thus it provides comment upon why Sue's remarriage therein seems 'like a re-enactment by the ghosts of their former selves' (p. 389). For Phillotson, too, is denying his former integrity—leaving 'crude lovingkindness' to 'take care of itself' (VI, IV, p. 379). Such are the qualities being rejected. For that rejection Jude dies. Through Hardy's use of fog, ugly Marygreen and decaying Christminster are related to traditions which have reinforced destructive attitudes for centuries.

In *Jude*, Hardy's use of a 'dream-country' environment is comparatively limited. Nonetheless, it is significant. It illuminates Jude's character development. (See Chapter 2.) It also illuminates developments in the web of relationships. Through these, Hardy encourages consciousness of the infeasibility of certain traditional attitudes. For example, through projecting certain attitudes on to Tess and suggesting their development, Hardy shows the artificiality of distinguishing between the sexual and the spiritual woman; through a similar method, *Jude* shows how frustrating it is if women do correspond to these social moulds. Both novels show how such distinctions exacerbate the problems inherent in the 'immortal puzzle'.

The contrast between what Arabella and Sue call love (V, V,

151

p. 313) is partly a product of such distinctions. With Arabella, Jude can feel that he is 'living for the first time: not wasting life'—that 'it was better to love a woman than to be a graduate or a parson; ay, or a pope!' (I, VII, p. 68.) He readily responds to her as to 'a complete and substantial female animal' (I, VI, p. 59), even after her return from Australia. Yet 'he knows well, too well, in the secret centre of his brain, that Arabella was not worth a great deal as a specimen of womankind' (I, IX, p. 78). By contrast, he responds to Sue as 'more or less an ideal character, about whose form he began to weave curious and fantastic day-dreams' (II, II, p. 108).

Hardy emphasizes that Jude is a 'straightforward' man. Both Arabella and Sue recognize this (I, VII, p. 69; IV, I, p. 225). He is capable of both passion and restraint. While recognizing the limitations of social conventions, he would marry Sue for good reasons. Thus, even his conflicts and contrasts are reasonable. On his account, there should, it seems, be no hindrance to resolving the 'puzzle' once he recognizes the danger of basing 'a permanent contract on a temporary feeling which had no necessary connexion with affinities that alone render a life-long comradeship tolerable' (I, XI, p. 90).

Sue shares such affinities. She can be a 'congenial friend' (II, IV, p. 119), 'something to love' (p. 117), even, while he is ill, an 'anchor' to which 'to cling' (p. 118). At moments, simultaneous physical reactions betray a reciprocal intensity of emotion: the clasping of hands in the empty classroom (IV, I, p. 223); their response to the cry of the rabbit caught in the gin (IV, II, p. 235); their simultaneous looking back (IV, III, p. 237). These incidents, in three consecutive chapters, culminate in that consequent kiss which proves the 'turning-point in Jude's career'. They develop 'complete mutual understanding, in which every glance and movement was as effectual as speech for conveying intelligence between them' such that they seem 'almost the two parts of a single whole' (V, V, p. 311). Phillotson recognizes the 'extraordinary sympathy, or similarity, between the pair'. 'They seem to be one person split in two.' As it is 'not an ignoble, merely animal, feeling between the two' it seems 'that their affection will be enduring' (IV, IV, p. 250).

However, Sue's character is complex. While Jude is experiencing a 'sense of degradation at this revived experience with'

Arabella, Sue appears almost as a projection of his 'anima': 'she stood like a vision before him—her look bodeful and anxious as in a dream.' However, 'her little mouth' is 'nervous', and the eyes which speak 'reproachful inquiry' are 'strained' (III, IX, pp. 205–6). She is like Jude 'at heart, but not at head' (IV, I, p. 223). Her confused, nervous disposition sets her apart from Jude's straightforward sensitivity. She prefers railway stations to cathedrals because they harbour no traditions. She feels crushed by cathedrals (III, I, p. 153), by ruins (III, II, p. 156), by old houses and 'the weight of so many previous lives there spent' (IV, I, p. 223). She abhors 'the Government stamp' which continues to validate the traditions perpetuated in these places. Yet, despite her heightened awareness of society's limitations, she is 'enslaved to the social code' (IV, V, p. 262). Indeed, she is a product of it. She insists that Jude should identify her with 'those pretty lines . . . from Shelley's "Epipsychidion" ' (IV, V, p. 265). Yet they epitomize that long tradition of perverting the lover's natural instinct to idealize the woman he loves. Considering, too, her sexual fastidiousness, her type does seem, at least in part, to be a product of that tradition. She seems to illustrate the ultimate destructiveness of that type. Hence, she scarcely seems to have a human identity of her own. She seems 'a sort of fay, or sprite—not a woman' (VI, III, p. 373), a 'spirit', 'disembodied creature', a 'dear, sweet, tantalizing phantom—hardly flesh at all' (IV, V, p. 265). (See, too, IV, VI, p. 269; VI, IX, p. 413.) Hence her 'curious unconsciousness of gender' (III, IV, p. 169), despite her apparently paradoxical love of being admired by men. Her very inconsistencies reflect her relationship to society. Society seems to have made her what she is. It has punished her for being so, and, having drained her of the strength to resist its pressures, driven her to conform to ill-fitting 'social moulds'.

Nonetheless, social law is not entirely to blame. To a large extent it reflects Nature's cruelty (V, VI, p. 327; V, VIII, p. 338).[6] The behaviour of individuals, mistakes which can only be seen as such in retrospect, and blind chance, all play their part. Hence, Jude attributes their sufferings to 'Man and senseless circumstance'. The question is, what has prompted social law to develop thus, exacerbating rather than assuaging, Nature's cruelty, creating an apparently 'artificial system of things, under which the normal sex-impulses are turned into devilish domestic gins and springes' (IV, III, p. 238). Under this system, the school authorities only recognize 'relations based on animal desire' (III, VI, p. 188). The 'mood of the average husband and wife of Christendom' is, Hardy claims, 'antipathetic' and 'recriminatory' (V, V, p. 315). A 'dull, cowed, and listless manner' seems 'to substantiate' Sue's supposed marriage to Jude (V, VI, p. 317). When she reverts to a mood of amiable companionship, society 'won't believe' they are married (p. 322). Nonetheless, while Hardy remarks upon the failure to protest against the transitory feelings upon which Jude's marriage is based (I, IX, p. 78), he later shows how compatible and enduring a marriage to Sue could be—at least, 'Nature's own marriage' (VI, III, p. 371). Clearly, Hardy implies, couples should fight the system, not each other. Or, rather, he prompts them to reassess the system, to consider why things have got so bad, and how they might be improved.

This theme permeates his fiction. In *The Well-Beloved* it takes the form of a detailed study from the perspective of an individual artist. Elsewhere, Hardy explores the theme through a web of relationships. Except in *Jude*, that web derives largely from his use of a 'dream-country' perspective. Yet, even in *Jude*, a 'dream-country' serves some part in creating that web of 'impressions' upon 'the immortal puzzle'. Through it, Hardy encourages us to consider its complexities. If society took more account of these, considering, in particular, the destructive potential in sexuality, it could strive towards a more constructive, less artificial code. For all the darkness and misery of the human condition, it seems that compatibility is possible, and that those verses on charity may yet survive all that is destructive and vestigial in the traditions of Christendom (VI, VI, p. 381 and 395).

NOTES

1. Preface, *The Woodlanders* (1895).
2. Other aspects of Hardy's concept of a 'pure woman' have been discussed elsewhere. See, for example, (i) Kathleen Blake, 'Pure Tess: Hardy on Knowing a Woman', *Studies in English Literature*, Vol. 22 (Autumn 1982),

689–705; (ii) Mary Jacobus, 'Tess' Purity', *Essays in Criticism*, Vol. 26 (October 1976), 318ff. I suggest that Hardy's concept of a 'pure woman' embraced an ideal balance between sexuality and spirituality, unlike the dissociation suggested by Arabella and Sue. In striving to adapt his novel to the moral demands of his publishers, he may, paradoxically, have developed more acutely his concept of a 'pure woman'. Like Angel, Hardy seems to regard Tess as 'a visionary essence of woman' (III, XX, p. 170); unlike Angel, Hardy's vision consciously embraced Tess's secret.

On 23 September 1984, Radio 4 broadcast *The Real Tess*, written and narrated by Elizabeth North, about Hardy and the stage dramatization of *Tess*. Hardy was shown to regard Gertrude Bugler as 'the very incarnation' of Tess. A poem destroyed by F. E. Hardy showed how deeply involved with that 'incarnation' of Tess the 84-year-old Hardy had become. Bugler was evidently innocent of complicity. In regarding her as Tess's 'incarnation', he must surely have been thinking of the final version of the novel rather than the earliest version where she is more actively responsible for her relationship with Alec.

Bugler had previously played the parts of Bathsheba, Eustacia and Marty—all with that same group, the Hardy Players. Perhaps Hardy developed his concept of a 'pure woman' partly through exploration of these successive types.

His appreciation of Bugler also shows clear affinities with Pierston's relationship with the third Avice. On Bugler, see M. Millgate, *Thomas Hardy: A Biography* (Oxford University Press, 1982), pp. 293ff; 535; 556–57. See, too, M. Millgate & Richard Little Purdy (eds.), *Collected Letters*, Vol. i (Oxford University Press, 1978), p. 245: 'I am glad you like Tess—though I have not been able to put on paper all that she is, or was, to me' (1891).

3. F. E. Hardy, *Life* (Macmillan, 1975), p. 375.

4. Nonetheless, Hardy does show the community's disenchantment with Troy after Fanny's death. Despite the unthinking neglect of her coffin, they are no longer amused by his inverted morality; rather, they are impatient with him for the trouble caused to Oak, Bathsheba, and Boldwood, as their comments, around the time of Troy's death, reveal.

5. V, XXXV, p. 277. See too IV, XXXIV, pp. 259–60, where Hardy emphasizes that 'all visitors to the mansion' find the portraits grotesque to the extent that they 'haunt the beholder afterwards in his dreams'. The effect is emphasized by 'their being builded into the wall' so that 'they can't be moved away.' Moreover, 'the unpleasantness of the matter was that, in addition to their effect on Tess, her fine features were unquestionably traceable in these exaggerated forms.' While in a stable frame of mind, Angel simply regrets his own lack of forethought. After her confession, he allows a candlelight view of them to destroy his inclination to forgive her (p. 277).

6. See too, *Jude*, I, II, p. 34, where lovemaking, whether legalized or not, seems to result in cruelty. See W. R. Goetz, 'The Felicity and Infelicity of Marriage in *Jude the Obscure*', *Nineteenth-Century Fiction*, Vol. 38, No. 2 (September 1983), 189ff, especially 208.

4

Man and Society

Chapter 2 showed Hardy using a 'dream-country' to help suggest the development of characters. Chapter 3 showed him using a 'dream-country' to help probe the complexities of their sexual relationships. Both showed that relationships between individuals and society were also important issues in Hardy's fiction.

Archetypal settings prove to be foci for Hardy's impressions of human society. He uses the friendly Christmas festivities of Mellstock to initiate us into the society of *Under the Greenwood Tree*. He uses the negation of tradition in modern Marygreen to suggest the harshness of the society against which Jude struggles. In *Far from the Madding Crowd*—Norcombe Hill; in *The Return of the Native*—Egdon Heath; in *The Woodlanders*—the path through the woods; in *Tess*—the Maydance; in *The Well-Beloved*—the island of stone: in each of these novels, an initiatory setting provokes peculiarly significant perspectives upon human society. The characters and their relationships might be said to dramatize those perspectives. At the same time, Hardy continues to develop his use of archetypal settings, such as Bathsheba's shearing-supper and shearing-barn and the equivocal harvest supper, to suggest the extent to which the behaviour of the individual and the community inter-relate.

In *The Mayor of Casterbridge* that inter-relation is prominent.[1] That 'dream-place' Casterbridge[2]—the capital of Hardy's Wessex—is, in this novel, 'the pole, focus, or nerve-knot of the surrounding country life' and has been for centuries. (IX, p. 65. See, too, IV, p. 33 and IX, p. 61.) Its survival depends upon preserving that 'primitive habit of helping one another in time of need' (XXVII, p. 195). Yet it also preserves a reputation as an 'old, hoary place o' wickedness' (VIII, p. 56). Henchard's character is similarly paradoxical.

As Hardy draws attention to Henchard's limitations, he also draws attention to the limitations of society. At first, Henchard's strivings to transcend his limitations inspire and affirm an archetypal respect for 'yer gospel oath' among the community (V, p. 39). (See, too, II, p. 22.) His 'word' is his 'bond'. (IX, p. 68. See too XXXI, p. 222.) His honesty is attested to even at his bankruptcy (XXXI, p. 220). Even his overthrow is not entirely the fault of sinister qualities; it is completed by 'the heavy failure of a debtor whom he had trusted generously' and a 'blunder of misrepresentation' (XXXI, p. 219). On the other hand, his reputation is already being questioned when Farfrae arrives. Farfrae's proffered corn-cure salvages Henchard's reputation for a while. However, with his fall he has 'lost his good name' (XL, p. 284). He is trusted no more. Yet Abel Whittle's loyalty ensures that we do not forget that Henchard helped others in time of need (XV, p. 103 and XLV, p. 332). Moreover, Henchard's final devotion to Elizabeth Jane is genuine, if ill-timed. Hardy encourages a sentimental reaction to the dead bird to emphasize a final impression that Henchard's overt, impulsive harshness is compensated by deeply generous qualities. In this he seems superior to the society which rebuffs him. Thus Hardy encourages us to question society's assessment of character. Society may appreciate noble qualities. It may even sympathize with his fall (XXXI, p. 221). Yet the appreciation of the crowd is limited, transient and superficial, and social success is fragile.

Hardy also prompts us to consider the extent to which sexual relationships affect that inter-relation between the individual and society. Curiously, Casterbridge folk regard Susan as a 'ghost' or 'skellinton'—as if they perceive, unconsciously, what she is to Henchard. They recognize that kindly motives must underlie his present choice, and respect him less for it (XIII, pp. 86–9). The culmination of their cruel tendency is the ritual which leads to Lucetta's death. Her lodging, at 'the node of all orbits' (XXIV, p. 166), overlooking the market-place and town-pump, seems to reflect the extent to which her apparently private problems are to prove part of Casterbridge and the human condition it represents. It reflects, too, the irony that Henchard's sexual relations are thrust before the public eye after he believes he has fully discharged his responsibilities towards Susan and recompensed Lucetta. The irony is particularly acute considering that he has striven to avoid women, that they might not compromise his ambitions for financial success and social status (I, p. 12; XIII, p. 85). Nonetheless, he did marry young; and he did become involved with Lucetta. And, ultimately, sexual jealousy proves the catalyst for his fall. He cannot escape his sexuality—nor its impact upon his relationship with society.

The pattern of his sexual relationships only illustrates a general pattern in his life: 'that idiosyncrasy of Henchard's which had ruled his courses from the beginning . . . had mainly made him what he was' (XLII, p. 303). Every detail of his story seems to relate, often jarringly, to Casterbridge and its inhabitants. Every tactless remark, every mistake, small or large, seems to backfire. His behaviour apparently influences that of his waggoner (XXVII). Even apparently good fortune proves otherwise. Farfrae saves Henchard from the community's anger about the 'unprincipled bread' (IV, p. 35); yet he proves the unwitting instrument of Henchard's destruction in business as well as in love, ultimately cleaning him 'out of all the character and standing which he has built up in these eighteen year' (XVI, p. 110). However, long before this, that socially disadvantageous marriage gave Nance Mockridge courage to voice her suspicion of 'a bluebeardy look about 'en' which will 'out in time' (XIII, p. 88). This suggests more than a shrewd instinct for those latent aspects of Henchard's character which will ultimately lead to his social destruction. Her words also suggest the emergence of an instinct to find grounds to defrock the successful denizens of society. Elizabeth Jane's kindness and willingness to serve prove lever enough (XX, p. 134). The degraded furmity-woman (XXVIII, p. 203) and Jopp (XXXVII, p. 269) feel the instinct more bitterly. In Mixen Lane, that 'mildewed leaf in the sturdy and flourishing Casterbridge plant' (XXXVI, p. 255), that bitterness develops to tragic proportions.

In the subculture of Mixen Lane, Hardy shows the struggle to survive in defiance of social failure (XXXVI, p. 255). Moral degeneration is difficult to avoid. At the town pump Hardy presents the dilemma of conflict between poverty and archetypal respect for the dead. However, the use of pennies for drink suggests that excuses are being made for moral degeneration (XVIII, p. 122). Henchard is not poor, and he, too, fails to respect Susan's dying wishes (XIX, p. 126). Poverty and morality are not necessarily the two sides of one coin. Nonetheless, the clientele of 'The Three Mariners', too, is understandably sensitive to the moral dilemmas imposed by poverty. Farfrae is shocked by Coney's claim that 'the best o' us' are 'hardly honest sometimes . . .' (VIII, p. 56). Hence, the company denies that claim. However, what 'Maister Billy Wills says' is clearly acknowledged often enough when naïve foreigners are not there to distract and entertain them.

Even the incomes of farmers and cornfactors are at the mercy of uncertain harvests. Thus

> the rural multitude saw in the god of the weather a more important personage than they do now. Indeed, the feeling of the peasantry in this matter was so intense as to be almost unrealizable in these equable days. Their impulse was well-nigh to prostrate themselves in lamentation before untimely rains and tempests, which came as the Alastor of those households whose crime it was to be poor. (XXVI, p. 185)

Hardy even begins his Preface by emphasizing this. Yet he does not present the skimmity-ride as a traditional demonstration of moral indignation by a society craving to appease the weather-god and so to ensure a good harvest.[3] Rather, it is a thoughtless game played by Casterbridge's degenerates. Nonetheless, by exposing thus the moral chink in the armour of the town's first lady, Mixen Lane mocks a society where material success is valued highly and associated with good character, regardless of factors beyond the individual's control (XXXVI, p. 259; XXXVII, pp. 267–69; XLII, p. 300). In this sense, the rite exorcises bitterness.

Dealer Buzzford's jumbled history of Casterbridge as 'a old hoary place o' wickedness' (VIII, p. 56) suggests a common theme of rebellion; it seems that Hardy has used Mixen Lane to draw it towards consciousness. In a town where folk leave houses unlocked with 'no thought of umbrella stealers' (IX, p. 63), it is hard to imagine crime on the scale that Buzzford suggests. Rather, 'wickedness' seems more likely to be authority's term for the people's rebellion against inhumane treatment. That hostility is revived by the 'growed wheat' (IV, p. 35). It constitutes our first impression of Casterbridge folk.

Were it not for the seriousness of a town having no decent bread, their attitude might be dismissed lightly as a little healthy grumbling. After all, their reception of the 'Royal Personage' shows no inkling of rebellion; only Henchard 'disdained to dress as well as he might' (XXXVII, p. 265). Yet the visit is fleeting. The conversations and attentions of Caster-bridge folk are soon centred upon themselves. At this, Lucetta's 'triumphant time' (p. 267), she makes it clear that she 'meant to know [Henchard] in public no more' (p. 265). Yet, as her pride swells, feeling intensifies against her, and scandal about them spreads 'like a miasmatic fog through Mixen Lane, and thence up the back streets of Casterbridge' (p. 267). Invisibly, Caster-bridge is preparing for the exhibition which really interests the community. At the trial of the furmity-woman (XXVIII, p. 201) Hardy has already made the constabulary seem comic and foolish. Here he has them hide their staves for fear of the crowd (XXXIX, p. 281). By the time 'the rusty-jointed executors of the law' have fumbled their way to Peter's Finger (p. 282) all is concealed. Simply by planning carefully, Mixen Lane can render the law and its officers ineffectual. They have shown their power—and their potential for rebellion.

Normally, however, Casterbridge folk accept the framework of society. Hardy uses the town's Roman characteristics to emphasize their obliviousness to that rebellious potential. They accept and are unmoved by the ubiquitous evidence of Roman occupation (XI, p. 74); it seems too remote in time to relate to their lives. Yet no one argues when Buzzford relates their rebelliousness 'in the time of the Romans' to the comparatively recent Duke of Monmouth's rebellion, and to Casterbridge's present reputation; the very nature of Buzzford's mistake suggests that Casterbridge still perceives, if unconsciously, the continuity of the type of authority which the Romans imposed.

Thus Hardy suggests that Roman civilization influences their lives more than they are consciously aware. The 'curious feature' of 'the burial-ground of the old Romano-British city' is 'its continuity as a place of sepulchre' (XX, p. 135). The road upon which so much drama is set still adheres to 'its Roman foundations' (XXIX, p. 205). Henchard's kindly meant and yet empty ritual courtship, pursued in a cottage 'near the Roman wall' (XIII, p. 84), suggests a sense of adherence to outworn social codes. Carvings of Apollo and Diana over Henchard's hearth recall sexual ideals which are mocked by the complexity of the problem discussed there (XII, p. 80). Indeed, 'Casterbridge announced old Rome in every street, alley, and precinct. It looked Roman, bespoke the art of Rome, concealed dead men of Rome.' 'One of the finest Roman Amphitheatres, if not the very finest, remaining in Britain', is 'accessible from every part of the town' and 'close to the turnpike road'.

> It was related that there still remained under the south entrance excavated cells for the reception of the wild animals and athletes who took part in the games. The arena was still smooth and circular, as if used for its original purpose not so very long ago. The sloping pathways by which spectators had ascended to their seats were pathways yet.

Only a carpet of grass disguises all this.

Yet 'a true impression of this suggestive place could be received' (p. 74). At dusk, its 'melancholy, impressive, lonely' atmosphere attracts 'furtive' appointments and inspires 'intrigues'. Lovers never meet here. But Henchard secretly meets here with both his wronged women, in sorrowful circumstances. He also spies on Elizabeth Jane from here (XLII, p. 305). Its 'sinister' history as a place of execution and the supposed sightings of ghosts of Hadrian's soldiery apparently 'watching the gladiatorial combat' clearly affect Casterbridge folk more than they consciously recognize. Hardy seems to suggest that, despite the supposed ideals of civilized society, its authorities have failed to change or impress human nature. Memories of a violent judicial system seem, rather, to provoke further crime and violence (p. 75). As the 'vastness' of the place and its suggestions become apparent 'by degrees' Hardy seems to suggest, as if in a dream, flickerings of a kind of vision of human society, incorporating those latent subversive feelings which Casterbridge folk are normally happy to keep buried, until provoked.

Similarly, it is dusk when Elizabeth Jane 'really' sees High-

Place Hall for the first time (XXI, p. 140). This later
monument to civilization also suggests 'intrigue' (p. 142).
Lucetta, civilization's representative, is unaware of that door,
'older even than the house itself' (p. 146). The 'keystone' of the
arch above it is a 'ghastly' mask. Its 'comic leer' is disfigured
from 'generations' of stonethrowing (p. 142). It leads to an alley
through which

> it had been possible to come unseen from all sorts of quarters in
> the town—the old play-house, the old bull-stake, the old cock-
> pit, the pool wherein nameless infants had been used to dis-
> appear. (p. 143)

Lucetta's house suits her aims and social condition (p. 141–42).
The alley seems, however, to suggest an image of those
dangerous undercurrents in human society of which she is
unconscious (XXXV, p. 251; XXXVII). Thus, through Lucetta,
Hardy draws attention to the continuing paradox of a human
society whose actual nature can contrast with that in which its
successful denizens believe.

One effect of Henchard's story is to draw attention to this
discrepancy. 'The mournful phases of Casterbridge life' are
'embodied' in a scene which is also in 'lugubrious harmony'
with Henchard's 'domestic situation' on learning Susan's
secret (XIX, pp. 128–29). While Casterbridge society still
respects him as its proud and successful Mayor, he feels he has
lost everything. From this perspective, Casterbridge seems
dominated by a gaol which, 'like a pedestal lacking its statue',
seems 'incomplete' without 'the corpse of a man' (p. 129)
hanging above. 'The river—slow, noiseless, and dark' runs
'like the voice of desolation' through 'a back-hatch' of the mill
'attached' to the ruined Priory; it seems to suggest the course
of human life dominated by a harshly punitive system of
authority.

The Church, too, seems to dominate Casterbridge. It tolls the
curfew bell 'with a peremptory clang'. Immediately, business
life responds with a 'clatter of shutters through the whole length
of the High Street'. It is echoed by the characteristic bells of
gaol and almshouse. While the clock-maker shuts up shop, his
clocks join in 'like a row of actors delivering their final speeches
before the fall of the curtain'. Yet the church bell persists, long

162

past the hour, with 'chimes . . . stammering out the Sicilian Mariners' Hymn' (IV, pp. 33–4).

However, the 'lower parts' of the 'grizzled Church, whose massive square tower rose unbroken into the darkening sky' are 'illuminated by the nearest lamps sufficiently to show how completely the mortar from the joints of the stonework had been nibbled out by time and weather' (p. 34). The mill persists. So do 'trees which seemed old enough to have been planted by the friars' (XXXI, p. 221). But the Priory is gone—its rubble transformed into Jopp's cottage. Nowhere in this novel does the church represent a living tradition. It is referred to as the place where Henchard marries. Its bells ring for Farfrae's wedding. It is the place from which the musicians come for what we witness as the real tradition—the drink around the 'great sixteen-legged oak table, like the monolithic circle at Stonehenge in its pristine days' (XXXIII, p. 231). They discuss the sermon; but 'the general tendency' is 'to regard it as a scientific feat or performance which had no relation to their own lives'. Because the Church is in partnership with authority, Casterbridge folk feel obliged to profess Christian beliefs. Yet they 'believed so little' in the Church and believed so much in Conjuror Fall, that they support him 'unseen' (XXVI, p. 187).

Hardy is not advocating any earlier pagan religion.[4] Conjuror Fall simply forecasts the weather through observing signs in Nature (XXVI, p. 188). He can predict Henchard's arrival through his understanding of human nature. But Hardy rejects religious beliefs which mislead humankind in the quest for understanding. There is no 'sinister intelligence bent on punishing' Henchard, though many of 'his kind' might think so (XIX, p. 128). Nor has anyone 'been roasting a waxen image . . . or stirring an unholy brew . . . to confound' him (XXVII, p. 191). Nor has Farfrae any 'glass that he sees next year in' (XXVI, p. 184). Rather, Hardy suggests, 'Character is Fate . . . and Farfrae's character was just the reverse of Henchard's.' Henchard himself acknowledges it (VII, p. 52). Perhaps his failures are characteristic of 'a vehement gloomy being who had quitted the ways of vulgar men without light to guide him on a better way' (XVII, p. 117).

For a while Henchard believes he has such a light. Hardy's perspective on Providence is ever ironic, and trust in it exposed

as illusory. Henchard's 'intervention' has a 'natural' explanation. However, having been diverted from 'desperate
intentions', the generally fatalistic Henchard is uncharacteristi-
cally jerked into superstitious trust that he is in 'Somebody's
Hand'. His sudden assumption of extreme guilt—'Who is such
a reprobate sinner as I?'—in Authorized Version tones rather
than his own betrays the origin of the superstition in supposedly
Christian teachings. Yet Hardy perceives that those teachings
are denied by experience. The cruel irony of Henchard's
resultant conviction that he is being 'kept . . . alive', just as the
action accelerates towards his ignominious death, shatters any
delusion the reader may have that, if such a power exists, it is
beneficent (XLI, p. 299).

Hardy illustrates this further in *The Woodlanders*. Fitzpiers is
believed to be in league with the devil (I, p. 10; III, p. 18; IV,
p. 33). By sending his books to the parsonage by mistake, and
through Fitzpiers' own actions, Hardy encourages the idea that
he illustrates the antithesis of Christian values. Yet, just when
Fitzpiers has revealed his most wicked thoughts to Melbury,
'the mercy of Providence' saves his life (XXXV, p. 264). With
the law as it stands, of course, 'Providence' is also protecting
Melbury; but, considering Melbury's provocation, this leads us
to question the law as well as Providence. After Giles's death,
Fitzpiers' life is saved again. In inverse proportion to justice,
'Providence' has sided with him completely, Grace partially,
and Tim Tangs, whose married life he has ruined through
distracting Suke's emotions, not at all. As a further reward, the
wife Fitzpiers has wronged returns to him immediately as a
consequence of the shock. Thereby she causes trouble and
worry to those who really care for her (XLVII, p. 369). If
'Providence' is beneficent, it is misdirected. This novel seems to
clamour in protest against those whom 'Providence' would
protect.

Rather than Providence, Hardy acknowledges 'a back'ard
current in the world'. Hence, 'we must do our utmost to
advance in order just to bide where we be' (*DR*, XXI, p. 401).
Egbert's grandfather is evicted because his patron's daughter
'left off hindering' the scheme (*AILH*, p. 57). Gabriel Oak is
notable for striving against that current. Thus he plays the rôle
of guardian angel towards his beloved Bathsheba. But Tess's

guardian angel fails her (*Tess*, I, XI, p. 107). Angel Clare could have taken upon him that function. He could have danced with her. He could have protected her. Having deserted her, he failed to return in time as Providence, by definition, should. Yet neither she nor her friends could have summoned him more fervently. This novel seems to clamour in protest on behalf of those whom 'Providence' would neglect.

In *Jude*, Hardy criticizes the idea of Providence even more directly. In Melchester, 'Providence' supplies restoration work for Jude while he awaits 'a call to higher labours' which are clearly inappropriate for him (III, I, p. 150). When 'Providence' intervenes again, 'a growing impatience of faith, which he had noticed in himself more than once of late, made him pass over in ridicule the idea that God sent people on fools' errands' (III, X, p. 216). When Jude tells Sue of that 'special Providence' which brought Arabella back to him (IV, II, p. 232), the irony is bitter, his disbelief clear.

Yet, even in his earlier fiction, Hardy illustrates the extent to which society believes in an unbelievable Providence. 'It's Providence!' Farfrae exclaims. 'Should anyone go against it?' (*MC*, IX, p. 68). Yet while Farfrae remains oblivious, Henchard immediately rejects Jopp with a dangerous tactlessness. Thus Hardy suggests that an apparently providential arrangement involves opening up a chink in Henchard's armour. Honoured once more, Farfrae concludes that they 'are ruled by the Powers above us! We plan this, but we do that' (XXXIV, p. 243). Poor Lucetta's perspective is painfully different. Yet she too can speak of an 'obstacle' being 'providentially removed' (XXIV, p. 173). She seems not to notice that it would have been more helpful if 'Providence' had not interfered. Elizabeth Jane seems unaware of the extent to which experience has influenced her belief in Providence; she takes care not to tempt 'Providence to hurl mother and me down, and afflict us again as He used to do' (XIV, p. 91). In *The Woodlanders* it is seen as 'tempting o' Providence' to keep Grace at school so long (IV, p. 30). And yet people continue to believe that it is good 'to act the part of Providence sometimes' (*W*, XX, p. 152). In *Far from the Madding Crowd* a 'happy Providence' frequently seems to prevent the worst from happening (VIII, pp. 68, 72; XV, p. 115; XLVI, p. 318); its power seems rather limited, and the epithet 'happy' prompts the question of how often experience has shown 'Providence' to promote unhappiness. The expressions are common; their logic is indefensible. Experience has modified the idea of Providence. Yet Church and society still encourage that 'simple faith' in 'Providence' (*Tess*, I, XI, p. 107).

Tess's experience shows that the belief is so contrary to the way of the world that it reduces resistance to destructive influences. Joan, representative of 'her own long family of waiters on Providence' (I, V, p. 66), encourages 'that reckless acquiescence in chance, too apparent in the whole d'Urberville family' (*Tess*, V, XXXVII, p. 297). Thus the d'Urberville home provokes criticism of Wordsworth's related pantheistic belief in 'Nature's holy plan' (I, III, p. 51). Tess retains her 'rather automatic orthodoxy' despite 'its obvious unreality' (IV, XXVI, p. 205). Yet, when she seems to be experiencing 'good fortune', she expects it to 'be scourged out of me afterward by a lot of ill'; for she has learnt from experience that 'that is how Heaven mostly does' (IV, XXXII, p. 247). She is also angry that 'books will not tell' why life is unjust (III, XIX, p. 165), and why, contrary to natural justice, Alec may be regarded as 'on the side of the Spirit, while she remained unregenerate' (VI, XLV, p. 353).

This conflict between faith and experience is common in Hardy's fiction. Much seems to confirm Henery's complaint that

> your lot is your lot, and Scripture is nothing; for if you do good you don't get rewarded according to your works, but be cheated in some mean way out of your recompense. (*FFMC*, XV, p. 112)

A rich parson gives the impression of having earned 'holy gold rings . . . by praying excellent well', though the genuine Parson Thirdly is poor (*FFMC*, XXXIII, p. 226). The workfolk seem to accept without comment that vicious 'acts of piety' are 'natural to the saintly inclined' (*FFMC*, VIII, p. 72). Jude's view is exceptional. Most, like the carter, simply accept that they 'never could understand religion' (*Jude*, I, III, p. 44).

Most conclude that faith is not worth the trouble. Many Egdon folk live so far from their church, and ' 'tis such a mortal poor chance that you'll be chose for up above', that 'going to church, except to be married or buried, was exceptional' (*RN*, I,

X, p. 96). If 'one of the Egdon folk' does go 'some rum job or other is sure to be doing' (*RN*, III, II, p. 184): the illustration involves witchcraft. Hence, 'in name they were parishioners, but virtually they belonged to no parish at all' (*RN*, II, IV, p. 128). In lighter tone, Mellstock folk appreciated a parson who left them alone, excused them from church-going, and did not ask for money for missionary purposes with which they did not sympathize (*UGT*, II, II, p. 91). With ironic humour, Hardy conveys Shaston's relief at being too poor to be Christian (*Jude*, IV, I, p. 220ff).

Faith in the Christian religion seems dead. Priory (*MC*, XXXI, p. 221) and 'abbey had perished, creeds being transient' (*Tess*, V, XXXV, p. 276). To Sue, Melchester's railway station replaces the cathedral as 'the centre of town life now' (*Jude*, III, I, p. 153). Christian's shadow resembles a coffin (*RN*, II, VI, p. 148). Elizabeth Jane notes the absence of miracles nowadays (*MC*, XLI, p. 297). Prayer has become a complicated and farcical business (*Jude*, I, III, p. 40). Christian tradition does not confront the 'groaning' of 'all Creation'; it is absorbed with petty points of doctrine (VI, II, p. 357). In ignorance, it comments upon Jude's tragedy with a recital of 'Truly God is loving unto Israel'. And it comments upon his death-bed catechism with a chorus of 'Hurrah!' (*Jude*, VI, XI).[5] Thus, Christminster and society lie. The lie may not be deliberate. Nonetheless, it leads to incomprehension and alienation; it is as if 'some disaster cleft Thy scheme/ And tore us wide apart,/ So that no cry can cross.'[6] Hence, it leads to total disbelief, and to that 'chronic melancholy which is taking hold of the civilized races with the decline in belief in a beneficent Power' (*Tess*, III, XVIII, p. 156).

Contrary to Hardy's early hopes, there is little 'evidence that the Church will go far in the removal of "things that are shaken" '.[7] Yet he long continues to believe that a move towards religious truth may be possible through his poetry.[8] It expresses those 'obstinate questionings . . . in the exploration of reality' which are 'the first step towards the soul's betterment, and the body's also'[9]: 'if way to the Better there be, it exacts a full look at the Worst.'[10] 'The shouts of the many and strong', repeated so often as to seem 'to be somewhat true', make him seem like 'one shaped awry' who 'disturbs the order' to no avail.[10] Yet he remains hopeful of 'binding Satan fast' within a hundred years.[11] Out of 'the graveyard of dead creeds' seems to come 'New promise'.[12] Out of 'a strangeness in the air' seems to come 'a Voice', revealing at last 'What earth and heaven mean',[13] and 'a stirring thrills the air' promising 'deliverance'.[14]

For many years Hardy believes in an imminent 'informing' of 'the Will' through 'Consciousness . . . till It fashion all things fair!'.[14] He draws attention to that neglected 'resource' of 'the human heart'—'loving-kindness'[15]—which, 'operating through scientific knowledge', may reduce pain 'to a minimum'. The Great War shatters this hope. The later poetry shows how far.[16] Even in times of optimism he recognized its precariousness, for it depends upon that

> modicum of free-will conjecturally possessed by organic life when the mighty necessitating forces—unconscious or other—that have 'the balancings of the clouds', happen to be in equilibrium, which may or may not be often.[17]

Nonetheless, much that is positive and enduring in the character of his fiction derives from exploring the limits of that 'modicum of free-will'. Troy could have done much for Fanny, especially with Boldwood's help. Rather, he makes one pathetic, futile and belated effort at 'reversing his course' (*FFMC*, XLVI, pp. 317–18). The 'grotesque' gargoyle, which 'laughed' as it 'vomited' upon Fanny's grave, may seem to justify Troy's illusion that he has been struggling against hopelessly antagonistic forces. Yet, in this instance, the solution is simple: despite her own pain, Bathsheba asks Oak to fill in the hole and to get the leadwork turned to prevent 'a repetition of the accident'; she then replants the flowers so that they 'thrive' (pp. 320–21). Hardy uses the incident to illustrate a pattern of behaviour; Troy uses the idea of supernatural control as he might nowadays use the Welfare State—as an excuse to under-estimate his free will and his potential for improving the human lot.

Hardy's characters frequently under-estimate their freedom to defy what seem to be demonic powers. Melbury does not intend to evade responsibility towards his daughter. However, he blames 'the devil' for tempting him, 'in the person of Fitzpiers', to break 'his virtuous vow' (*W*, XXXI, p. 234). Their combined influence on Grace increases the 'psychic' intensity of her 'premonition that she could not resist him if he came', although she feels neither 'love, nor ambition, rather a fearful consciousness of hazard in the air' (XXII, p. 164). Later, however, she is to recognize that fear need not have intimidated her. Rather, her instincts offered her the freedom to obey her impulse to refuse her hand (*W*, XXIX, p. 216). Hardy dismisses the illusion of 'Providence'. He dismisses, too, illusions of a malevolent 'President of the Immortals' of pagan, fatalistic 'Aeschylean phrase' (*Tess*, VII, LIX, p. 449). He encourages consciousness of the extent to which humankind can control its course.

Yet he also acknowledges much as yet beyond human comprehension or control. In this respect, *The Fiddler of the Reels* might be regarded as a study of an important theme of his fiction.[18] It shows how difficult it can be to judge whether Car'line 'had' or 'fancied she had, no power' (*SS*, p. 150) to resist the fiddler's 'weird and wizardly . . . power over unsophisticated maidenhood' (p. 135) as intensified by Music and Dance.[19] Thus, while Hardy explores possibilities for the exercise of 'that modicum of free-will', he also explores the nature and extent of antagonistic forces, such as the dark and confusing complexities of relationships; the difficulty of recognizing mistakes until too late; the difficulty of changing patterns of behaviour even then. Melbury is possessive, but he means no ill. He makes mistakes. Their repercussions spread through the Great Web. He cannot stop them. A change in the law might help. Human society en masse can have more power than the individual. Yet it, too, has its limits.

In his autobiography, Hardy includes numerous references to psychological complexities and evidence of apparently irrational powers as yet beyond our ken. (See Appendix 1.) Such incidents are frequently the subject of his short stories and narrative poems. *The Withered Arm* is based upon an incident which Hardy believes to be true.[20] It exemplifies Hardy's efforts 'to explain or excuse the presence of evil and the incongruity of penalizing the irresponsible'.[21] When Gertrude is 'overlooked' (*SS*, p. 43) by 'an enemy' (p. 42), Rhoda is horrified to find that she can 'exercise a malignant power over people against my own will' (p. 36). Yet the Squire's cruel indifference seems to render her unconscious will inevitable and observable to villagers who see her as a witch. The Squire seems untouchable. Instead, his blameless wife suffers the reflection of Rhoda's pain. Only when the third victim—her innocent son—is to be hanged as 'an example' (p. 53), at the same age as she was when she bore him, does the instigator of the trouble involve himself. By then he is powerless to intervene. Yet the web of pain initiated by his cruelty does not simply involve temporal forces; it also involves apparently supernatural factors, as yet inadequately defined by religious codes and beyond our control.

Thus the power of authority to propagate evil seems unlimited, while its power to initiate good is fettered. Even Mrs. Charmond—'the divinity who shaped the ends of the Hintock population' (*W*, XV, p. 111)—is subject to the trials of the human condition (*W*, XXXVI, p. 275). Similarly, Henchard's career dramatizes the emergence of human frailty from an astonishingly transient veneer of social power. Only as Mrs. Charmond's pride crumbles does a capacity for 'loving-kindness' become manifest (*W*, XXXVI, p. 275). Only when 'weariness of the world' drives Henchard from Casterbridge, does he really learn to love (*MC*, XLIV, p. 318). Jude's one final hope is that the verses on Charity 'will stand fast when all the rest that you call religion has passed away' (*Jude*, VI, IV, p. 381). Yet while the qualities in which Hardy invests such hope for humankind remain associated with weakness and social failure, it is hard to imagine society embracing them. In contrast to Jude, Phillotson comes to believe that 'in an old civilization like ours, it was necessary to act under an acquired and cultivated sense of . . . justice and right . . . and to let crude loving-kindness take care of itself' (p. 379).

Sometimes, however, those attitudes and values which thwart the kinder instincts of humankind seem less intractable. In his early novels, Hardy focuses upon the ups and downs of a few major characters. In the later novels, he is more and more concerned to show the limitations society imposes upon them. The rural community seems to be of fading significance. However, some of its attitudes and values contradict, and to some extent counteract, those of society. This is particularly clear in his short stories.

In *The Three Strangers*, the christening party at the shepherd's house suggests a scene of archetypal affectionate fellow-feeling.

Though 'not three miles from a country-town' (*SS*, p. 1), it seems far away; the difficult countryside inbetween, and the serene acceptance of an archetypal human condition here, endorses this impression. While the settlement itself 'partially broke the force of wind and rain' (p. 6), the festivities prove a wonderful defence against the cruelties and discomforts of Nature as symbolized in the storm (p. 5). The cruelties of the Law prove more intrusive. As the hangman gradually reveals his identity, the community

> instinctively . . . withdrew further and further from the grim gentleman in their midst, whom some seemed to take for the Prince of Darkness himself, till they formed a remote circle, an empty space of floor being left between them and him—'circulus, cujus centrum diabolus'. (p. 17)

The home has been invaded by a further image of their separation from society.

With the sounding of the gun from the gaol, the men become involved in pursuit of the convict, breaking up the party. However, Hardy shows how superficial their apparent allegiance to the Law may be. They only respond because they fear that 'it would look very much like connivance if they did not' (p. 19). The hangman, having initiated the action, leaves them to it; his behaviour illustrates that of the legal authorities who appoint constables from among their own folk to track down their own people. The constable seems to make constructive use of his employers' assumption that he is stupid. It is impossible to prove that he does not really have the faith he claims in his symbol of office. His argument that he must return home for his staff at least succeeds in delaying action for a little while. At the same time, his apparently awesome respect for the Law succeeds in mocking its pretensions (p. 18). On the other hand, his convoluted explanation to the magistrate (p. 23), and his confused language on arresting the suspect (p. 21) are probably genuine enough. Even so, Hardy achieves a sense of mockery here, too, particularly when confusing 'the name of the Father' and 'the Crown' (p. 22).

Hardy's treatment is not, however, entirely humorous. The crying of the constable's betrothed (p. 18) and of the baby (p. 19) emphasize the disturbing nature of the incident. The women 'seemed glad of an excuse to' part company with the pursuers in order, by contrast, to 'comfort the baby'. The country folk fear the Law enough to appear to seek assiduously for the sheep-stealer. They resist it enough to examine 'their own lofts and out-houses' less closely than they might. Unconsciously, they have already harboured the convict in the very heart of the shepherd's home. They do not regret it. Rather, he has 'won their admiration' as well as their sympathy, for they believe 'the intended punishment' to be 'cruelly disproportioned to the transgression' (p. 25).

Most of the characters are dead at the time Hardy relates the tale. Yet the story remains as alive as ever (p. 25). Thus it preserves a sense of archetypal, affectionate fellow-feeling coming to terms with, if not overcoming, the Law's cruelty. In this there appears to be hope for humankind.

In *The Distracted Preacher*, Hardy draws us into sympathy with another closely knit village community, through the archetypal affections of the preacher and Lizzy (p. 70). Again, the folk mock the Law by defying it, while pretending otherwise (p. 109). They drive the determined Latimer to despair that 'you may serve your Government at too high a price' (p. 113). He fears the folk, rather than they him (p. 98). They perceive the government officials as 'too stupid ever to really frighten us'—only to 'make us a bit nimble' (p. 115). Their resistance inspires respect. It is strong and highly organized, and yet relatively harmless (p. 112)—especially in contrast to the ferocity of the Law against convicted smugglers.

Hardy's apparent sympathy with the community is confirmed by the footnote (p. 120). Through the comical aspect of 'the tremendous sniffing' (p. 100) Hardy deflects us from respecting Latimer's conscientiousness. Through Lizzy's arguments, Hardy suggests that their survival is too crucial to compare with respect for 'a king who is nothing to us' (p. 111). 'Almost everybody in Nether-Moynton lives by' smuggling (p. 88). 'If those Coastmen had got off with the tubs, half the people in the parish would have been in want for the next month or two' (p. 112), including Lizzy and her mother (p. 114): 'I know my mother, but the king I have never seen. His dues are nothing to me. But it is a great deal to me that my mother and I should live' (p. 114). Hardy also emphasizes the value of smuggling as a traditional way of life which binds the community in cords of fellow-feeling (pp. 64, 73, 114). By comparison, the system of Law and Authority symbolized by Caesar is not exactly 'dead' (p. 88); rather, perhaps, it persists as it ever did, striving to impress itself upon a hopelessly resistant race of people, as in Casterbridge (*MC*, VIII, p. 56 and XXXVII). Only superficially does it succeed.

In *Jude*, Hardy emphasizes the influence that the Church has on Society. In *The Distracted Preacher*, however, the parishioners' own values override those of the Church. The first impression is that, as in *Far from the Madding Crowd* (XXXIII, p. 226), they simply wish to 'play fair'. This attitude in itself undermines that united respect for King and Country signified by the Church and preserved in Lizzy's sampler (*SS*, p. 67). Later Hardy shows that the parson has been persuaded to connive with the villagers in order to keep his congregation (pp. 91, 104). They use his church as sanctuary both for their tubs and for themselves (pp. 64, 103). Even 'the soundest church-going parishioners in the country' are, Hardy suggests, 'indifferent' to 'their true and appointed parson' (p. 59). His joking tone softens the implications of rebellion. But as Lizzy's lover gradually comes to terms with the fact that her conscience really does not uphold the law (p. 66), Hardy demonstrates the latent power of the values she represents.

Those smuggling exploits upon which this story is based exemplify that long history of resistance to Church and State (*MC*, VIII, p. 56). Centuries after the original Roman invasion, the 'conventional, proud but efficient' Roman Church ousted the Celtic Church. It co-operated with 'the power of kings and the relative orderliness of their system of government' to their mutual benefit. Together they 'really could determine what their subjects did'.[22] Yet resistance was strong, if subtle.

> In England, the Church did not succeed in its claim to exercise exclusive jurisdiction in matrimonial cases until the eleventh century. For hundreds of years after that, poor people continued to marry without benefit of clergy

and to ignore the 'more niggling and constrictive' of the Church's laws 'governing what constituted a legitimate marriage'.[23] Even in Tess's day 'people marry sister-laws continually about Marlott' (*Tess*, VII, LVIII, p. 446). The 'Church's fierce moral condemnation' and 'official uncharitableness towards' cases such as hers seem never to have been 'wholeheartedly endorsed' by the poor. Tess's friends do not perceive the seriousness of it (II, XIV), even at that time in history when those official attitudes were at their peak.[24]

Mixen Lane shows how barbarous the common people can be. Yet official barbarity can be even worse (*MC*, VIII, p. 56). The characters seem confused by its association with religion. This distorts both memory and understanding. Matthew seems to be a 'prophet' who encouraged blood-curdling oaths (*FFMC*, XXXIII, p. 227). They have superstitious ideas about the power of prayer (for example, *FFMC*, VIII, p. 69; *RN*, I, III, p. 38). So confused are they about differences between God and Satan that superstitions about both can be associated with the same relic (for example, *Tess*, II, XIV, p. 358–59). All this adds to the sense that something is wrong with the Church's teachings. Even Tess's vicar seems to recognize that 'ten years of endeavour to graft technical belief on actual scepticism' have worn away at the 'nobler impulses' of 'the man' (*Tess*, II, XIV, p. 132). Some of Hardy's short stories elaborate impressions in his novels that those 'nobler impulses' are yet strong enough to survive and to motivate the subtly subversive values and attitudes of the country folk.

However, reorganization of the countryside seems to have achieved what harsh penal laws could not—the disintegration of such communities. Hence Hardy's concern, as expressed in *The Dorsetshire Labourer*, to preserve their traditions while improving their quality of life. Hence his concern, in his fiction, to preserve their values.

Of course, Hardy generally presents his country folk as being quite unaware of any such potential. In *The Return of the Native* they are apparently exhibiting loyalty to King and Parliament. Really, Hardy says, they are perpetuating pre-Roman religious rites—reaching out to be the 'fettered gods of the earth' in a spirit of 'Promethean rebelliousness' against 'foul times, cold darkness, misery and death' (*RN*, I, III, p. 23). But this subversion is quite unconscious; after all, Hardy is imposing this construction upon a gathering as serene as that of *The Three Strangers* (*SS*, p. 3). The characters do not seriously consider why 'the impulses of all outlandish hamlets' should be 'pagan still', or how they have 'survived medieval doctrine' (*RN*, VI, I,

p. 390). But through direct comment and through his use of Egdon, Hardy suggests their unconscious awareness of how 'civilization' is their 'enemy' (*RN*, I, I, p. 14). The single clear white Roman road over a heath littered with evidence of pre-historic occupation seems to symbolize the extent to which Hardy feels that civilization has impressed the people.

While his short stories may draw attention to the constructive potential of these communities, their values are often far from sound or attractive. Mixen Lane illustrates this. Egdon in a storm can seem unfathomably frightening; so can Susan Nunsuch. Even the brave Caesar feared Egdon's 'sinister condition' (*RN*, I, VI, p. 60). In leaving before the autumnal equinox he would avoid that surge of 'Promethean rebelliousness' (I, III, p. 23) culminating in Bonfire Night. Hardy seems to suggest that he, too, sensed the precariousness of his authority and the powerful, dangerous, unfathomable depths of the people he was striving to subdue. Perhaps the main function of the 'dream-country' of Hardy's fiction is to suggest and explore this paradoxical human condition.

In his fiction, as in his poetry, Hardy acknowledges the unchanging destructive impetus of time. In *The Clasped Skeletons*, Hardy notes how fossils once 'met the gleam of day' and 'breathed this atmosphere'.[25] In *The Mayor of Casterbridge*, upon Susan Henchard's return, Hardy emphasized aspects of the scene which had remained unchanged—not only since 'the previously recorded episode'—but 'for centuries untold' (*MC*, III, p. 23). Even in the first episode he noted the thick ubiquitous dust, suggestive of the ultimate fate of all creation (*MC*, I, pp. 7–9). Then 'what is length of time? But dream!'[25]

Among time's unchanging aspects is our resistance to changing its destructive impetus. Nonetheless, the affection symbolized by 'the clasped skeletons' has persisted, enshrined in the love stories of successive generations and civilizations.[25] The apparent 'reciprocity' between Michael and Susan may be illusory. The 'atmosphere of stale familiarity' may be 'typical'. 'In contrast' to Michael's cruelty, the reciprocal affection of the horses may shame the human race (*MC*, I, p. 18). However, a less harsh perspective is offered when Henchard re-enacts the scene after his fall; now it appears that he had been angry about his social and financial position and not, directly, with his marriage. The 'act of simple affection' (*MC*, III, p. 24) betwixt Susan and Elizabeth Jane reminds us, much earlier, that the capacity for affection has survived. So do Henchard's recuperative acts. Thus Hardy suggests that there is still latent within the human condition a capacity for 'loving-kindness'.

Thus, as in his poetry, Hardy uses images of the past to suggest the potential of the human condition as well as its past history of destruction. Remembering 'a woman' who defended a child, 'not of her own', against 'a man's senseless rage', Hardy sees the 'barrows, bulging as they bosoms were/ Of Multimammia stretched supinely there'.[26] He uses a similar image (*MC*, XLV, p. 330) just before drawing attention to Henchard's ability to show and to inspire kindness. The emotional intensity of Whittle's 'deep sadness' and sacrifice contrasts with the response of Farfrae and Elizabeth Jane (pp. 330, 333). In the context of Henchard's death, upon the heath, far from society, Hardy illuminates that capacity for 'loving-kindness' in one of the feeblest members of society.

Hardy acknowledges the dehumanizing effects of civilization in his own life. Only when separated from destructive influences in the world by death, Hardy claims, can he be 'more myself'.[27] He knows 'some liberty' on those 'heights in Wessex, shaped as if by a kindly hand/ For thinking, dreaming, dying on' where 'I seem where I was before my birth, and after death may be.' There he feels able to distance himself from those 'crises' which remind him that

> Down there I seem to be false to myself, my simple self that was,
> And is not now, and I see him watching, wondering what crass cause
> Can have merged him into such a strange continuator as this,
> Who yet has something in common with myself, my chrysalis.[28]

In his fiction, of course, Hardy dramatizes and illuminates 'crises' and their 'crass cause'. Even so, in the 'dream-country' of his fiction, he is like a spirit exploring a time dimension.

In his fiction, as in his poetry, Hardy's exhortations on 'loving-kindness' are far from final; besides the limitations of society and of human nature, many as yet inexplicable and irrational aspects of our apparently ill-fated universe impede us.

Through Henchard, Hardy seems to project into the novel his own fear and striving to analyse the atmosphere of a strange, threatening world. Henchard could feel 'in the air around Lucetta . . . an antagonistic force. . . . When he had tried to hang near her he seemed standing in a refluent current.' Hence, to him, 'her windows gleamed as if they did not want him; her curtains seemed to hang slily, as if they screened an ousting presence' (*MC*, XXVI, p. 181). So sensitive to atmosphere is Conjuror Fall that he can predict the likely visit of Henchard as well as the weather (*MC*, XXVI, p. 187). Through Henchard's fall, Hardy dramatizes the transience and instability of the human lot which prompts the people's peculiar sensitivity to the weather and to the atmosphere it generates (p. 185). Henchard's superstitious reactions may be explicable in terms of character. Yet people are full of imperfections. Hence, such reactions are common (*MC*, XIX, p. 128; XXVI, p. 184; XXVII, pp. 191–92). Moreover, Hardy does present the weather as the ultimate image of that 'ironical sequence of things' (XIX, p. 128) which does seem bent on trying Henchard at his weakest moments.

Hence, from the time of Henchard's fall, he pervasively influences our perspective upon the environment. Hardy uses a sense that 'the low land grew blacker, and the sky a deeper grey' until 'the landscape looked like a picture blotted with ink' to convey the effect upon Henchard of news that Farfrae has 'gone into my house' (XXXII, pp. 225–26). Although Elizabeth Jane speaks privately to Farfrae, it is on account of Henchard. When Hardy says 'it was not yet light' we can hardly avoid thinking of that danger of which she is trying to make Farfrae aware; 'a chorus of tiny rappings' through the 'dense fog' in a town 'silent as it was dark' suggest an atmosphere vibrant with that awareness (XXXIV, p. 239). The whole community seems to know, and to respond (p. 241). Later, another 'idea' connected with him spreads 'like a miasmatic fog through' Casterbridge (*MC*, XXXVII, p. 267). Its implications are serious; they culminate, incidentally, in Lucetta's death. Thus, all Casterbridge seems implicated in that 'slow wind making its moan' through Yalbury Wood, which appears, ostensibly, to suggest Henchard's feelings alone (XL, p. 284).

His 'time of emotional darkness of which the adjoining

woodland shade afforded inadequate illustration' (p. 286) relates intrinsically to the situation in Casterbridge. When Henchard calls 'in the steely light of dawn', Lucifer seems to be 'fading into day' on having culminated Casterbridge's time of disorder with Lucetta's death (p. 288). Henchard is now an outcast to society. Yet at this very time Hardy uses a 'dream-country' environment to draw attention to the sense in which Henchard represents the human condition. Thus, even in this novel, where the 'dream-country' may seem comparatively insignificant. Hardy uses it to convey a sense of his poetic vision of the human condition underlying the disguises of society.

In conclusion, it is difficult to decide what the 'dream-country' is and what it is not. In a sense, the entire fiction is the product of that poetic vision. In another sense, the 'dream' aspects could be considered illusory and expendable. Perhaps we could say that the 'dream-country' is the territory of the poet exploring a time dimension, considering relationships between man and society, considering what the human condition might be independent of society's destructive aspects. Perhaps the vision he strives to express is of a society derived from revelation of 'what earth and heaven mean' (see note 13)—a vision in which he is to lose hope.

Increasingly, Hardy develops his use of mythic manifestations, symbolism, ballads and traditional tales in his struggle to suggest 'impressions' of this human condition. Thus Hardy embraces a vast web of developing ideas and suggests a nexus of human feelings and behaviour. Increasingly, too, he uses direct comment to suggest stages in awareness as characters strive to come to terms with their perceptions.

Perhaps it is because the true origin of Hardy's 'dream-country' is his poetic vision that he is not dependent upon a stimulating physical environment to create a vivid and important 'dream-country'; the apparent barrenness of environment in *Jude*, and the secondary interest in the environment shown by Pierston, illustrate this. Yet, in focusing upon Wessex, and upon Casterbridge in particular, he shows that his poetic vision is not restricted to an exploration of his own heart; rather, the poet's heart explores and embraces the strivings of a human community. His driving purpose is to seek a way towards the easing of their pain.

NOTES

1. R. P. Draper discusses Casterbridge's 'organic relationship with its inhabitants' in 'The Mayor of Casterbridge', *Critical Quarterly*, Vol. 25, No. 1 (Spring 1983), 63ff.
2. F. E. Hardy, *Life* (Macmillan, 1975), Ch. XXX, p. 351.
3. See, for example, Christina Hole (ed.), *Encyclopedia of Superstitions*, section on 'Rough Music'. Hardy had noted 'accounts of at least three skimmity-rides . . . in Dorset newspapers in 1884' (*Life*, p. 169, 4 December 1884). He mentions Thomasin's unfounded fear of one in *The Return of the Native*. In *Far from the Madding Crowd* he shows the sense in which sexual irregularities could affect an agricultural community. (See Chapter 3.) Hardy does not treat the skimmity-ride in this way, despite the link between Henchard's sexual jealousy and his gamble with harvest weather. Rather, he describes it as a 'rough' and dangerous 'joke' causing more trouble even than the instigation of riots which, Longways suggests, is a common consequence (XXXVII, p. 268).
4. Hardy has little evidence for comparison anyway. One of the characteristics of Roman occupation was their exceptional success at obliterating indigenous cultures, cutting off their history, and subjugating the peoples to their own laws. See, for example, Felix R. Paturi, *Prehistoric Heritage* (Macdonald & Jane, 1979), pp. 98–104. It is now commonly accepted that the Romans were far from honest about the achievements of the indigenous Britons when they did refer to them in their records. Imperialist invaders in modern times have behaved likewise. For example, the contemporary struggles in Zimbabwe have highlighted the attitudes of Cecil Rhodes and his followers, within the last century, and the eventual re-emergence of the subjugated cultures. Even their tribal feuds seem to be carrying on from where they left off a hundred years ago.

   The Roman devastation was so great, and so long ago, that Hardy has comparatively little recourse to evidence of the socio-religious beliefs of the Britons. However, Wessex remains littered with their landmarks. Hardy seems to use these as silent witness to the extent of the Roman devastation. (See *MC*, II, p. 20; XIII, p. 84; XVI, p. 106; XVI, p. 111; XLIII, p. 309.) Modern archaeology regards them in a strikingly similar light. (*Horizon*, B.B.C. 2, 24 January 1985 and 27 January 1985, 'Decoding Danebury'.)
5. Hardy's poetry illuminates the perversity in the theological arguments. See, for example, 'A Dream Question', *Complete Poems* (Macmillan, 1979), No. 215, p. 261; 'God's Education', Ibid., No. 232, pp. 278–79; 'A Christmas Ghost Story', Ibid., No. 59, p. 90 (1899).
6. 'The Bedridden Peasant', Ibid., No. 88, p. 125.
7. 'Apology to Late Lyrics and Earlier', Ibid., Note 1, p. 561.
8. Ibid., p. 561.
9. Ibid., p. 557.
10. 'In Tenebris II', Ibid., No. 137, p. 168.
11. 'A Hundred Years Since', Ibid., No. 941, pp. 951–52.

12. 'The Graveyard of Dead Creeds', Ibid., No. 694, pp. 724–25.
13. 'There Seemed a Strangeness', Ibid., No. 695, p. 725.
14. 'Last Chorus', from 'The Dynasts', Ibid., No. 934, pp. 943–44.
15. 'A Plaint to Man', Ibid., No. 266, pp. 325–26.
16. See, for example, Ibid., Nos. 248, 591, 696, 904, 918, 919.
17. 'Apology to Late Lyrics and Earlier', Ibid., p. 558.
18. See Appendix 2.
19. See too *DR*, VIII, p. 166–69. Manston achieves a similar effect with his organ. Tess is similarly fascinated by Angel's harp-playing (*Tess*, III, XIX, pp. 161–62). However, the fiddler seems deliberately to paralyse the will of his victim, suspending character and judgement. In Hardy's poem, 'The Fiddler', *Complete Poems*, No. 207, p. 248, the fiddler recognizes and delights in this power, though he does not use it for his own ends. Here it affects 'many a heart'.
20. Preface to *Wessex Tales*, p. vi. Compare p. viii: 'However, the stories are but dreams, and not records.'
21. 'Apology to Late Lyrics and Earlier', *Complete Poems*, p. 557.
22. James Campbell (ed.), *The Anglo-Saxons* (Phaidon, 1982), Ch. 3, pp. 46, 61.
23. Ferdinand Mount, *The Subversive Family: An Alternative History of Love and Marriage* (Cape, 1982), Ch. 1, p. 19.
24. Ibid., Ch. 8, pp. 132–35. Alan Macfarlane, 'Illegitimacy and Illegitimates in English History', quoting 'Bastardy and its Comparative History', ed. Peter Laslett *et al.* (London, 1980), pp. 75–6.
25. 'The Clasped Skeletons', *Complete Poems*, No. 858, pp. 873–74.
26. 'By The Barrows', Ibid., No. 216, p. 262.
27. 'When Dead', Ibid., No. 689, p. 721.
28. 'Wessex Heights' (1896), Ibid., No. 261, p. 319.

Appendix 1:

Hardy and the Supernatural

Hardy chose to include an astonishing number of references to the supernatural in his biography. Even while insisting to Archer that there was no 'evidence' for belief in telepathy, Hardy offered an instance of his own mother's telepathic experience. He dismissed such instances as 'too trifling' to be construed as 'evidence'.[1] Yet, on a train bound for London, Hardy himself experienced 'a curious instance of sympathetic telepathy'. He found himself writing 'the first four or six lines of "Not a line of her writing have I" ', about a woman's death. 'The woman whom I was thinking of—a cousin—was dying at the time, and I quite in ignorance of it.'[2] His second wife tells of 'a night on which he could not sleep, partly on account of an eerie feeling which sometimes haunted him, a horror of lying down in close proximity to "a monster whose body had four million heads and eight million eyes" '.[3] On finding that the site of his new home, Fordington Field, 'was steeped in antiquity', he 'thought the omens gloomy'.[4] Hardy 'never in his life allowed himself to be weighed, as he said he considered that to be unlucky'.[5] It does seem likely, then, that Hardy 'had a temperamental leaning towards the use of premonitions, omens, ghosts and prophecies'[6]; he could hardly fail to incorporate these into his art, considering the nature of his art.

Hardy suspected that some tales, such as 'some of Holder's stories' could be 'rather well-found than well-founded'. Even Holder himself 'could not quite guarantee' the truth of one.[7] And yet this was the one that Hardy chose to recount. Perhaps this was because it aroused interesting insights into the human condition. For example, Hardy uses the archetypal association

181

of demonic activity with a 'night of terrific lightning and thunder'[8] in Chapter XXXVII of *Far from the Madding Crowd.* Moreover, the tale suggests the workfolk's suppressed sense that the Church represents an imposed human authority, unwelcome because it does not embrace the kindest instincts of humankind. (See Chapter 4.) The tale provides an acceptable form for preserving this idea.

Often, on the other hand, literal authenticity makes it difficult for Hardy to ignore supernatural incidents.[9] The age of the tale may also be significant. Someone, sometime, seems to have become aware of the archetypal associations between disturbances in the world of Nature and disturbances in the life of man, and embodied that awareness in a story. Consequently, listeners are aroused to appreciate those archetypal associations. They, too, think them important enough for the tale to be handed down as worldly wisdom for the benefit of future generations. Hardy seems inspired to incorporate this sense of renewing suppressed wisdom into his fictional art.

NOTES

1. Archer, 'Real Conversations', *The Critic*, XXXVIII (April 1901), 309–18.
2. F. E. Hardy, *Life* (Macmillan, 1975), Ch. XVIII, p. 224. The poem, which he finished after her death, was 'Thoughts of Phena—At News of her Death', *Complete Poems*, No. 38, p. 62.
3. F. E. Hardy, Ch. X, p. 137.
4. Ibid., Ch. XIII, p. 163.
5. Ibid., Ch. XIII, p. 174.
6. Ruth Firor, *Folkways in Thomas Hardy* (University of Pennsylvania Press, 1931), p. 304.
7. F. E. Hardy, Ch. XII, p. 156.
8. See, for example, E. & M. A. Radford, *Superstitions of the Countryside*, ed. & revised by Christina Hole (Arrow Books, 1978), p. 111. Even the recent striking by lightning of York Minster, despite the preponderance of conductors, provoked nationwide speculations regarding the possibility of Divine Wrath against the Church and/or the people of Britain.
9. F. E. Hardy, Ch. IX, p. 126.

Appendix 2

Many of Hardy's short stories might be regarded as studies in important aspects of his fiction. In Chapter 4 I show how this could be said of *The Fiddler of the Reels*. Subsequent discussion shows how *The Withered Arm*, *The Three Strangers*, and *The Distracted Preacher* could all be seen to illuminate his novels.

Perhaps the example most relevant to this thesis is *The Interlopers at the Knap*. Here Hardy makes close use of the natural environment to suggest the nature of Darton's 'pilgrimage' (*WT*, p. 181). He is setting off to marry Sally, whom he does not love. His deepest feelings are suggested by the 'tedious' journey along 'the north road . . . in the gloom of a winter evening' (p. 179). In the interests of a straightforward life he has deceived himself into reasoning that she is 'simple' (p. 181) and easy to live with. Correspondingly, he 'placidly' takes 'the straight road' (p. 184) at the signpost; he is unaware that his bride's home is along the winding path.

Later, after the storm and a period of meditation, he 'suddenly opened his eyes' (p. 199) to the significance of seeing the woman he truly loved in the dress consciously intended as Sally's wedding gown. In that moment of truth, he recognizes the correlation between his emotional disturbance and 'the stars' which are 'flickering coldly, and the dampness which', having 'just descended upon the earth in rain now sent up a chill from it' (p. 202). But the moment passes.

His second journey along the road is 'heartily' undertaken. Hence it seems 'not half its former length' (p. 210). However, Hardy uses Nature to illustrate Darton's unconscious state of mind. Darton is enthusiastic, though he goes but to ask Sally's hand, rather than to an actual wedding; and circumstances have changed greatly since he asked her last. Over-confident, he misinterprets his certainty that he has 'made no mistake this time' as a sign that he will not 'be able to mistake, thank Heaven, when I arrive' (p. 210).

For his third journey, he deliberately waits for 'a bright day late in May—a day when all animate nature was fancying, in its trusting and foolish way, that it was going to bask under blue sky for evermore'. Clearly, Hardy is using the environment to illustrate Darton's illusion: thus, 'though Spring had come, and heavenly blue consecrated the scene, Darton succeeded not' (p. 217).

Yet Nature is not tricking him; he is misinterpreting Nature. Hardy is using the environment to show the limitation of Darton's self-knowledge; Darton does not adequately recognize the extent to which his impressions of Nature may be projections of his unconscious. On his first journey, his unconscious selects aspects of the environment which might illustrate his true feelings. On the second journey, it emphasizes aspects of the environment which illustrate the falseness of his hearty manner. But in each case, Hardy suggests, he cannot or will not heed it. On his third journey, he tries to manoeuvre his unconscious to tie in with Nature, heedless that he cannot thus force himself to love, and heedless, too, that Sally's love has passed, as will the fine weather.

This kind of use of environment is important to Hardy. In his novels it contributes much towards suggesting the development of character. (See Chapter 2.) Its use reaches its zenith in *Tess*, where it highlights Tess's cruel struggle to renew her life against a climate of opinion which refuses to allow it. (See Chapter 3.)

Bibliography

Works by Thomas Hardy:

FICTION

(AILH)   *An Indiscretion in the Life of an Heiress* (Hutchinson, 1976)
(DR)   *Desperate Remedies* (Macmillan, 1975)
(UGT)   *Under the Greenwood Tree* (Macmillan, 1977)
(FFMC)   *Far from the Madding Crowd* (Pan, 1980)
(RN)   *The Return of the Native* (Macmillan, 1958)
(MC)   *The Mayor of Casterbridge* (Macmillan, 1968)
(W)   *The Woodlanders* (Macmillan, 1973)
(WT)   *Wessex Tales* (Macmillan, 1960)
(Tess)   *Tess of the d'Urbervilles* (Macmillan, 1978)
(Jude)   *Jude the Obscure* (Macmillan, 1978)
(WB)   *The Well-Beloved* (Macmillan, 1979)
   A Changed Man and Other Tales (Macmillan, 1966)
(SS)   *Selected Stories* (Macmillan, 1977)

NON-FICTION

Complete Poems, ed. James Gibson (Macmillan, 1979)
Hardy's Personal Writings, ed. Harold Orel (Macmillan, 1967)
Collected Letters, ed. M. Millgate and R. L. Purdy (Macmillan: Vol. I, 1978; Vol. II, 1980)
The Dynasts (Macmillan, 1965)

Works by other authors:

ALLOTT, MIRIAM, *Novelists on the Novel* (Routledge Paperback, 1965)
ARCHER, WILLIAM, 'Real Conversations', *The Critic*, XXXVIII (April 1901)

ATKINSON, R. J. C., *Stonehenge* (Pelican, 1960)

BAILEY, J. O., *Thomas Hardy and the Cosmic Mind* (University of Carolina Press, 1956)

BLAKE, KATHLEEN, 'Pure Tess: Hardy on Knowing a Woman', *Studies in English Literature*, Vol. 22 (Autumn 1982)

BUTLER, LANCE ST. JOHN (ed.), *Thomas Hardy After Fifty Years* (Macmillan, 1977)

CAMPBELL, JAMES (ed.), *The Anglo-Saxons* (Phaidon, 1982)

CREIGHTON, T. R. M., 'Some Thoughts on Hardy and Religion', from *Thomas Hardy After Fifty Years*. See BUTLER, LANCE ST. JOHN

CROSSLEY-HOLLAND, KEVIN, *The Norse Myths* (André Deutsch, 1980)

DEWAR, H. S. L., Introduction to Hardy's paper on 'Some Romano-British Relics found at Max Gate, Dorchester', *Dorset Monographs*, No. 6, The Dorset Natural History and Archaeological Society (Dorchester, 1966)

DRAPER, R. P., 'The Mayor of Casterbridge', *Critical Quarterly*, Vol. 25, No. 1 (Spring 1983)

EVANS, C., 'Dreams: A Functional Theory', *Trans-Action* (Washington University, 1967)

——, *Landscapes of the Night* (Gollancz, 1983)

FIEDLER, L. A., 'Archetype and Signature', *Perspectives on Poetry*, J. L. Calderwood & H. E. Tolliver (eds.) (Oxford University Press, 1968)

FIROR, RUTH, *Folkways in Thomas Hardy* (University of Pennsylvania Press, 1931)

FOWLES, JOHN, 'Hardy and the Hag', from *Thomas Hardy After Fifty Years*. See BUTLER, ST. JOHN

FRYE, NORTHROP, 'Credo', *Kenyon Review*, XIII (Winter 1951)

GOETZ, W. R., 'The Felicity and Infelicity of Marriage in *Jude the Obscure*', *Nineteenth-century Fiction*, Vol. 38, No. 2 (September 1983)

GREGOR, IAN, *The Great Web* (Faber and Faber, 1974)

GRIMAL, PIERRE (ed.), *Larousse: World Mythology* (Hamlyn, 1974)

HARDY, F. E., *The Life of Thomas Hardy* (Macmillan, 1975)

HAWKINS, G. S., *Stonehenge Decoded* (Souvenir Press, 1966)

——, *Beyond Stonehenge* (Hutchinson, 1973)

HITCHING, F., *Earth Magic* (Picador: Pan Books, 1978)

HOLE, C., *Encyclopedia of Superstitions* (Hutchinson, 1961)

Bibliography

JACOBUS, MARY, 'Tess's Purity', *Essays in Criticism*, Vol. 26 (October 1976)

JAFFÉ, A., 'Symbolism in the Visual Arts', from *Man and his Symbols*. See JUNG, C. G.

JUNG, C. G., *Archetypes of the Collective Unconscious*, Collected Works, Vol. 9i (Princeton University Press, 1968). This, and all Jung's works quoted here, translated by R. F. C. Hull.

——, *Individual Dream Symbolism in Relation to Alchemy*, Collected Works, Vol. 12 (Routledge, 1968)

——, *Integration of the Personality* (Routledge & Kegan Paul, 1940)

——, *Modern Man in Search of a Soul* (Routledge & Kegan Paul, 1966)

——, *Dreams* (Princeton/Bollingen Paperbacks, 1974)

——, (ed. & conceived by) *Man and his Symbols* (Picador: Pan Books, 1980)

KRAMER, DALE (ed.), *Critical Approaches to the Fiction of Thomas Hardy* (Macmillan, 1979)

LODGE, DAVID, *The Language of Fiction* (Routledge & Kegan Paul, 1966)

——, '*Jude the Obscure*: Pessimism & Fictional Form', from *Critical Approaches to the Fiction of Thomas Hardy*. See KRAMER, DALE

MAPLE, E., *Superstitions and the Superstitious* (W. H. Allen, 1971)

MILLER, J. HILLIS, *Fiction and Repetition* (Basil Blackwell, Oxford, 1982)

MILLGATE, M., *Thomas Hardy: A Biography* (Oxford University Press, 1982)

MOUNT, FERDINAND, *The Subversive Family: An Alternative History of Love and Marriage* (Cape, 1982)

NEUMANN, ERICH, *The Great Mother: An Analysis of an Archetype* (Princeton/Routledge & Kegan Paul/Bollingen, 1974)

PATURI, F. R., *Prehistoric Heritage* (Macdonald and Jane, 1979)

RADFORD, E., and M. A., *Superstitions of the Countryside* (ed. C. Hole) (Arrow Books, 1978)

RANK, OTTO, *Psychology and the Soul* (A. S. Barnes, New York, 1961)

RYAN, M., 'One Name of Many Shapes: *The Well-Beloved*', from *Critical Approaches to the Fiction of Thomas Hardy*. See KRAMER, DALE

SCHWARZ, D. R., 'Beginnings and Endings in Hardy's Major Fiction', ibid.

SUMNER, R., *Thomas Hardy: Psychological Novelist* (Macmillan, 1981)

VON FRANZ, M. L., 'The Process of Individuation', from *Man and his Symbols*. See JUNG, C. G.

WIMSATT, W. K., *The Verbal Icon: Studies in the Meaning of Poetry* (University of Kentucky Press, 1982)

WOOLF, VIRGINIA, *Collected Essays* (Hogarth Press, 1966)

Index

189

Index